DOMESTIC INDIVIDUALISM

The New Historicism: Studies in Cultural Poetics
Stephen Greenblatt, General Editor

DOMESTIC INDIVIDUALISM

*Imagining Self in
Nineteenth-Century America*

GILLIAN BROWN

UNIVERSITY OF CALIFORNIA PRESS
BERKELEY   LOS ANGELES   OXFORD

University of California Press
Berkeley and Los Angeles, California

University of California Press, Ltd.
Oxford, England

© 1990 by
The Regents of the University of California

Library of Congress Cataloging-in-Publication Data

Brown, Gillian.
    Domestic individualism : imagining self in nineteenth-century
America / Gillian Brown.
        p.   cm. — (The New historicism : 14)
    Includes bibliographical references (p.   ) and index.
    ISBN 0-520-06785-1 (cloth)
        1. Domestic fiction, American—History and criticism.   2. American
fiction—19th century—History and criticism.   3. Stowe, Harriet
Beecher, 1811–1896—Political and social views.   4. Hawthorne,
Nathanial, 1804–1864—Political and social views.   5. Melville,
Herman, 1819–1891—Political and social views.   6. Individualism in
literature.   7. Self in literature.   I. Title.   II. Series.
PS374.D57B7   1990
813'.309—dc20   90-11143
                                                           CIP

Printed in the United States of America

9 8 7 6 5 4 3 2 1

The paper used in this publication meets the minimum requirements of
American National Standard for Information Sciences—Permanence of Paper
for Printed Library Materials, ANSI Z39.48–1984. ⊚

To My Mother and Father

Contents

Illustrations

Acknowledgments

Many individuals, at different points and in many different ways, have participated in, and sustained me through, the process of writing this book. For their particular contributions, I would like to thank:

Walter Benn Michaels, Julia Bader, Catherine Gallagher, Michael Paul Rogin, Eric Sundquist, Steven Greenblatt; Marianne Dekoven, Richard Poirier, Myra Jehlen, William Keach, Miriam Hansen, Judith Walkowitz, Martha Howell, Cora Kaplan; Heather Faith Brown, Jennifer Hammett, Sonia Hofkosh, Edward Mitchell-Hutchinson, Stuart Culver, Priscilla Wald, Richard Grusin, Lynn Wardley, Mary Ann O'Farrell, Cathy Popkin; Caroline Bynum, Amy Kaplan, T. Walter Herbert, Jane Tompkins, Elizabeth Fox-Genovese, Emory Elliott; Alex Chism, Doris Kretschmer, Pamela MacFarland, and Jane-Ellen Long. I have been as fortunate in my parents as in my colleagues and friends. These pages owe much to the beneficent domesticity that Laurence and Beverly Brown have tirelessly provided for their seven children. To Howard Horwitz, whose critical care has enhanced this book as well as all other things, goes my deepest gratitude.

I only wish that I could express my appreciation to another participant in the making of this book who did not live to see its completion. I hope that this book in some manner perpetuates the spirit of the conversations on aesthetics and domesticity I had with David Bombyk when I first embarked on this study.

My research for this book has been facilitated by the courtesy and helpfulness of the librarians of various institutions: the Library of Congress, the Schlesinger Library on the History of Women in America, the University of California Bancroft Library, the New York Historical Society, the Cooper Hewitt Museum Library, and the Columbia University Burgess Library Rare Book Room. This study also has been aided by the institutional support of an American Council of Learned Societies Fellowship and a Henry Rutgers Research Fellowship, as well as by generous grants from the Rutgers University Research Council.

I am grateful for permission to reprint two of the chapters in this book which had been published previously. Chapter 1 first appeared as "Getting in the Kitchen with Dinah: Domestic Politics in *Uncle Tom's Cabin*" in the *American Quarterly* 36 (copyright 1984 by the American Studies Association). Chapter 6, "The Empire of Agoraphobia," was published in *Representations* 20 (copyright 1987 by the Regents of the University of California) and reprinted in R. Howard Bloch and Frances Ferguson, eds., *Misogyny, Misandry, and Misanthropy* (University of California Press, 1989).

Introduction

The title of this study joins two heretofore rarely linked traditions: nineteenth-century domestic ideology and possessive individualism. In proposing this conjunction I mean to illuminate the character and function of the nineteenth-century rise of domesticity as a development within the history of individualism. To see domestic ideology as a passage in liberal humanism is not simply to acknowledge the historical and philosophical contexts of this ideology of femininity and personal life. This historicization also, and to my mind more significantly, demonstrates the role of domestic ideology in updating and reshaping individualism within nineteenth-century American market society.

It is the organizing premise of this book that nineteenth-century American individualism takes on its peculiarly "individualistic" properties as domesticity inflects it with values of interiority, privacy, and psychology. I shall be concerned with these domestic dimensions of individualism and individualistic functions of domesticity as they appear primarily but not exclusively in 1850s' novels, stories, and essays by Stowe, Hawthorne, and Melville, as well as in other cultural forms and practices such as abolitionism, interior decorating, architecture, mesmerism, communitarian reform, child-rearing, and even illness. Reading these various forms as definitions and redefinitions of selfhood reveals a self continually under construction, or at least renovation. And the materials that become the features of the self—its properties—thus represent a history of proprietorship and invention, the processes of ownership and production sustaining the self.

The reconstructions of the individual analyzed in the readings that follow assume, extend, and sometimes alter the logic of possessive individualism. C. B. Macpherson has identified the "possessive" nature of the individualism associated with the rise of the liberal democratic state. According to this concept of self evolving from the seventeenth century, every man has property in himself and thus the right to manage himself, his labor, and his property as he wishes. As Macpherson stresses, this is a market society's construction of self, a self aligned with market relations such as exchange value, alienability, circulation, and competition.[1] Though the term *individualism* does not come into use until the late 1820s,[2] when market society and forms of the modern liberal state are well established, the principles it encompasses were already instated. That is, by the mid-eighteenth century the notion of individual rights promulgated in the political philosophies of Hobbes and Locke comprised an article of cultural faith. Drawing on this tradition, the American Declaration of Independence and the Constitution extended property rights to include self-representation and designed a government which would protect this democratic right to self-determination.

Welded to the market activities generally available only to white men, possessive individualism obviously reflects a masculine selfhood. Yet in the nineteenth century, this form of individualism comes to be associated with the feminine sphere of domesticity.

Visiting the United States in the 1830s, Alexis de Tocqueville observed disapprovingly that American democracy nurtured an individual whose "feelings are turned in upon himself." Tocqueville elaborated the domestic accents of this self-interest: "Individualism is a calm and considered feeling which disposes each citizen to isolate himself from the mass of his fellows and withdraw into the circle of family and friends; with this little society formed to his taste, he gladly leaves the rest of society to take care of itself."[3] What concerns Tocqueville here is what he takes to be the withdrawal from political and civic responsibilities that underwrites individualism—its domestic constitution. I shall return later to his assumptions about the isolationism of domesticity; for the moment I want to pursue how Tocqueville's characterization of domesticity as a withdrawn "little society" to which "feeling" "disposes" the individual echoes the nineteenth-century rhetoric of home as a "haven in a heartless world."[4]

The domestic circle in which Tocqueville locates American individualism emerged as a sphere of individuality in tandem with market economy expansion. Domestic ideology with its discourse of personal life proliferates alongside this economic development which removed women from the public realm of production and redirected men to work arenas increasingly subject to market contingencies. To counter "this perpetually fluctuating state of society," Catharine Beecher exhorted women to "sustain a prosperous domestic state."[5] The domestic doctrine Beecher helped to define held women and the home as the embodiment and the environment of stable value. Maintaining a site of permanent value, the domestic cult of true womanhood facilitated the transition to a life increasingly subject to the caprices of the market. The confidence of encomiums to the virtues of womanhood and home simultaneously sublimated and denied anxieties about unfamiliar and precarious socioeconomic conditions and about the place of the individual within those conditions. In the midst of change the domestic sphere provided an always identifiable place and refuge for the individual: it signified the private domain of individuality apart from the marketplace.[6]

What I am calling domestic individualism thus denotes a self-definition secured in and nearly synonymous with domesticity. The nineteenth-century self-definitions this book explores locate the individual in his or her interiority, in his or her removal from the marketplace. Hence Stowe can identify the fate of slaves and the power of women with the state of home, political economy with domestic economy. Hawthorne likewise imagines good housekeeping as self-protective and revivifying. From a somewhat different perspective, Melville alternately images domestic influence as self-constricting and as not self-constricting enough. This theme is taken up by Charlotte Perkins Gilman at the end of the century in "The Yellow Wallpaper" and *Women and Economics,* which critique the domestic confinement of women and advocate their free circulation in spheres of their choosing. Although the feminist critique of domestic ideology rejects the situation of women in the home, it nonetheless retains in its aspirations for women's enfranchisement and self-determination the domestic definition of self. Arguing in 1892 for woman suffrage, Elizabeth Cady Stanton reproduces this composite of the individual when she aligns women's "birthright to self-sovereignty" with the fundamental "solitude of self" "our republican idea" of "the individuality of each human soul" constitutes. Nowhere is the tradition of self-proprietorship more alive than in Stanton's belief that "to deny the rights of property is like cutting off the hands."[7] The faculties of hands, which dictionary definitions list as those of grasping, producing, possessing, controlling, and authorizing, recapitulate the proprietary character of individualism.

Since domesticity secures this character for the individual, its selective allotment of rights and places in society is the real target of the feminist domestic critique. This means that women in the nineteenth century are in the peculiar position of wanting to be in a sphere they already both do and do not inhabit. For if the individual rights Stanton wants for women—"the rights of property," "political equality," "credit in the marketplace," "recompense in the world of work," "a voice in choosing those who make and administer the law"—by definition reside in domesticity,[8] the domestic sphere seems, then, to be the best place for women. The domestic confinement feminists protest should guarantee the democratic rights they want. This is precisely the logical maneuver by which opponents of woman suffrage were able to argue that women's rights existed in their domestic sphere, rationalizing the illogic of women's disenfranchisement by appealing to the entitling function of domesticity.

What the feminist movement for women's political and economic autonomy highlights, therefore, is the sexual division of individualism within domesticity.[9] This domain is at once the separate sphere of women and the correlative to, as well as the basis of, men's individuality. It is thus the case that the nineteenth century advanced and delimited individualism by identifying selfhood with the feminine but denying it to women. What women wanted was, quite literally, themselves. This paradoxical feminization of self that excludes as it encompasses women shapes the well-worn gender distinctions deeded to us by the nineteenth century. The measure of its success as a model of the subject can be indicated by the persistence with which the domestic and the individualistic have figured in American literary tradition as antinomies, despite Tocqueville's recognition of their alignment.

Individualism and domesticity have both long figured as thematics of nineteenth-century American culture, but as distinct and oppositional trajectories. Thus two disparate literary movements seem to emerge in the 1850s: on the one hand the American Renaissance, represented in the "classic" works of Emerson, Whitman, Hawthorne, Melville, and Poe;[10] and on the other hand the Other American Renaissance, inscribed in the works of Stowe and such writers as Susan Warner, Fanny Fern, Harriet Wilson, and Elizabeth Stuart Phelps, who are only recently receiving the critical attention long given their white male contemporaries.[11]

This gender division has persisted with remarkable neatness and clarity throughout American literary criticism. Recall how myths of the origins of American culture describe second-generation Adamic and oedipal stories: new Edens, sons in exile, estrangement from women. According to Leslie Fiedler, "the figure of Rip Van Winkle presides over the birth of the American imagination, and it is fitting that our first successful home-grown legend memorialize, however playfully, the flight of the dreamer from the shrew."[12] In this androcentric, if not misogynist, account of American culture, literature records the battle between the masculine desire for freedom and the feminine will toward civilization: the runaway Huck Finn versus the "sivilizing" Widow Douglas. The paradigm of the dreamer's flight from the shrew defines the domestic as a pole from which the individual must escape in order to establish and preserve his identity. Huck lights out for the territory in order to avoid what Ann Douglas calls "the feminization of American culture," to flee from the widow's sentimental values that epitomize, in Henry Nash Smith's words, "an ethos of conformity."[13]

Feminist reinterpretations of the domestic dispute this scenario by reversing its terms, making the domestic figure herself a runaway, a rebel. According to the new feminist literary history, women figured in the American imagination not as shrews to be dreamed away, but as producers and embodiments of the American dream of personal happiness. In the feminist exegesis of American cultural archetypes, the housewife, whom the prototypical canonical literature (and criticism) would evade, signifies a reformist rather than conformist ethos. As the Angel in the House, the woman at home exemplified ideal values and presided over a superior, moral economy. In sentimental literature, as Nina Baym puts it, "Domesticity is set forth as a value scheme for ordering all of life, in competition with the ethos of money and exploitation that is perceived to prevail in American society." Dedicated to "overturning the male money system as the law of American life," domesticity constitutes an alternative to, and escape from, the masculine economic order.[14]

Against the self-interest of the typically male individualism Tocqueville analyzed, the subculture women image is based on self-denial and collectivity—the ethos of sympathy customarily and disparagingly called sentimentalism. In this view, women thus claim and typify an anti-market (if not anti-masculine) individualism. Contrary to Tocqueville's narrow account of domesticity as the depoliticization of the individual, such domestic novels as *Uncle Tom's Cabin* demonstrate that the alignment between individualism and domesticity might structure dispositions other than self-interest, such as self-denial and self-protection.

Building upon and complicating feminist revisionary treatments of domestic ideology in the first part of this book, I trace through "Stowe's Domestic Reformations" a nineteenth-century update of possessive individualism, the domestic enclosure of the rights of women and blacks. But my argument in these chapters, as well as in the others that engage other aspects of self-sovereignty in literature not generally considered "domestic," contextualizes rather than confirms the feminist reversal of canonical theories of American literature.

Indeed, as I have been thus far suggesting, the feminist restoration of a domestic reform tradition displays the limitations of a masculinist critical practice, but hardly amounts to a reversal of nineteenth-century American male individualism. For the account of market manhood to which domestic reformers object images a self by definition already domesticated, insofar as its character is secured and authenticated by the domestic ideology of home. Conceived as withdrawn to himself, the individual shares the definitive principle of domesticity: its withdrawal from the marketplace. While women's deployment of domestic ideology directs it to genuinely reformist ends and counters prevailing dispositions of power that disenfranchise women, their domestic reforms, instead of projecting an antithetical model of selfhood, further domesticate an already domesticated selfhood. Moreover, as will become manifest in the readings of Hawthorne and Melville, the androcentric bias in American literary criticism is integrally related to and rooted in domestic ideology. To think of the domestic as reformist or revolutionary, therefore, is to register only one of its operations.

Focusing on texts in dialogue with their immediate culture and their larger cultural traditions, I mean to demonstrate a scope of domestic ideology hitherto unacknowledged even by feminist studies that link the domestic to a conception of female selfhood. Far from an account of the female subject, domesticity signifies a feminization of selfhood in service to an individualism most available to (white) men. This means that domesticity doubly binds, in obviously different ways, men and women, blacks and whites, to the same self-definition. From various perspectives and to varying degrees, nineteenth-century American literature reflects and helps to shape or alter this definition. I therefore make no attempt to distinguish between classic and feminist or revisionary American literary canons. I have chosen texts that may or may not fit these categories (in some cases previously unread materials) for their various expositions of the problematic of domestic individualism.

My study provides no schematic configuration or specific theory of American literature. Rather, it emphasizes the convergence of literary works with social practices as a way of underscoring the depth and breadth of imaginative work that literary artifacts and

social formations such as domesticity and its representations perform. The readings I present, though generally historical, are occasionally also speculative, moving forward in time, sometimes
into the present. In the final chapter, for example, I read "Bartleby
the Scrivener" alongside "The Yellow Wallpaper" and an 1870
story from *Godey's Lady's Book*, explicating the agoraphobic logic
of these fictions, which anticipates our contemporary accounts of
both agoraphobia and anorexia. By relating the connections
among these various forms and by pursuing these relations across
centuries, I mean to suggest, not just the imaginative productivity
of domesticity, but the cultural endurance of domestic individualism and the power of American literature in promoting that
tradition.

I have weighted this book with an insistence on convergences,
on affiliations and shared identities such as the rather striking
affinities between housekeeping and abolitionism, interior decorating and racism, architecture and romance, mesmerism and
commerce, cannibalism and literary relations, anorexia and anti-
consumerism. This generally deconstructionist approach obviously does not do away with distinctions as it uncovers the affinities
among different categories. My emphasis is not meant in any way
to deny differences, whether generic, racial, sexual, economic, or
political, but to illuminate how the deployment of difference—in
this case, the sexual and spatial divisions domestic ideology en-
gendered—operates and gains force by concealing the common
purposes that different or even oppositional objects or practices
serve. In other words, I am interested in how domestic ideology,
as a system of differences, works to maintain cultural coherence
through differences.

At the same time, however, the fact that domestic ideology
helps form cultural coherence does not mean that it represents a
monolithic design. The domestic construction of individualism, as
my readings will indicate, reflects myriad interests and historical
particulars. For example, domesticity in the context of nineteenth-
century abolitionism signifies a reformist politics, while in the
context of woman's suffrage it appears as a reactionary institution.
Though in these cases domesticity denotes certain political orches-

trations, on the part of abolitionists or misogynists, this book does not unfold a unitary politics of domesticity: no single system emerges in the operations of the domestic. Its effectiveness as a strategy of self is just that: not a totalizing force, but a working machinery, one that has served and continues to serve many purposes.

In the succeeding chapters, the recurrent paradigm of difference that I shall be considering is the distinction between self and market, as well as its variant forms: home/market, body/market, mind/ body, work/body.[15] There appear in these discussions themes, terms, and concepts made familiar by cultural critics from Marx to Veblen and from Benjamin to Baudrillard, and by psychoanalytic theorists from Freud to Lacan. Revisions and critiques of both these traditions, by contemporary feminists such as Sarah Kofman and Luce Irigaray, as well as by new materialists such as Elaine Scarry, Walter Benn Michaels, and Susan Stewart, also hover over and shape my readings of nineteenth-century domestic artifacts. These various (and sometimes vastly different) interpretive enterprises figure in my study not as theories that authorize my reading practice but as themselves practices, that is, as engagements with and formulations of the same problematics of self-definition I am treating. Moreover, one aim of my representational history of the domestic is to suggest some ways that domestic formations have worked to set in place the conceptions of identity and work that materialists and psychoanalysts have classified and theorized.

As this book explores how the individual and ideas of the individual incorporate economic realities, the vocabularies of economic and psychoanalytic analyses often merge. The conventional limits of such terms as economy, psychology, or domesticity mark the delineations between public and private life that domestic ideology so effectively implements. Indeed, the domestic processes through which the nineteenth-century individual internalized as well as distinguished himself from market capitalism dissolve the definition of economy as the political economy in which the individual lives. In my presentation of the cohabitation of the individual with the economic, material conditions and mental states accordingly coalesce. Chapter 3, for instance, examines in part the relation between housework, hysteria, and alienation; Chapter 6 investigates consumerist domesticity, agoraphobia, and anorexia. This investigation of domestic ideology thus delineates both the complexity and the contingency of cultural forms.

Finally, what is made can be made or arranged otherwise, or even disposed of, but disposal of artifacts, we now have urgent reason to know, creates new problems and dangers. The self-protective scope continually adjusted by new individualistic forms, however, might lead us to find new and safer ways of self-definition and disposal. It is in the reformulation and manipulation of domestic boundaries, after all, that the self this book studies both changes and endures.

Part One

Stowe's Domestic
Reformations

Chapter One

Domestic Politics in
Uncle Tom's Cabin

Getting in the Kitchen with Dinah

"More notorious and undeniable than any other" "abuse of the system of slavery," Harriet Beecher Stowe believed, was "its outrage upon the family."[1] Nowhere in *Uncle Tom's Cabin* is this domestic violation so marked as in the careless condition of the Southern kitchen. Dinah's kitchen in Little Eva St. Clare's New Orleans home "looked as if it had been arranged by a hurricane blowing through it."[2] In Dinah's domestic arrangements, "the rolling pin is under the bed and the nutmeg grater in her pocket with her tobacco—there are sixty-five different sugar bowls, one in every hole in the house" (1: 304); she "had about as many places for each cooking utensil as there were days in the year" (1: 297). This promiscuous housekeeping scandalizes the St. Clares' Northern cousin Ophelia, offending her domestic propriety as much as slavery disturbs her moral sense. Ophelia finds that Southerners not only neglect their "awful responsibility" for the souls of their slaves but also let their households operate "without any sort of calculation to time and place" (1: 255, 297). In Ophelia's New England home "the old kitchen floor never seems stained or spotted; the tables, chairs, and the various cooking utensils never seem deranged or disordered" (1: 227). There, "everything is once and forever rigidly in place" (1: 226).

In a vain attempt to remodel Dinah's kitchen in the New England style, Augustine St. Clare once installed "an array of cupboards, drawers, and various apparatus, to induce systematic regulation" (1: 298). But after discovering that "[t]he more drawers and closets there were, the more hiding-holes could Dinah make for the accommodation of old rags, hair-combs, old shoes, ribbons, cast-off artificial flowers, and other articles," St. Clare washed his hands of kitchen affairs (1: 298–99). As long as he need not view "the hurryscurryation of the preparatory process," he can enjoy Dinah's "glorious dinners" and "superb coffee." Dinah, St. Clare advises Ophelia, should be judged "as warriors and statesmen are judged, by her success." For St. Clare, the vital point is that "Dinah gets you a capital dinner" (1: 304). Just as he represses the unsavory aspects of his domestic economy, St. Clare prefers to ignore the problems of the state Dinah represents. Worrying about the evils of slavery, he warns Ophelia, is "like looking too close into the details of Dinah's kitchen" (2: 8).

But Ophelia cannot disregard slavery any more than she can dismiss kitchen details. As she tells St. Clare, "You would not take it so coolly if you were housekeeper" (1: 303). Although he rhetorically asserts the correspondence between Dinah's kitchen and the slave economy, St. Clare fails to recognize the intimacy between domestic and political issues, missing the lesson of his own effort at home improvement. He could not alter Dinah's kitchen because "[n]o Puseyite, or conservative of any school, was ever more inflexibly attached to time-honored inconvenience than Dinah" (1: 298). The time-honored inconvenience to which Dinah is attached is not merely backward kitchen technology but the political economy that enslaves her. Her habits manifest less her eccentricities than "the spirit of the system under which she had grown up"; Dinah simply "carried it out to its fullest extent" (1: 298). Neither redecorating Dinah's kitchen nor keeping it out of sight can satisfy good housekeeping standards, because kitchen problems cannot be remedied without reference to the system the kitchen articulates in its modes of household production. Housekeepers like Ophelia, whose business is knowing the causes and cures of domestic disorder, understand the political nature of Dinah's housekeeping and therefore recognize the political connection between Dinah's kitchen and slavery. Since kitchens both provide for families and display the systems of political economy with which domestic economy intersects, the responsible housekeeper observes the significance of kitchen things and seeks the best governing system for an orderly domesticity.[3]

What makes Dinah's imperious and "erratic" kitchen government incompatible with proper domestic economy is its reference to her desire rather than to a "systematic order" (1: 295–96). Dinah's kitchen runs by whim, its condition varying with her "irregular" moods, which "reigned supreme" (1: 302, 296). Though usually "studious of ease in all her arrangements" (1: 297), "she had, at irregular periods, paroxysms of reformation." But even these occasional reformatory "clarin' up times" can achieve no better domestic order than Dinah's laziness produces; her diligent as well as her dilatory phases enact a capricious personal economy instead of the "systematic pattern" that is necessary to Ophelia's efficient domestic economy (1: 302, 303). Indeed, the variable state of Dinah's kitchen exhibits the antithesis of domestic economy: the fluctuating marketplace. The reign of desires without "logic and reason" (1: 296) other than personal interest and the uncertainty it creates characterizes the market economy from which nineteenth-century domestic economy distinguished itself. Exponents of domesticity defined the home as a peaceful order in contrast to the disorder and fluctuations occasioned by competitive economic activity in the marketplace. "Our men are sufficiently money-making," Sarah Josepha Hale advised readers of the *Ladies Magazine*. "Let us keep our women and children from the contagion as long as possible."[4] The contagion of the market had already entered the Southern home where Ophelia finds desire and disorder—the impetus and pulse of the marketplace—in the kitchen.[5]

Slavery disregards this opposition between the family at home and the exterior workplace. The distinction between work and family is eradicated in the slave, for whom there is no separation between economic and private status. When people themselves are "articles" subject to "mercantile dealings," when "the souls and bodies of men" are "equivalent to money" (2: 317), women can no longer keep houses that provide a refuge from marketplace activities. Slavery, according to *Uncle Tom's Cabin,* undermines women's housework by bringing the confusion of the marketplace into the kitchen, the center of the family shelter. The real horror that slavery holds for the mothers of America to whom Stowe addressed her anti-slavery appeal is the suggestion that the family life nurtured by women is not immune to the economic life outside it.[6]

More than the tragedy of the slave mothers who "are constantly made childless by the American slave trade" (2: 316), the security of free white American mothers and the family institution they guard concerns Stowe. While the slave economy does not threaten American mothers with selling their children, it does limit their authority and efficacy when it creates households with "no time, no place, no order" (1: 304). In a home governed by Ophelia's exemplary New England domestic economy there is "nothing lost, or out of order; not a picket loose in the fence, not a particle of litter in the turfy yard." Instead of hurryscurryation, "the air of order and stillness, of perpetuity and unchanging repose," characterizes the model American home (1: 226). The Southern slave system produces what Ophelia terms "shiftlessness," haphazard "modes of procedure which had not a direct and inevitable relation to the accomplishment of some purpose." Dinah's shiftlessness, because it is indifferent to the carefulness and regulation necessary to the integrity of the home, appears "the sum of all evils" (1: 229).

In fashioning her abolitionist protest as a defense of nineteenth-century domestic values, Stowe designates slavery as a domestic issue for American women to adjudicate and manage. The call to the mothers of America for the abolition of slavery is a summons to fortify the home, to rescue domesticity from shiftlessness and slavery. Someone has to get in the kitchen with Dinah to eliminate hurryscurryation. The chaos in Dinah's kitchen signifies the immanence of the dissolution of domesticity's difference from the marketplace. Hence, in Stowe's politics of the kitchen, abolishing slavery means erasing the sign and reminder of the precariousness of the feminine sphere.

To read *Uncle Tom's Cabin* as Stowe's manifesto for family integrity is, of course, no twentieth-century innovation. Ever since George Sand noted in her 1852 review that "this book is essentially domestic and of the family," readers of *Uncle Tom's Cabin,* especially feminist readers, have continually noticed the novel's politicization of domesticity. In her history of literary women Ellen Moers reinforces this reading tradition, recognizing Stowe's anti-slavery appeal as "proudly and openly a woman's work" on behalf of "domestic polity." "Surely no other woman writer," Moers declares, "has ever recorded the rattle and clutter of domestic life . . . with such confidence that upon these female matters rested the central moral issue before the nation: slavery."[7]

Subsequent feminist responses to *Uncle Tom's Cabin* vary in their confidence as to whether the political reform of slavery could be established upon domestic principles. Ann Douglas believes that *Uncle Tom's Cabin* invokes the sentimental virtues of the home, which, in her view, "provided the inevitable rationalization of the economic order." The novel therefore "in no way hinders" the system of slavery it protests. Countering Douglas's characterization of popular sentimental literature as women's "dirty work" for the advancement of industrial capitalism, Jane Tompkins emphasizes sentimental literature's feminist critique and revision of American society. According to Tompkins, "the popular domestic novel of the nineteenth century represents a monumental effort to reorganize culture from woman's point of view," and "of these efforts *Uncle Tom's Cabin* is the most dazzling exemplar."[8] The domestic values celebrated by *Uncle Tom's Cabin* and popular domestic novels represent an alternative, moral, feminine organization of life which could radically reform American society.

Tompkins's account of sentimental power offers an important reevaluation of sentimentalism, reinstating the polemical force and literary merit of the novel which Douglas dismisses. But Tompkins's argument for *Uncle Tom's Cabin's* literary value as a "political enterprise" overlooks the fact that Stowe's polemic for a regenerating domesticity is a critique of conventional domestic ideology as well as an attack on slavery and the marketplace.[9] What makes *Uncle Tom's Cabin* a particularly striking domestic novel is that Stowe seeks to reform American society not by employing domestic values but by reforming them. The domestic ideology from which *Uncle Tom's Cabin* derives its reformative force is, when understood historically, a patriarchal institution. The novel addresses this relation between patriarchy and sentimental ideals by explicitly thematizing the intimacy and congress between economic and domestic endeavors, between market and kitchen systems. Therefore the domesticity Stowe advocates must be understood as a revision and purification of popular domestic values—domestic values which Stowe regards as complicit with the patriarchal institution of slavery. Stowe's domestic solution to slavery, then, represents not the strength of sentimental values but a utopian rehabilitation of them, necessitated by their fundamental complicity with the market to which they are ostensibly opposed.

The association of *Uncle Tom's Cabin* with the cult of domesticity is thus more complicated than feminist interpretations have yet suggested. Stowe's critique of American society is even more radical than Tompkins realizes, precisely because it addresses the problematic status of sentimental values noted by Douglas; that is, domestic ideology's "continuation of male hegemony in different guises."[10] In the chronology of Stowe's abolitionist argument the alliance between domestic and market values necessitates and occasions *Uncle Tom's Cabin*'s revisionary politics. It is because sentimental power is undermined by the fact that it incorporates the values it purports to supersede that Stowe calls for the reform of kitchens as a precondition to women's reform of market economy.

Good Housekeeping

"A living impersonation of order, method, and exactness" (1: 229), Ophelia embodies the ideal domestic economy delineated by Stowe's older sister Catharine Beecher in her popular 1841 *Treatise on Domestic Economy*.[11] Ophelia's service to "systematic regulation" (1: 304) exemplifies Beecher's dictum that "there is no one thing more necessary to a housekeeper, in performing her varied duties, than *a habit of system and order*" (*Treatise*, 144). If Ophelia is,

1. Kitchen Design. Catharine Beecher and Harriet Beecher Stowe, *The American Woman's Home*, 1869.

as Stowe describes her, "the absolute bond-slave of 'ought'" (1: 230), her mistress is Beecher and her housekeeping ethics derive from Beecher's systematic domestic economy. (See Beecher's kitchen design, Figure 1.) Under the slave economy's "shiftless management," Dinah "washes dishes with a dinner napkin one day and a fragment of an old petticoat the next" (1: 304). Beecher's advice on the care of kitchens specifies the materials Dinah ought to use: "Keep a supply of *nice* dishcloths hanging near the sink, hemmed and furnished with loops. There should be one for dishes that are not greasy, one for greasy dishes, and one for pots and kettles. These should all be put in the wash every washing day." Furthermore, "[u]nder the sink should be kept a slop-pail, and on a shelf, close by, should be placed two water-pails, one for hard and one for soft water. A large kettle of warm soft water should always be kept over the fire, and a hearth-broom and bellows be hung beside the fireplace. A clock, in or near the kitchen, is very important, to secure regularity in family arrangements" (*Treatise*, 367).

Beecher regards women's responsibility for "regularity in family arrangements" as a patriotic and religious duty. By performing their household tasks, or, in Beecher's political terms, sustaining "a prosperous domestic state," women become agents in accomplishing "the greatest work that was ever committed to human responsibility"—"the building of a glorious temple, whose base shall be co-extensive with the bounds of the earth, whose summit shall pierce the skies, whose splendor shall beam on all lands" (*Treatise*, 14). To Americans "is committed the grand, the responsible privilege, of exhibiting to the world, the beneficent influences of Christianity, when carried into every social, civil, and political institution"; and "then to American women, more than any others on earth, is committed the exalted privilege of extending over the world those blessed influences, that are to renovate degraded man, and clothe all climes with beauty" (*Treatise*, 12–13).

The manifest destiny of American women to domesticate and Christianize the world can be realized through the work they perform in their homes. Uniformity and neatness in the kitchen matter profoundly, since these habits create a standard of harmony for America. For Beecher, good housekeeping is a political practice and the home a model political province. Through maternal functions the boundaries of the domestic province expand to encompass the nation. As mothers, women determine the characters "of the mass of people" upon whom "the success of democratic institutions" depends. "The mother writes the character of the future man; the sister bends the fibres that hereafter are the forest trees; the wife sways the heart whose energies may turn for good or evil the destinies of a nation" (*Treatise*, 13). Maternal influence travels with every individual, and in America, where individuals moved often and extensively, socially and geographically, maternal power held sway over a limitless domain.

Stowe includes the Southern states in the limitless domain of mothers and housekeepers, for "south as well as north, there are women who have an extraordinary talent for command, and tact in educating" (1: 295). She imagines a Southern domestic order in keeping with Beecher's household economy on the Shelby Kentucky plantation. Mrs. Shelby belongs to the superior class of housekeepers Beecher envisions. Such women "are enabled with apparent ease . . . to produce a harmonious and orderly system." If such housekeepers "are not common at [*sic*] the South, it is because they are not common in the world" (1: 295). The Kentucky home seems a standard of domestic excellence; it becomes both the memory of home Uncle Tom cherishes and an Edenic image. In front of Tom's cabin on the Shelby plantation "a neat garden patch" with "strawberries, raspberries, and a variety of fruits and vegetables, flourished under careful tending." The garden enveloped the cabin; its begonias and roses, "entwisting and interlacing, left scarce a vestige of the rough logs to be seen" (1: 38).

Slavery, the snake in the garden, compromises this Edenic home. Topsy, during her religious instruction from Ophelia, inquires if "dat state" our first parents "fell out of" was "Kintuck" where "we came down from" (2: 51). Topsy's ironic confusion of words and origins emphasizes the conditionality of the happy system of the Shelby housekeeping. Kentucky is lost not just to Tom but to domesticity, because the slave economy always subjects the home and family to market contingencies. Although Tom's wife, Chloe, the Shelby plantation cook, "was a trained and methodical one, who moved in orderly domestic harness," in the best Beecher tradition, neither her "anxious interest" in kitchen preparations nor Mrs. Shelby's tactful supervision can prevent the sale of Tom (1: 296). Even the order of the best housekeeper is precarious in the slave economy; the "kindest owner" is subject to "failure, misfortune, or imprudence, or death" (1: 24). When Mr. Shelby needs to make mortgage payments he sells Tom, along with Eliza's son Harry. This failure of domestic practices to sustain both black family unity and the white mistress's authority points not only to the slave economy's disregard of domestic values but to domesticity's dependence on the whims of whatever economic practice it adjoins.

Beecher explicitly sought the conjunction of domestic economy with American economic advancement that so worries Stowe in *Uncle Tom's Cabin*. Their brother, Henry Ward Beecher, preached that "[t]he spirit of our people, and, I think, God may say *the public spirit of the world,* is for amelioration, and expansion and social change."[12] Catharine perceived that social change included negative as well as positive effects, noting that "[p]ersons in poverty, are rising to opulence, and persons of wealth, are sinking to poverty" (*Treatise,* 16). As Henry proffered a religious rationale to his upwardly mobile Brooklyn parishioners, Catharine advanced an ideology of womanhood that also matched the expanding economy and the changing fortunes of individuals.[13] For her definition of women's role in America, she appropriated Tocqueville's observation that "American women support these vicissitudes with a calm and unquenchable energy" (*Treatise,* 23). In a country where "[e]verything is moving and changing," the virtue of women lies in their ability to harmonize with fluctuations; as Beecher again cites Tocqueville, "It would seem their desires contract, as easily as they expand" with the changing fortunes of their husbands (*Treatise,* 23). Because women's desires always mirror the effects of masculine ones—they expand with economic gains and contract with economic losses—women embody a model of stability achieved through complete self-denial. In Beecher's domestic economy, women's exemplary self-denial perfectly complements the economy in which their men work.[14]

Stowe's portrait of an old Kentucky home discloses the problem with this complementary alliance: the very market conditions Beecher's domestic economy supports can render domestic efforts irrelevant. If good housekeeping under slavery protects the home only so long as market circumstances permit, then domesticity's influence in Northern capitalist society is likewise limited. As long as the marketplace, of which the slave trade is the worst version, exists, the domestic sphere remains vulnerable. Stowe's worry about the dangers of capitalism to family values echoes slavery advocate George Fitzhugh's belief that "[t]he Family is threatened, and all men North or South who love and revere it, should be up and a-doing."[15] In the minds of slavery apologists, the North failed in its parental responsibility for its wage laborers; slave labor power offered a more truly familial and stable society than the diffuse, precarious lifestyle produced by the money power of Northern capitalism. Slave power signified to abolitionists similarly chaotic, undisciplined living conditions. Slave-masters like Simon Legree exemplified the extremes of capitalistic masculine self-advancement when not domesticated and regulated in a wage-labor system. Stowe, anxious about the dehumanization she discerned in both systems, originally subtitled her novel "The Man That Was a Thing."[16]

But the critique in *Uncle Tom's Cabin* of antebellum America also questions what the slavery debate took for granted: the character of domesticity. Nineteenth-century advocates of domestic values assumed the integrity of the family state, believing the home to be inviolate from the marketplace.[17] Indeed, the home was to reform the marketplace; as Beecher put it, the purpose of women's housework was "to be made effectual in the regeneration of the Earth" (*Treatise,* 14). The rhetoric of feminine difference and spiritual mission in which Beecher presented her domestic economy concealed the cooperative, accommodating function of domesticity revealed by Stowe in the insufficiency of the Shelby housekeeping. Domesticity's applicability to both slave and capitalist economies causes Stowe uneasiness about the virtues of domesticity as a replacement economy. Domesticity itself requires reformation.

The ultimate adversary to mothers and housekeepers is not slavery, not even capitalism, but the masculine sphere of the marketplace. The most effective way to save the home from the marketplace, to prevent domesticity from consorting with either slave power or money power, is to abolish the marketplace altogether. In the name of domesticity, *Uncle Tom's Cabin* attacks not only the patriarchal institution but nineteenth-century patriarchy, not only slave-traders but the system and men who maintain "the one great market" upon which trade depends (1: 109).

Stowe recognized the power for women in the alliance her sister forged, but she also perceived the limits of women's power in a patriarchal domesticity. She sought a more radical and extensive power, to be obtained through the replacement of the market economy by a matriarchal domestic economy.[18] *Uncle Tom's Cabin* revises Beecher's domesticity, disjoining it from patriarchal economic practices and severing it from service to any institution other than itself. Instead of ensuring industrial capitalism and supporting the government that passed the Fugitive Slave Law, the domestic might constitute an alternative system: an economy of abundant mother-love built on an excess of supply rather than the excess of demand and desire upon which both the slave economy and Northern capitalism operated. *Uncle Tom's Cabin* perfects and ensures domesticity in matriarchy. Mothers and mother figures initiate escapes from slavery and determine family safety. As domesticity becomes for Stowe a feminist deployment of nineteenth-century femininity, housekeeping in *Uncle Tom's Cabin* becomes not merely politically significant but a political mode, not representative of any economic order but itself an economic order.

Women and Politics

The ideal kitchen in *Uncle Tom's Cabin* functions smoothly under the aegis of "motherly loving kindness" (1: 196). Rachel Halliday's kitchen in the Indiana Quaker settlement that shelters runaway slaves is, like Ophelia's, "without a particle of dust"; but more than orderliness, its "rows of shining tins, suggestive of unmentionable good things to the appetite," indicate the value of abundance and generosity in Stowe's utopian domestic economy (1: 195). Ophelia, Stowe explains in her *Key to Uncle Tom's Cabin,* despite her "activity, zeal, unflinching conscientiousness, clear intellectual discriminations between truth and error, and great logical and doctrinal correctness," "represents one great sin": the lack of the Christian "spirit of love."[19] Rachel embodies and dispenses that spirit of love, "diffusing a sort of sunny radiance" over meal preparations. Making breakfast under Rachel's supervision is "like picking up the rose-leaves and trimming the bushes in Paradise," a vision of perfect, happy labor (1: 204). "There was so much motherliness and full-heartedness even in the way she passed a plate of cakes or poured a cup of coffee, that it seemed to put a spirit into the food and drink she offered" (1: 205). Rachel's domestic acts appear sacramental, her meals a communion reminiscent of Edenic unity:

Everything went on so sociably, so quietly, so harmoniously, in the great kichen,—it seemed so pleasant to everyone to do just what they were doing, there was such an atmosphere of mutual confidence and good-fellowship everywhere,—even the knives and forks had a social clatter as they went on the table; and the chicken and ham had a cheerful and joyous fizzle in the pan, as if they enjoyed being cooked. (1: 205)

The spirit of mother-love creates a domesticity in the image of paradise: a world before separations, a domestic economy before markets.

Eliza, Harry, and George Harris, the runaway slaves reunited in the Halliday sentimental utopia, discover that "[t]his, indeed, was a home,—*home*—a word that [they] had never yet known a meaning for" (1: 205). Rachel's "simple, overflowing kindness" defines the perfect home, and that kindness includes helping runaway slaves. This defiance of the Fugitive Slave Law demonstrates the commitment of the Quaker community to God's love and familial feeling over man's law. In Rachel's kitchen the boys and girls share domestic duties under their mother's guidance while their father engages in "the anti-patriarchal operation of shaving" (1: 205). Godlike mothers generate and rule this family state by their love. In Stowe's model home, domesticity is matriarchal and antinomian, a new form of government as well as a protest against patriarchy and its manifestations in slavery, capitalism, and democracy. Her domestic advice carries an addendum to the household practices Beecher assigned to women: the duty of women to oppose slavery and the law that upholds it. "It's a shameful, wicked, abominable law," Mrs. Bird, another concerned housekeeper in *Uncle Tom's Cabin,* tells her senator husband, "and I shall break it, the first time I get a chance" (1: 121). She gets her chance when Eliza collapses in the Bird kitchen after she escapes from

Kentucky by crossing the frozen Ohio River. *Uncle Tom's Cabin* politicizes women's domestic role at the very moment of sentimentalizing that role, urging women to stop slavery, in the name of love. Love and protest, maternal duty and political action, compose Stowe's reformulated domestic virtue.

According to domestic logic, women were naturally suited to participate in the anti-slavery movement. As Stowe wrote in her "Appeal to the Women of the Free States of America on the Present Crisis in Our Country," "God has given to women a deeper and more immovable knowledge in those holier feelings which are peculiar to womanhood, and which guard the family state."[20] The public practice of this moral gift seems to follow inevitably from Beecher's assumption of women's moral role in democracy. Yet Beecher, though opposed to slavery, could not support women's participation in political agitation. In her "Essay on Slavery and Abolition with Respect to the Duties of American Females," she argues that the abolition movement draws women away from the noncombative sphere designed for them in "the Divine Economy." Instead, women are "to win everything by peace and love . . . this is all to be accomplished in the domestic and social circle." "In this country, petitions to Congress . . . fall entirely without the sphere of female duty."[21] Women's political activism would be a fall from domestic purity, and hence from domestic power and its superior political influence through self-subordination and moral exemplification. While Beecher could never condone slavery, she also could never depart from patriarchal law in order to abolish a paternalistic institution.

Abolitionists and domestic feminists were quick to grasp the inconsistency of an ideology of feminine virtue that precluded the exercise of that virtue. In reply to Beecher, Quaker activist Angelina Grimke published a series of public letters in which she objected that Beecher's injunction to women to abide by the law and to stay within their own sphere meant *"Obeying man* rather than God." If women do not voice their opinions to their representatives in Congress, "they are mere slaves known only through their masters."[22] Grimke here interprets the passivity of women in politics as slavery; in another pamphlet, "Appeal to the Christian

Women of the South," she accords Southern women familial responsibility for the abolition of slavery. Women "do not make the
laws," but they "are the wives and mothers, sisters and daughters
of those who do."[23] Angelina's older sister Sarah puts the case more
strongly: the Southern white woman who lives daily with the slave
system suffers moral contamination by witnessing the continual
violation of her black sisters. "Can any American woman look at
these scenes of shocking licentiousness and cruelty, and fold her
hands in apathy, and say 'I have nothing to do with slavery'? *She
cannot and be guiltless.*"[24] The passive, apathetic woman is both a
slave and a slave-mistress, degraded and degrading. In the Grimkes'
analysis, Southern domesticity not only fails to create a peaceful
home environment but lowers the status of white women.[25] From
this realization follows their rejection of the limits of the domestic
sphere and their commitment to women's rights.[26]

Contemporary activist women such as Elizabeth Cady Stanton
and Susan B. Anthony also discerned the bonds of patriarchal
domesticity in the patriarchal institution and thus defined abolition
as a feminist cause. After the Civil War, Stanton supervised the
rewriting of the Bible from women's point of view in order to
counter the Christian domestic tradition of encouraging women's
self-sacrifice and obedience to patriarchal authority. Stanton regularly introduced anti-Bible resolutions at suffrage conventions,
prompting former slave Frederick Douglass on one occasion to
defend self-sacrifice. Feminist Lucy Coleman immediately addressed the discrepancy between self-denial and the quest for freedom: "Well, Mr. Douglass, all you say may be true; but allow me
to ask you why you did not remain a slave in Maryland, and
sacrifice yourself like a Christian for your Master, instead of running off to Canada to secure your liberty like a man?"[27]

While Stowe also propounds the feminist-abolitionist critique
of domesticity and slavery, she does not reject Christian self-
sacrifice as an effective reformist mode. Because Stowe regards
self-denial as political, she celebrates in the deaths of Little Eva and
Uncle Tom the very self-abnegation Stanton and Coleman de-
nounce. In her own biblical commentary, *Woman in Sacred History,*
Stowe praises "that pure ideal of a sacred woman springing from

the bosom of the family, at once wife, mother, poetess, leader, inspirer, prophetess."[28] This notion of femininity as maternal, literary, political, and mystical conjoins domestic and feminist values, incorporating both self-denial and self-assertion in the ideal woman. *Uncle Tom's Cabin* retains the Christian domestic tenet of feminine self-abnegation in order to elaborate a maternal power commensurate to the task of abolishing slavery. The novel presents Beecher's triad of maternal virtues in specifically Christian terms: self-denial as martyrdom, exemplification as typology, household unity as eternal life. Little Eva is saintlike, Uncle Tom is Christlike; homes are heavenly and family reunions are eschatological. This religious interpretation of ideal maternal practices merges motherhood with Christianity. The self-sacrifice of women or slaves, then, signifies redemption and eternal life. *Uncle Tom's Cabin* allies this conventional feminine mode with the civil disobedience of Rachel and Mrs. Bird and the dramatic escapes from slavery, first by Eliza and then by Cassy, that comprise the activist female model Stowe proposes. For Stowe, domestic self-denial and feminist self-seeking can be complementary manners. The debate between Beecher and the Grimkes that Coleman and Douglass rehearsed is irrelevant to Stowe because for her maternal power manifests itself in both sacrifice and rebellion, temporality and eternity.

In Stowe's abolitionism, domestic conventions work in two directions, simultaneously pointing to the sentimental solution of the afterlife in heaven and to a radical plan of immediate action to secure better temporal conditions. Tom and Eva die in set pieces that memorialize their Christian virtues; Eliza, Harry, George, and Cassy rebel and escape to Canada in a dramatic and often melodramatic narrative that affirms the necessity of active protest. Stowe's application of sentimental and feminist styles of belief and practice demonstrates the contradictory position in which domesticity places women by regarding them simultaneously as the embodiment of transcendent principles and as the primary support of the social system. She resolves this contradiction by interpreting the identification of femininity with ideal values as women's access to critical, subversive stances. Feminine virtue establishes the feminine vantage on social revision. Mrs. Bird's maternal feelings motivate and justify her critique of slavery and the laws that bolster it. The realization of the potential power of motherhood and the arrival of woman as a revisionary social critic—as "mother, poetess, leader, inspirer, prophetess"—depend on the full exercise of what Stowe called women's faculty. Faculty, Stowe explains in her fictional portrait of Catharine Beecher in *The Minister's Wooing,* is the New England term for savoir faire and refers specifically to domestic economy and household talents: "To her who has faculty, nothing shall be impossible."[29]

In order to politicize her readers, Stowe assumes the role her sister prescribed. *Uncle Tom's Cabin* urges a departure from the passivity assigned women by culture, a departure which is also a return home, to the ideal matriarchal home. The book's household angel, Eva, dies and returns to heaven. Killing the Angel in the House means for Stowe the apotheosis of the angelic, domestic tradition of femininity—both the finish of patriarchal domesticity and the ascension of maternal power. Virginia Woolf's observation on the need of women writers to destroy the images and characteristics of domestic femininity foisted upon them by social tradition becomes inverted here to signify a literary act empowered by and empowering domesticity. Stowe's domestic feminism reconstructs the family, retaining the Angel in the House and revising history under her aegis. Abolition in *Uncle Tom's Cabin* is accordingly conveyed and understood through mothers.

Maternal Economy

Mrs. Shelby, upon learning of her husband's sale of Tom and Harry, immediately perceives the violation of her domestic values; she wonders how, after teaching her slaves "the duties of the family," she can "bear to have this open acknowledgement that we care for no tie, no duty, no relation, however sacred, compared with money?" (1: 57). When Mr. Shelby admonishes her for feeling "too much" about their slaves, Mrs. Shelby asserts the predominance of the emotions of the heart over the masculine economics of the mind: "Feel too much! Am I not a woman,—a mother?" (1: 110). Her sentiments echo the thought of an 1836 anti-slavery speech that declared abolitionism an inherent maternal trait. "A woman not an abolitionist! No. This truth has a lodgement in the heart of every female that understands it, and deserves the name of a mother and a wife."[30] Shelby exasperatedly notes that his wife is "getting to be an abolitionist" (1: 58). He respects her "piety and benevolence," and even indulges "a shadowy expectation of getting into heaven through her superabundance of qualities" (1: 26), but insists that she doesn't "understand business;—women never do and never can" (2: 54). She cannot help him economize because "there's no trimming and squaring" his business affairs as if they were "pie crusts." Consistent with Shelby's disregard of domestic ideals, the state of his business is, like Dinah's kitchen, "all scamper and hurry-scurry" (2: 54).

In place of this chaotic, hurry-scurry masculine economy in which slaves are sold to pay their master's debts, Stowe urges the "harmonious and systematic order" (1: 295) created by Mrs. Shelby's "high moral and religious sensibility and principle" (1: 26). Women offer a preserving rather than a desiring version of economics, family protection rather than ventures endangering family stability. Ophelia, with the efficiency and diligence typical of her housekeeping, demands a legal deed for her possession of Topsy so that she can "save her from all the chances and reverses of slavery" (2: 137). Stowe's domesticity, then, ideally functions as an alternative to the slave-holding economy, not as a congruent, affirmative practice, but as a different ethic of possession.

Stowe's rejection of the masculine political economy finds its most explicit and emphatic expression in George Harris's renunciation of America and filial duty to its laws: "I haven't any country, any more than I have a father." When commanded by his master to forget his marriage to Eliza and to cohabit with another slave woman, George runs away to Canada, "where the laws will own . . . and protect" him (1: 167). He wants the familial structure he has been denied since childhood, the company of the mother and sisters from whom he was separated. Despising the values of his white male ancestry, George chooses the feminine economy of mother-love: "My sympathies are not for my father's race, but for my mother's. To him I was no more than a fine dog or horse: to my poor heart-broken mother I was a *child*" (2: 299–300). To defend the familial relation, the rights of women as it were, George seeks another country.

George's final decision to emigrate with his reunited family to Liberia bespeaks the hope that blacks might form a republic and nationality of their own and restates the ideals of the American family. Like women, blacks are "affectionate, magnanimous, and forgiving." The "mission" of the new republic of freed slaves is, like domesticity, "essentially a Christian one": "to spread over the continent of Africa" the "sublime doctrine of love and forgiveness" (2: 302–3). While the emigration of American blacks might suggest a convenient solution to white fears about the possible retribution of freed blacks, Stowe's imagination of "this new enterprise" articulates less about fears of blacks than about fear of men (2: 301). Stowe's transplantation of heroic blacks such as George and Eliza to Liberia colonizes Africa for domesticity. American men have no part in this enterprise. To feminize the world, Stowe banishes from the future all men of business such as Shelby and Legree and the slave traders. In Stowe's utopian world after slavery and markets, the men who live, and those who are reverently remembered, support domestic values.[31] The Shelby son frees his slaves to save them from "the risk of being parted from home" (2: 309); Uncle Tom preaches Christian virtues; George Harris restores his family. The removal of masculine economic desire through the disappearance of slave-masters is the necessary condition for the ascendance of domestic economy.

Stowe's domestic economy interprets the Beecher tenet of self-denial as women's independence from desire and from their mirroring function for masculine desire. Domesticity imbues femininity with the "superabundance of qualities" Mrs. Shelby exhibits in her benevolence. This feminine virtue forms the foundation of a feminine economy that redefines the notion of possession. Women's plenitude obviates desire. The celebrated stillness of nineteenth-century women is thus neither a hysterical renunciation of life in order to register their complaint against women's prescribed role in society, nor a historical condition summarizing the effect of women's exclusion from executive power in their society, but an annunciation of women's self-sufficiency and a claim to their immunity from desire.[32] The lack of desire reflects the imagined state of possession, that is, the condition of satiety and fulfillment, the goal of the pursuit of happiness. The nondesiring woman is therefore the embodiment of perfect ownership. In her self-sufficiency she escapes the fluctuations attendant upon desire and achieves the ideal of the masculine economy: complete self-possession and satisfaction. In Stowe's domestic logic of possession it becomes possible to own without having desired.

Stowe's divorce of desire from possession militates against conditions of insufficiency or incompletion. She perfects ownership by nullifying desire, the sign of the temporality of ownership. Process and its disorders disappear in the best of New England kitchens, where "nothing ever seems to be doing or going to be done." "In some silent and mysterious manner" "the family washing and ironing is there performed" and "pounds of butter and cheese there brought into existence" (1: 226–27). In the Edenic order and abundance of Rachel's kitchen "the work of getting breakfast" is so "cheerful" and harmonious that domestic labor already represents the stillness and satiety to which it is directed.

Stowe replaces the master-slave relation with the benign proprietorship of mother-child, transferring the ownership of slaves to the mothers of America. Women prefer familial ties to market relations, caring for the welfare of their dependents—children and slaves—rather than for the profits wrought from them. In Stowe's matriarchal society, slaves are synonymous with children because they lack title to themselves and need abolitionist guardianship—which is to say, maternal aid. Maternal supervision, the ideal form of owning in Stowe's reformed property relations, follows the pattern of divine care. "One good, loving woman" like Rachel can solve "difficulties spiritual and temporal" just as God's superabundant love fills the needs of humanity (1: 197). Uncle Tom wants not emancipation but this protective ownership: "the Lord's bought me and is going to take me home,—and I long to go. Heaven is better than Kintuck" (2: 280). By imitating God's parental economy, mothers approximate heaven in their homes.

Stowe's identification, in her model of domestic economy, of maternal power with God rejects any aspiration to ownership beyond the motherly functions of reproduction and preservation, suggesting an economy without markets and a life devoid of the problems caused by masculine desire. She fittingly situates this utopian life in heaven, the home to which Tom and Eva happily return. Tom dies uttering his longing to go home to heaven where there is "nothing *but* love!" (2: 281). The child Eva also experiences intimations of immortality as domestic bliss; she has visions of heaven's landscape and she knows she is going home to "our Saviour's home" (2: 88). Eva's father's death, entitled "Reunion," likewise brings him home: "Just before the spirit parted, he opened his eyes, with a sudden light, as of joy and recognition, and said '*Mother*' and then he was gone!" (2: 143). Eliza, just before reuniting with her husband, dreams of a heavenlike place, "a beautiful country, a land, it seemed to her, of rest, . . . and there, in a house kind voices told her was a home, she saw her boy playing, a free and happy child" (1: 203–4). She awakes in the next best place to heaven, Rachel's home. The designation in *Uncle Tom's Cabin* of heaven as home implies a return to maternal bonds; this also implies a mother God, even though Stowe retains the traditional name of God the father.

Death or some form of escape enables homecomings and family reunions. As much as divine love and maternal care, death generates the domestic economy that maintains family unity. Eva's death epitomizes loving self-sacrifice for the family. As she tells Tom, she is "glad to die" to "stop all this misery" of slavery (2: 88). She exemplifies her father's observation that "[y]our child is your only true democrat" (1: 257) and the popular theme in anti-slavery literature that "[c]hildren are all born abolitionists."[33] Named for St. Clare's saintly mother, Evangeline, Eva emblemizes the virtues of motherhood as well as those of childhood. Indeed, Eva is the child who is mother to the woman, Stowe's ideal of feminine potential, an angel. Ophelia realizes that Eva "might teach [her] a lesson" in loving Topsy (2: 95). Tom recognizes Eva as "one of the angels stepped out of his New Testament" (1: 213). The domestic pieties popularized by Beecher and domestic novelists culminate in Eva's redemptive death for the sins of slavery.[34]

In Stowe's abolitionist employment of sentimental motifs, death recreates the family by sheltering it in heavenly matriarchy. Families in *Uncle Tom's Cabin* begin not in the transmission of paternal traditions but in the separation from patriarchal origin. Mothers, or God, heal the rupture; they restore and reconstitute the family away from the fallen world. Dying therefore becomes the ultimate domestic act in this book of many domestic activities. Such detemporalization of slavery and femininity seems to ignore or sentimentalize the problem of social injustice by opting for the rewards of the next world; however, Stowe returns from the myth of heaven to the myth of Sisyphus, to the problem of human efforts.

Revolt of the Mothers

The landscape of Simon Legree's plantation, the last Southern residence Stowe describes, seems more foreign and fantastic than heaven because it is completely nondomestic, unkempt, and un-governed.

What was once a smooth-shaven lawn before the house, dotted here and there with ornamental shrubs, was now covered with frowsy tangled grass . . . littered with broken pails, cobs of corn, and other slovenly remains. . . . What was once a large garden was now all grown over with weeds, through which, here and there, some solitary exotic raised its forsaken head. (2: 179)

Here Tom meets Cassy, the slave woman with plans for freedom that do not involve martyrdom. Very much an actress in human affairs rather than divine or supernatural ones, Cassy confronts the issue of how to find temporal power in femininity and slavery. Cassy, kept for the pleasure of her various owners, signifies the other side of domesticity or, rather, life without the romance and virtue of domesticity. In contrast to the ideals of family unity and redemptive death embodied in Mrs. Shelby, Eliza, Rachel, and Eva, Cassy's experience dramatizes the condition of domestic violation unrelieved by Christian hope, a darker version of Eliza's plight.

Cassy's life is a textbook on domestic violation: she has lost her children to the slave trade and her sexual integrity to her various masters. She has even murdered her last child in order to prevent another separation and loss. In this act Cassy proves the destructive maternal capability that figures alongside maternal generativity in Stowe's abolitionist deployment of femininity. The possibility for murder as well as nurture inheres in the maternal power Stowe advocates as a humane alternative to Northern money power and Southern slave power. Cassy represents outraged domesticity; violated by slavery, she protects her child from slavery by her own violence. Once called "a good angel" by her first master, Cassy now evokes from Legree the epithet "she-devil" (2: 208, 214). But if a fallen angel, Cassy nonetheless recalls motherly feeling; she ministers to Tom after his beatings and she protects Emmeline, Legree's newest concubine. Stowe describes Cassy, like Eva, as always gliding in her movements and working "by magic" (2: 193). In Cassy, however, unworldliness bespeaks madness, not spirituality.

Legree interprets this insanity as deviltry, a force in opposition to himself, "for Cassy had an influence over him from which he could not free himself" (2: 215). Cassy's deviltry intimidates Legree because of his susceptibility to superstition; and as Stowe observes, "No one is so thoroughly superstitious as the godless man. . . . Life and death to him are haunted grounds, filled with goblin forms of vague and shadowy dread" (2: 256). The structure of superstition and madness in which Legree and Cassy live houses the ramifications of the lack of faith. In this house that is not a home, the prevalent feature is the absence of domesticity and maternal influence. There does not even appear to be a kitchen. Legree's superstition derives from his rejection of his mother's love. Maternal absence haunts him with a continual fear of maternal presence; "That pale, loving mother,—her dying prayers, her forgiving love,—wrought in that demoniac heart of sin only as a damning sentence, bringing with it a fearful looking for of judgment and fiery indignation" (2: 218).

Legree's fear that "the form of his dead mother should suddenly appear to him" (an inversion of Tom's joyful visions of Eva in heaven) reveals the power of motherhood, which without belief in goodness seems witchery (2: 220). Legree's mother had left him a lock of her hair as a deathbed blessing; Legree burnt the hair, yet believes it has rematerialized when he discovers in Tom's belongings Eva's farewell token, a golden curl.[35] Legree's immersion in such Gothic phenomena signifies life without motherly influence, which is equivalent to life without God. This absolute bastardy marks the homelessness of both the slave and the slave-master.

Cassy's alienation and insanity, "the strange, weird, unsettled cast to all her words and language," articulate the suppression of maternal feeling rather than the absence of mother and replacement of mother with devil experienced by Legree (2: 257). Cassy finally asserts her motherliness in her flight with Emmeline to the North, where she reunites with her daughter Eliza. To effect this escape she poses as the ghost of Legree's mother and thus symbolically dies for freedom. A strategic and pragmatic imitation of Little Eva occurs: a woman's death which is not a death but a return of the mother, the mother of Legree and the mother in Cassy. Cassy's theatrics explore women's subversive possibilities, illustrating "that the most brutal man cannot live in constant association with a strong female influence, and not be greatly controlled by it" (2: 257). Cassy and the memory of Mrs. Legree so radically control Legree that Cassy's ghostly impersonation of his mother scares him into a fatal drinking bout. The redemptive, generous motherhood of ideal domesticity is here transformed to a murderous maternity in service to Stowe's activist feminine program for abolition.

Through Cassy's stratagem, Stowe instructs women to exploit their idealized status: to domesticate and literalize their spirituality, to enact Eva's saintly mission by taking immediate abolitionist action. Stowe certainly did not expect her readers to perform either Eva's martyrdom or Cassy's murder. In her letter to Gamaliel Bailey, editor of the *National Era,* announcing the plan for the serial *Uncle Tom's Cabin,* Stowe wrote, "[T]he time is come when even a woman or child who can speak a word for freedom and humanity is bound to speak." She hoped in particular that "every woman who can write will not be silent." The situation of America in 1851 reminded Stowe of the Carthaginian women who "in the last peril of their state cut off their hair for bowstrings to give to the defenders of their country."[36] Simon Legree's mother bestowed her hair for the reformation of her son; this maternal cord of sustenance enslaves him to his superstitions, chains him to drink—the nineteenth-century sign of the homeless—and finally destroys him. *Uncle Tom's Cabin* urges that all women, like Cassy, pull their strings.

Emancipation waited another decade after *Uncle Tom's Cabin,* and Stowe's grandniece Charlotte Perkins Gilman was still designing matriarchal utopias in the early twentieth century.[37] Yet these facts, instead of qualifying the influence of the novel, attest to the scope and ambitiousness of Stowe's domestic project. *Uncle Tom's Cabin* reinterprets domesticity as a double agentry in which women simultaneously act within society as its exemplars (Mrs. Shelby, Eva) and at the boundaries of society as its critics and revolutionaries (Rachel, Mrs. Bird, Cassy). Stowe envisions the revolt of the mother: the imaginative emergence of repressed feminine potential, what we might call the gothicization of the sentimental mode, the transformation of Eva into Cassy. Domestic traditions culminate in Cassy as well as in Eva; homemakers and housekeepers evolve into activists when their sustaining convention, the integrity of women and their homes, is threatened. In immediate political terms this means the enlistment of mothers in the abolitionist movement. Once it is enforced by powerful institutions—the presidency, Congress, the army, and domesticity—abolition takes effect. Stowe's larger goal, the advent of mother-rule, requires a feminized world and domestic economy, the post-patriarchy of Liberia or a reformed America. The consolidation of domestic hegemony relies on the acceptance of Stowe's proposition that patriarchy be replaced with matriarchy for the good of the family.

Stowe's utopia of family unity awaits, then, not an afterlife at the end of conventions, but its own conventionality. The institutionalization of Stowe's domesticity is obviously a more problem-

atic matter than abolition, because it involves the erasure of masculinity. For familial peace, a piece of maternal love, of heavenly
property, men as we know them cannot exist. Men must become
like women, dedicated to the family and detached from the desire
that constitutes marketplaces. In the Quaker community that exhibits Stowe's domestic economy of mother-love, the men, in an
"anti-patriarchal" gesture, shave their beards and subordinate the
laws of men to the laws of God and mothers.[38] *Uncle Tom's Cabin*
sacrifices the beards of the fathers, the slave-masters, and the un-
regenerate sons to the history of a matriarchal family. Stowe seeks
to weave a new civilization with the female hair that can alternately protect and terrify.

But the fact that Stowe retains the name of the male God
throughout her matriarchal design suggests that her imagination
of a feminized world still requires the sanction of male authority,
or at least of the modes associated with masculine power. Her
utopian female dominion seems uncannily familiar, not only because it invokes popular domestic ideals, but because it resembles
masculine practices of power. Stowe borrows from patriarchal
authority the prerogative of dispatching human destinies, the same
prerogative exercised by men and slave-masters. Finally, violence
in *Uncle Tom's Cabin* not only is executed by the slave economy
and masculine desire that endanger the family and home but is
embedded in the very foundation of the home. For Stowe, only a
house divided, a house divested of men, markets, and desire, can
be a home.

Chapter Two

Sentimental
Possession

Turning nineteenth-century American political economy inside
out, *Uncle Tom's Cabin* finds the lineaments of a matriarchal domestic economy in the seams of mother-love binding the patriarchal family.[1] The common thread running through these economies joins the sentimental property relations Stowe envisions to
a long-standing association of entitlement with property. That
Stowe retains the proprietorial imperatives of the masculine political economy she would replace indicates the continuity of her
domestic reformations with the liberal theory of freedom and
equality.

The sentimental power *Uncle Tom's Cabin* marshals against slavery invokes the liberal tradition of possessive individualism, in
which individual rights are grounded in the principle of self-
ownership.[2] Following this tradition of entitlement that underlies
the establishment of American democracy, Stowe identifies abolition with property relations, with sympathetic familial bonds.
Her abolitionist domestic economy advances a feminized ethic of
possession: the rights of blacks are secured in the sentimental
property relations she envisions. The movement from slavery to
freedom appears in Stowe's vision as the process of reclassifying
market articles as familiar objects, followed by another reclassifi-
cation in which whites and colors are sorted and finally neatly
separated. It is in this refinement of possessive individualism that

the power and limitations of *Uncle Tom's Cabin* and Stowe's matriarchal family state become most clear.

The sentimental accents that Stowe places on ownership stress
a domestic and maternal organization of the dynamic of possession, which she advances as an alternative to slavery. Under this
accentuation, the concept of possession takes on affective dimensions: in addition to denoting ownership and the owned object (or
property), possession encompasses the states of being possessed
and of being propertied—what might be considered the inspira-
tion with which ownership invests its objects, and with which
objects invest their owners. Elaborating the investment logic of
possessive individualism, Stowe develops an aesthetics of property relations that proves to be as characteristic of a certain racism
as it is of abolitionism.

Sentimental Things

At the end of *Uncle Tom's Cabin,* Stowe counsels her readers to
redress the wrongs of slavery; in this effort there is one crucial
thing "that every individual can do,—they can see to it that *they
feel right*" (2: 317). Stowe links her domestic politics to a sentimental aesthetics in which the right feeling inheres in a nurturing
attitude toward one's possessions and responsibilities. This careful
proprietorship characterizes the exemplary maternity that Stowe
proposes as a corrective to the slave economy. Thus Tom's mistress, Mrs. Shelby, is described as "getting to be an abolitionist"
when she feels what her husband deems "too much" about their
slaves (1: 58). The sale of Tom undermines her own maternal and
benevolent treatment of slaves, her teaching of "the duties of families" to them (1: 110). Maternity as a model for a different system
of possession is embodied most notably in Rachel Halliday, whose
"motherliness and full-heartedness" offer a home to runaway
slaves, whose domestic economy is so filled with "the spirit of
love" that "it seemed to put a spirit into the food and drink." Not
only slaves but the very household items such as the food that
enjoys "being cooked" in Rachel's kitchen seem happily enthralled
by her "over-flowing kindness" (1: 204–5).

Good motherhood and good housekeeping manifest the proper relation between caretakers and their charges, whether households, children, or slaves. Thus, Stowe's abolitionist protest against the trade in human beings which separates and destroys families opposes not so much the proposition that humans are things, but the fact that they are treated as transferable, as commodities.[3] Stowe does not abrogate but domesticates property and possessions; she takes what she perceives as the affective life of property and tries to isolate it from the conditions of property. The love and care of household things with which Stowe imbues *Uncle Tom's Cabin* are what differentiate motherhood from slaveholding, maternal possessions from market articles, and it is this domestic reformulation, rather than eradication, of ownership and property that ideally protects the individual rights of blacks. It also explains what have remained the troubling contradictions of *Uncle Tom's Cabin:* the novel's simultaneous advancement of domestic feminism, anti-slavery, and racism.[4] The difficulty in accounting for the novel's sentimental power stems not only from an androcentric bias against sentimentality but also from the disconcerting fact that Stowe's sentimentalism forwards both abolitionism and racism. The freed slaves in *Uncle Tom's Cabin* find their home, not in a matriarchal or newly liberalized America, but in Africa. This double movement that at once emancipates and segregates blacks needs to be understood as a feature of the logic of sympathetic proprietorship, and as symptomatic of a problem within possessive individualism.

As much as Stowe's feminization of property relations both protests against the patriarchal institution of slavery and revises patriarchally inflected capitalist values, it also continues to define blacks as possessions, albeit protected and properly valued ones. If, as Philip Fisher has argued, sentimentalism has operated as a representational tactic for extending human rights to the disenfranchised,[5] it nevertheless retains the slave or woman or child within the inventory of human proprietorship. That is, the case for shared humanity and human rights is made, not in terms of equality, but in terms of the humanity vested in a subject by virtue of its possession, through an intimacy and identification developed in the history of a proprietorship. In *Uncle Tom's Cabin,* sympathy and mutuality arise in property relations. For example, Mrs. Shelby's experience of teaching her religion to her slaves is what endears them to her and makes their sale unacceptable; Eliza and Tom merit Mrs. Shelby's help in securing freedom because they have been part of her family and her Christian values. Her slaves number among her treasured possessions. It is through the proper valuation of their objecthood that slaves become entitled to the rights of individuals.

What Fisher has called the romance of the object in sentimentality is also a romance of possession, a phenomenology of sympathetic ownership. In the logic of sentimental possession, to be properly owned—mothered and nurtured and tended—is to be possessed of the mother's attributes (or those of the ideal owner she exemplifies, God), inspirited with love and generosity like the children, utensils, and food in Rachel's kitchen. Stowe's sentimentalism, then, does not reflect and generate the process of making a thing into a man, as Fisher asserts, but, rather, the process of making things into possessions. It is as property—as properly owned property—that slaves in *Uncle Tom's Cabin* become persons, better-placed things. The sympathetic humanization Fisher attributes to sentimentality operates by virtue of property relations, by shifts in the status of things and not in the transcendence of things. Possession makes what is owned a different kind of thing: a thing becomes a personal possession, supplemental and hence special to the owner. Possession might be said also to be a personification or, more precisely, a personalization of things which supplements and transmutes the thing's objecthood: once a thing becomes familiar through the association ownership entails, it seems (more) personal, more self-expressive of its owner.[6] As this extension of the proprietor into his or her valued articles, property reflects and represents the individual; as emblems of their owner, cherished things ratify the individual sovereignty of their proprietors. The narrative of the beloved thing is a narrative of entitlement because it projects the possessive principle of the owner's freedom: it restages self-possession, highlighting how personhood obtains in its objecthood. *Uncle Tom's Cabin* elaborates this dynamic as a story of the relations between mothers and slaves, between good owners and the objects they keep and sustain. Following the sentimental model of self-possession, the slave narrative of Harriet Jacobs appropriately tells the story of the relation between the freed black and her formerly enslaved self.[7]

The fundamental objecthood of personhood is also expressed in the emphasis in sentimentalism on objective correlatives for feelings and persons, in sentimental culture's proliferation of portraits, keepsakes, mementos, talismans, and souvenirs. *Uncle Tom's Cabin* both epitomized and contributed to Victorian paraphernalia of sentiment, inspiring dolls, toys, games, songs, poems, plays, and finally even the 1893 Columbian Exposition display of a cabin identified as Tom's.[8] When considered in the light of the integral relation between human rights and human possessions Stowe develops, the mass production of sentimental accessories signifies the widening sphere of democracy. And this liberal scenario, of course, forms a standard rationalization of market expansion; indeed, market growth historically has extended individual rights—for white men.[9] But for blacks, the market has represented a history of enslavement. The same market economy that circulates white freedom circulates black slaves.

In this context Stowe's sentimental abolitionism may seem a rather ineffective strategy of enfranchisement. If the sentimentalization of objects culminates in their market circulation (as in the commercialization of Tom's cabin, or, in the novel's own narrative, the sale of Tom), sentimental possession appears simply to be a sentimental account of property relations in a market society. In other words, sentimental possession may rationalize—by personalizing—market relations. On one level, this is certainly the case, as the *Uncle Tom's Cabin* industry spectacularly demonstrates; but recognizing the market character of sentimentalism is illuminating less as a qualification of Stowe's abolitionism than as a motivation for it. In objecting to the slave market's violation of the family, Stowe holds the market accountable for a failure of sentiment, for impeding or perverting the process of sentimental relations. The anti-market task she undertakes in *Uncle Tom's Cabin* is to make property relations more sentimental, or truly sentimental—to stop things from circulating.

Because the market has served only the rights of white men, Stowe seeks to purify possessive individualism, imagining the humanistic property relation as transcendent of market relations, as protected in domesticity. Her ethic of sentimental possession shares the liberal ideal of self-realization in property, but she would secure this goal by replacing market relations with familial ones. Excoriating the "mercantile dealings" in "the souls and bodies of men" (2: 316–17), *Uncle Tom's Cabin* moreover rejects the policy of securing freedom through market practices. Tom must die in order to "read [his] way to title clear/to mansions in the skies" (2: 246)[10] and to demonstrate the historical failure of the market to entitle blacks. Chloe's plan to buy back her husband with money earned from selling her pies is obviated by Tom's martyrdom, a radically extra-market form of domestic economy; once Tom has died he is free by virtue of being forever outside the market, for even Legree "don't sell dead niggers" (2: 282). Tom's martyrdom and the security it exemplifies inspire George Shelby to make all his plantation slaves "free men and free women" who shall not "run the risk of being parted from home" (2: 309). So Tom's way—getting out of the market—becomes the celebrated model of liberty in the novel. George accordingly exhorts the freed blacks: "Think of your freedom, every time you see UNCLE TOM'S CABIN; and let it be a memorial to put you all in mind to follow in his steps" (2: 310). The memorial cabin thus marks the emancipatory achievement of sentimental possession, of a possessive individualism removed from markets.

Defining self-possession in terms of a domestic space—whether the home in heaven where Tom "long[s] to go" or the cabin in "Kintuck"—reiterates the structuring assumption of possessive individualism, the grounding of freedom in private property. In Stowe's censure of the market and enclosure of freedom within the domestic sphere (spiritual or mundane), sentiment stays at home; by this logic, home fortifies individualism, rooting the principle of possession in interiority. As Tom passes "right in the door" of heaven he declares "What a thing 'tis to be a Christian!" (2: 280). The "glory" of being what *Uncle Tom's Cabin* defines as a Christian thing inheres in its inseparability from "the love of Christ" (2: 281). The Christian model of union Stowe invokes is elaborated in sentimental possession as the loving connection of the domestic circle. Home thus contains the ideal condition for self-possession: a sympathetic and secure proprietorship. The glory of sentimental things emerges in their domestic placement; the organization of drawers and cupboards and closets matters in Stowe's abolitionism because the coherence of these domestic compartments constitutes the extra-market condition of a stable individualism.

Sentimental Fetishism

Stowe's perfected possessive individualism measures self-possession by the quality of domesticity, by the extent of the domestic interior's difference from the market arena. The path Tom follows out of the market into memorial iconography runs through the domestic reformations Stowe continued to imagine after *Uncle Tom's Cabin*, in her household advice literature as well as her anti-slavery writings. Her recommendations for improved domestic economy elaborate sentimental possession as the antithesis and transcendence of market relations—as the superiority of enduring possessions to fashionable commodities. In a series of articles on domestic concerns Stowe wrote during the 1860s for the *Atlantic* and then published in collections,[11] she stresses that creating the right atmosphere and feelings requires a special mode of consumerism, an investment in objects for their independence from and defiance of fashion. The right stuff in a home is distinguished from market currency by its use and comfort (and these are always the same in Stowe's depiction). Household furnishings and decorative objects are thus regularly de-commodified in Stowe's domestic economy; in her insistence on use value she differentiates household possessions, the stuff of sentimental associations, from the ephemeral objects in the marketplace.

The recurrent theme in Stowe's recommendations for home decorations and furnishings is the "better value" of comfort, its permanence and its good influence. Her parable of "The Ravages of a Carpet" illustrates the follies of fashionable redecorating.[12] When the women of the Crowfield family decide to install a new parlor carpet, the "homelike and pleasant" character of the room changes. First the new purchase makes all the old furnishings—the "well-used set furniture" built of "heavy mahogany, guiltless of the modern device of veneering, and hewed out with a square solidity which had not an idea of change"—appear shabby and inadequate. So "in less than a year" these are replaced by "a new sofa and new chairs," "some dark green blinds," and "great, heavy curtains that kept out all the light that was not already excluded by the green shades." In the process, the "feeling of security, composure and enjoyment" about the room that made it "good to be there" vanishes or, as the narrator imagines, "the household fairies had left it,—and when the fairies leave a room, nobody ever feels at home in it." The family and their friends eventually follow the original carpet and familiar furnishings with "the marks and indentations" of "good times and social fellowship" to their new location in the father's study. There the warm atmosphere of their once comfortable parlor is reestablished.

The poet Lucy Larcom fondly describes this domesticating power of "household goods." She explains how "seeing our old furniture kept us from being homesick" in a new residence:

Filled up with these things, the little one-windowed sitting-room easily caught the home feeling and gave it back to us. Inanimate objects do gather into themselves something of the character of those who live among them, through association; and this alone makes heirlooms valuable. They are family treasures, because they are part of the family life, full of memories and inspirations. Bought or sold, they are nothing but old furniture. Nobody can buy the old associations; and nobody who has really felt how everything that has been in a home makes part of it, can willingly bargain away old things.[13]

Of all these familiar articles, Larcom most values her "mother's easy-chair": "I should have felt as if I had lost *her,* had that been left behind."

The Crowfield family furniture is likewise dear and priceless. The moral of Stowe's story about feelings and furniture, of course, is the incompatibility of fashion with true domesticity. In a related story in this series Stowe emphasizes this opposition as the difference between housekeeping and homekeeping. A well-kept house appears beautiful but no one wants to live in it and "nobody ever comes in to spend an evening." In this story about the dangers of purely conspicuous housekeeping (that is, house-keeping geared only to correct appearances), the orderly, perfectly appointed house is so inhospitable that it ruins the children who grow up in it: one son runs away to sea; another becomes "a perfect Philistine." As Stowe summarizes, "Silks and satins—meaning by them the luxuries of housekeeping—often put out not only the parlor-fire, but that more sacred flame, the fire of domestic love"; such housekeeping finally renders the family "*homeless.*"[14]

What make fashion and its analogue, a good appearance, inhos-pitable, as it were, are their impracticality and their currency. And these are in effect tautological for Stowe: because new furnishings are unfamiliar, they do not invite use. Fashionable items lie outside the domestic orbit of use value; they can *only* be commodities. In this rather remarkable resistance to commodity fetishism (which, as will become clear, takes the form of an objection not to fetish-ism but to commodities) Stowe defines household possessions as both useful and talismanic of use value, the cornerstone of an extra-market domestic economy. These things of sentimental value and regular use succeed and supersede domestic consumer-ism; Stowe's narrative of sentimental possession is a Christian purification of market economy in which commodities are tran-substantiated into possessions. Even though new objects must be purchased at the commencement of a household, Stowe counsels that these be things made to last, that they be selected for their potential as long-standing possessions, as parts of the family. They will be inspirited like the Crowfield family room or Rachel Hal-liday's kitchen, purified of their market origins. Use signifies an intimacy between persons and their possessions; this is why Stowe refers to our furniture as our "servants and witnesses."[15] The service and notarization familiar things perform make the differ-ence between a house and a home, a commodity and a possession.

It is this transformative capacity of sentimental possession that Stowe employs in her abolitionist renovation of American society. This redemptive power resides in the sentimental possession, the beloved domestic object, which is itself both transformed and transforming. In *Uncle Tom's Cabin,* a number of mothers' belongings—attributes and reminders of maternal love—figure crucially in the escapes of slaves. Eliza finds safety in Rachel Halliday's rocking chair, "motherly and old, whose wide arms breathed hospitable invitation, seconded by the solicitation of its feather cushions,—a real, comfortable, persuasive old chair, and worth, in the way of honest, homely enjoyment, a dozen of your plush or brocatelle drawing-room gentry" (1: 214). This chair's sentimental persuasions reverberate with the comforting "creechy-crawchy" of the "small flag-bottomed rocking-chair, with a patch-work cushion in it, neatly contrived out of small pieces of different colored woolen goods" on which Rachel sits. "It had a turn for quacking and squeaking,—that chair had,— either from having taken cold in early life, or from some asthmatic affliction, or perhaps from nervous derangement" (1: 215). Besides its own medical history, this chair bears witness to a familial history: "for twenty years or more, nothing but loving words, and gentle moralities, and motherly loving kindness, had come from that chair" (1: 215).

Just as Stowe tells us that "head-aches and heart-aches innumerable had been cured there,—difficulties spiritual and temporal solved there" (1: 216), she believes that slavery can be overcome through the mobilization of sentimental sympathies and associations. As she wrote her editor, she planned *Uncle Tom's Cabin* as a presentation of pictures of the horrors of slavery, for "there is no arguing with *pictures,* and everybody is impressed by them, whether they mean to be, or not."[16] The marketability of slaves, which Stowe represents as their homelessness, is perhaps most poignantly underscored by the "brilliant scriptural prints" and "portrait of George Washington" (in blackface) adorning Tom's cabin—the cabin that despite Stowe's title is not his, the "home" in which Tom is not a fixture. Neither Christianity nor the natural rights tradition in America established by the revolution and associated with George Washington protects Tom, because he is not really owned by them. His interior decorating is borrowed from patriarchal white culture, and these furnishings only invoke a sentimental power they do not possess because they are not fully possessed by Tom. Only the property owner can possess and securely be possessed by the insignia of liberal humanism. Slavery reveals the liberal tradition as a self-perpetuating entitlement of white men of means. Because Washington did not underwrite the rights of proprietorship for blacks, there is an exactitude as well as an irony in making a black Washington a household icon: by the logic of individualism that sentimental possession develops, testimonials to a similarly circular black natural rights tradition would protect Tom. Without that tradition, without the presumption of himself as already free, sentimental furnishings are only market reproductions, ineffective things.[17]

Similarly, the familial accoutrements the slave may come to "have"—such as Tom's "Kentucky home, with wife and children, and indulgent owners" or the "St. Clare home, with all its refinements and splendors" (2: 168)—cannot prevent the slave's sale to a Simon Legree. Indeed, the provisional nature of the slave's relation to sentimental objects—that is, the precariousness of being only an approximate sentimental object—curtails the slave's access to the aesthetics he acquires from kindly owners. "It is one of the bitterest apportionments of a lot of slavery, that the negro, sympathetic and assimilative, after acquiring in a refined family, the tastes and feelings which form the atmosphere of such a place, is not the less liable to become the bond-slave of the coarsest and most brutal." Stowe thus characterizes slave experience as the history of the furniture of commercial (and masculine) spaces: "a chair or table, which once decorated the superb saloon, comes, at last, battered and defaced, to the bar-room of some filthy tavern, or some low haunt of vulgar debauchery." Unlike Rachel's rocking chair, such a "table and chair cannot feel." Stowe emphasizes "the great difference" between this furniture and the slave is that "the *man* can" feel; even the legal definition of him as "chattel" "cannot blot out his soul, with its own private world of memories, hopes, loves, fears, and desires" (2: 168–69). Misplaced in the market, the slave is mistaken for and treated like insensible furniture. Stowe's redress of slavery would redeem the fates of both the slave and the furniture by securing the association between persons and the things they love, that is, by imaging a circulatory power in objects that certifies the private little world of the soul.

It is against the insecurity of market objects that Stowe dispatches her own salvific objects. Thus one significant detail in the emancipation of Eliza and her son Harry is the Bird family gift of their "poor little Henry's" things: the "little coats of many a form and pattern, piles of aprons, and rows of small stockings" that had been worn by their dead child (1: 153,154). These "memorials" to use are passed on to be of use again (1: 154), to help restore and fortify the slave family.[18] Similarly, the memorial lock of hair Simon Legree's mother left him operates to abet the escape of Cassy and Emmeline and to render him powerless. So powerful is this sentimental possession that its influence survives and strengthens in its disposal. Even though Legree has burned his mother's keepsake, it seems to him to reappear when he discovers the lock of Little Eva's hair that Tom keeps as a memento. Against his insistence that "[i]t would be a joke, if hair could rise from the dead," the narrator of *Uncle Tom's Cabin* declares "that golden tress *was* charmed; each hair had in it a spell of terror and remorse." The superstitious Legree is so frightened by the persistence of the token that he takes refuge in drink and fails to notice Cassy's escape preparations. In the economy of sentimental possessions and sympathy delineated by Stowe in this chapter appropriately called "The Tokens," the market the slave-trader epitomizes is overwhelmed by the power of objects.

While Stowe's sentimental aesthetics as well as her abolitionist politics would eliminate the market logic of commodities epitomized by fashion (or slavery), they nevertheless retain and refine a logic of fetishism often associated with commodities. Stowe's employment of fetishism as an anti-market tactic assumes a spiritual power in objects quite different from the mysterious vitality of objects that Marx was concurrently describing in his critique of market economy. For Marx, objects acquire a scandalously "mystical" character when they are stamped with market (exchange) value; appearing to have a life of their own apart from the persons who produced them, commodities seem vested with magical powers. The mystique of commodities conceals their true nature—their representation of human labor. Commodity fetishism hides the real character of the commodity, its life as labor, its origin in economic relations among persons. Subsequent Marxist analysts of the rise of consumer culture emphasize the repressed material history of the commodity—its severance from its producer—as the motivating condition for consumer spending: the commodity makes us want it for our self-completion. The corollary to this account of a constitutive relation between consumers and commodities is that the commodity wants us. As Walter Benjamin puts it, "If the soul of the commodity which Marx occasionally mentions in jest existed, it would be the most empathetic ever encountered in the realm of souls, for it would have to see in everyone the buyer in whose hand and house it wants to nestle."[19]

Stowe's sentimental fetishism invests domestic possessions with this sense of empathy between the object and its owner. In this light, sentimental possession and consumerism share a mythology of things in which possessions appear necessary and constitutive supplements to persons. But sentimentalism images an elevated and sanctified fetishism, a fetishism that transforms commodities. Indeed, from Stowe's domestic perspective commodities appear, as it were, insufficiently fetishized—because not yet owned. Far from concealing productive human relations in market relations, the fetishism of objects in Stowe's political economy projects the productive labor of housekeeping. That is, the liveliness of household things consists in their domestic functions; they take on a life of their own in their usefulness or service. Could sentimental possessions themselves speak, they would say, *pace* Marx: What belongs to us as objects is our disposition to usefulness.[20] In Stowe's nonexchange domestic economy, objects outside the market can and do speak. What Marx takes as the mystified conception of the commodity Stowe images as its true character and anti-market potential. The personification of objects, which for Stowe is a function of their removal from the market, makes them mediums of human history. Because household things take on lives of their own, they can take on the lives of their owners. The more "lively" the object, such as Rachel's vocal rocking chair, the more likely it is to convey familial material history.

The love of things Stowe advocates exceeds and even nullifies consumerist desire, by imagining a reciprocity between persons and their possessions, by seeing them as contiguous and congruent. Ownership, which takes things out of the market and keeps them in the home, confers this congruence. Whereas for Marx ownership reflects the market relations of property, and owners "exist" "merely as representatives of" commodities,[21] for Stowe ownership exhibits an extra-market set of relations. Or, more precisely, sentimental possession translates possessive individualism into a secure proprietorship by detaching it from the market. Fetishism is for Stowe a function of an enduring ownership, and it is this familiarizing spirit of proprietorship that Stowe would marshal against the market.

While this logic of fetishism in sentimental property relations might well suggest that feminine proprietorship and de-commodification—the domestic transformation of society and its members—could be accomplished by a concerted consumerism,[22] Stowe remains firm in her market antipathy and pointedly limits spending in her domestic economy, stressing the self-sufficiency of home. "The Ravages of a Carpet" demonstrates both the intrusiveness and the superfluity of the new carpet (first lauded as a "bargain") in the household; the room it transforms is finally never used. Any purchase that cannot be assimilated into the home's order of things is ill-fated; like the carpet, such things will not be used and domesticated. Stowe's revisionary domestic economy resembles the materialist ideal of a pre-market culture of use value, but images an even stronger version of self-sufficiency, a radical endogamy of possessions. The congruence and order of her ideal home free it from the market; sentimental fetishism reflects a culture so completely outside exchange values that even use value is imperceptible. That is, things like Rachel's rocking chair so closely correspond to the wills and feelings of their owners that they appear to *be* them rather than to be serving them. This radical congruence, however, obviously poses problems for the status of enfranchised blacks. The question of race in a domestic economy dedicated to consonance surfaces in Stowe's subsequent writings as a doubtfulness about de-commodification and as an even stronger market antipathy.

Sentimental Segregationism

The portrait of plenitude, intimacy, self-sufficiency, and congruence presented in Stowe's ideal domestic economy might recall the paternalistic myth of harmonious familial economy promulgated by slavery apologists,[23] who argued that the patriarchal institution provided blacks with homes, education, and Christianity. Such a continuity between domestic values and aspects of the slave system certainly occurred to Stowe, who worried in 1869 that "the essential *animus* of the slave system still exists." In an article called "A Family Talk on Reconstruction," she recognizes this same "desire to monopolize and to dominate" in the persistence of "the great aristocratic arrangement of American society" in the division of labor, and particularly in the relations of women to their domestic servants.[24] What begins in *Uncle Tom's Cabin* as an anti-slavery, anti-market protest culminates in a critique of labor relations and valorization of independent housekeeping. Reliance on servants threatens Stowe's revisionary economy by perpetuating aristocratic distinctions consigning physical labor to a lower class. Women with servants appear like "the noblemen of aristocracies," according to Stowe, because of a lack of "equal respect for physical and mental labor."[25] And for the same reason, women workers regard domestic service as a labor in which they are "assimilat[ed]" into "slaves." Slavery and domestic service upset the balance between mental and physical faculties in exemplary republican labor. So reconstruction of American society must contend with "one of the worst" results of slavery, "the utter contempt it brings on useful labor":

So long as everything is not strictly in accordance with our principles of democracy, so long as there is in any part of the country an aristocratic upper class who despise labor, and a laboring class that is denied equal rights, so long this grinding and discord between the two will never cease in America. It will make trouble not only in the South, but in the North,—every branch and department of labor,—trouble in every parlor and kitchen.[26]

The ultimate aim of abolition is thus the reformation of labor.

To equalize labor and eliminate the "laboring class" in America's emergent republican society, Stowe advocates the "dignity of labor," the dignity of "the lady who does her own work."[27] Stowe's endorsement of self-reliant labor correlates with "the doctrine of universal equality" in American society. Slavery is at odds with this work ideal for reasons of efficiency as well as morality: "People, having once felt the thorough neatness and beauty of execution which came of free, educated, and thoughtful labor, could not tolerate the clumsiness of slavery."[28] The inefficiency of inequality persists in systems that delegate work to others; the ultimate folly of the housekeeper not doing her own work is that her dependence makes her "completely the victim and slave of the person she pretends to rule."[29] Not only does this mean more work for the housekeeper but it robs her of her self-possession. Stowe's translation of the problems of slavery into the domestic service problem stresses the "constant changes" and "reign of Chaos" that typify the servant system.[30] Obtruding into the intimate relations between a housekeeper and her household, servants embody the same unpredictable and disorderly market forces that Stowe identified in Dinah's chaotic kitchen, the same threat to the housekeeper and the domestic sphere of freedom.

The solution to "the servant problem" lies in the proper training of the housekeeper.[31] "She who can at once put her own trained hand to the machine in any spot where a hand is needed never comes to be the slave of a coarse, vulgar Irishwoman." Women "who have been accustomed to doing their own work" "are certainly more sure of the ground they stand on,—they are less open to imposition,—they can speak and act in their own houses more as those 'having authority,' and therefore are less afraid to exact what is their just due, and less willing to endure impertinence and unfaithfulness." Training and experience are recommended as a stay against the undermining influence of servants who "are for the most part the raw, untrained Irish peasantry" "with all the unreasoning heats and prejudices of the Celtic blood."[32]

In addition to the housekeeper's self-possession, the democratic principles of equality are at stake in the servant problem. The abolitionist duty with which *Uncle Tom's Cabin* charged American women extends to protecting the rights of workers. "A servant can never in our country be the mere appendage to another man, to be marked like a sheep with the color of his owner; he must be a fellow-citizen, with an established position of his own, free to make contracts, free to come and go, and having in his sphere titles to consideration and respect just as definite as those of any trade or profession whatever."[33] Toward the Irish servant class, the "mistresses of American families, whether they like it or not, have the duties of missionaries imposed upon them"; in instructing Irish servants "in the mysteries of good housekeeping" "they are doing something to form good wives and mothers for the Republic." By "treating their servants in a way to lead them to respect themselves and to feel themselves respected," American women implement the democratic spirit of equality.[34]

Yet this projected assimilation of Irish servants into American domestic economy, following the ideals of sentimental possession, is not an option for emancipated slaves in *Uncle Tom's Cabin*. There it becomes clear that being the same color as one's owner or employer is in fact the condition of sentimentalization and upward mobility in Stowe's economy of assimilation. For freed blacks Stowe also urges education, in "reparation for the wrongs the American nation has wrought upon them," and as preparation for moving to "a refuge in Africa" (2: 318) rather than a place in American society. The history of Topsy illustrates how blacks ultimately remain outside the orbit of sentimental possession:

Miss Ophelia took Topsy home to Vermont with her, much to the surprise of that grave deliberative body whom a New Englander recognizes under the term *"Our folks."* "Our folks," at first, thought it an odd and unnecessary addition to their well-trained domestic establishment; but, so thoroughly efficient was Miss Ophelia in her conscientious endeavor to do her duty by her eleve, that the child rapidly grew in grace and in favor with the family and the neighborhood. At the age of womanhood, she was, by her own request, baptized, and became a member of the Christian church in the place; and showed so much intelligence, activity and zeal, and desire to do good in the world, that she was at last recommended, and approved, as a missionary to one of the stations in Africa; and we have heard that the same activity and ingenuity which, when a child, made her so multiform and restless in her developments, is now employed, in a safer and wholesomer manner, in teaching the children of her own country. (2: 304)

The fate of the emancipated black in Stowe's self-sufficient domesticity lies outside the protective envelope of sentimental possession, in the safety of "her own country."

Here emerges the segregationism of Stowe's domestic reformations. Although Stowe's proposal of self-reliant and self-possessed labor bespeaks a democratic reformation of work and social relations and her transformation of possessive individualism into sentimental possession entitles blacks to democratic rights, her sanitized model household ultimately excludes blacks. Stowe's democratization of labor through the elevation of "the habit of self-helpfulness" seals her ideal domestic economy from the trade in labor and humans signified by slaves and servants.[35] Because of the uncertainties of domestic service, labor itself ideally should be expunged from the domestic economy: "it should be an object in America to exclude from the labors of the family all that can, with greater advantage, be executed out of it by combined labor." The cooperative neighborhood laundries Stowe proposes eliminate the need for servants and enhance domestic order:

How much more neatly and compactly could the whole domestic system be arranged! If all the money that each separate family spends on the outfit and accommodations for washing and ironing, on fuel, soap, starch, and the other et ceteras, were united in a fund to create a laundry for every dozen families, one or two good women could do in firstrate style what is now very indifferently done by the disturbance and disarrangement of all other domestic processes in these families.[36]

This model of cooperative labor commercializes or, more accurately, recommercializes housework in a way that keeps the domestic sphere free of foreign elements. Stowe's solution to the servant problem is to fortify the home in a protected market of its own, to make domesticity independent of all commercial relations except those in congruence with itself.

This perfection of domesticity in a perfected version of market relations suggests that the ultimate goal of sentimental possession is a protectionist economy, a self-sustaining community. In ridding the home of servants and the market relations they embody, just as in ridding the nation of slavery, Stowe imagines the replacement of commodity relations with sentimental relations. Yet if Stowe envisions as an adjunct to the sentimental home a sentimental market, it is a uniformly white one. For the purified logic of possessive individualism Stowe uses to grant humanity and freedom to blacks requires the elimination or at least the invisibility of commodities, and hence of blacks. The race of the slave and that of the servant (always Irish in Stowe's depiction) mark their market histories. The Irish can eventually be assimilated, but blackness marks the slave as forever unassimilable. The only place for former commodities in Stowe's new domestic economy is as temporary furniture and family props, as talismanic figures such as the "glossy black" Uncle Tom becomes or as salvific figures such as Topsy, "one of the blackest of her race," becomes. Thus the metamorphosis of the black slave into treasured servant and witness to the (white) family or into Christian missionary and martyr and therefore into both familiarity and invisibility is, like repatriation, ultimately a way of making blacks disappear.

Even in a "well-trained domestic establishment" like the New England home to which Topsy goes before going to "her people" in Africa, freed slaves never become "our folks"; the congruence and intimacy of sentimental possession do not allow for miscegenation. While miscegenation would appear the most obvious and practical means of de-commodification and domestication, it is at odds with the ideal of sentimental possession because it involves mixing market and home. In *Uncle Tom's Cabin,* even the willing union of Cassy with a white man only issues in the sale of their children. Color, the telltale sign of the market, signifies the scandal of unprotected familial relations. This association of blackness with an unstable domesticity also appears in nineteenth-century representations of free blacks. For example, the genealogy of

Frado, the mulatto heroine of *Our Nig,* Harriet Wilson's 1859 autobiographical sentimental novel about a black servant in New England, begins with her (white) mother's seduction and abandonment by a white man. Disgraced by her unprotected (in all senses) sexual relation, the woman can never secure herself in marriage. In despair she lives with a black man who offers his protection, and Frado is the product of this extralegal relation. The mulatto child embodies not just this union but the shame of the original property violation. Color thus operates as a labeling of damaged goods, a confirmation of the precarious status of unprotected property.[37]

Miscegenation, however, may operate in a different direction, concealing the black mark of market goods.[38] In *Uncle Tom's Cabin,* many of the slaves achieve freedom by passing as whites, by exploiting their white paternity. But Stowe dismisses this potential of black to become white by reminding us of the blackness of blacks. At the moment in the novel when slaves become free and ready to pursue their entitlements, they appear simultaneously most self-possessed and most black. The closing pages of *Uncle Tom's Cabin* record an inventory of the finances and blackness of emancipated slaves "now resident in Cincinnati" (2: 320). Listing examples of the enterprise of free blacks as proof of her argument that it is a good investment for Americans to educate blacks for a new life in Africa, Stowe details both their proportion of blackness (significantly, either "full black" or no less than three-quarters) and their financial worth:

C—. Full black; stolen from Africa; sold in New Orleans; been free fifteen years; paid for himself six hundred dollars; a farmer; owns several farms in Indiana; Presbyterian; probably worth fifteen or twenty thousand dollars, all earned by himself.

K—. Full black; dealer in real estate; worth thirty thousand dollars; about forty years old; free six years; paid eighteen hundred dollars for his family; member of the Baptist church; received a legacy from his master, which he has taken good care of, and increased.

G—. Full black; coal dealer; about thirty years old; worth eighteen thousand dollars; paid for himself twice, being once defrauded to the amount of sixteen hundred dollars; made all money by his own efforts— much of it while a slave, hiring his time of his master, and doing business for himself; a fine, gentlemanly fellow.

W—. Three-fourths black; barber and waiter; from Kentucky; nineteen years free; paid for self and family over three thousand dollars; worth twenty thousand dollars, all his own earnings; deacon in the Baptist church. (2: 320)

These conjunctions of market value and color underscore the identity of blacks with commodities that Stowe retains even as her ethic of sentimental possession offers a way of transforming commodities into citizens. In doing away with the taints of the marketplace Stowe's purified domestic economy must ultimately do away with blackness, the mark of incongruity and exogamy. But in order for blackness to be expunged it must first be identifiable. Recalling and removing racial difference, Stowe's abolitionist vision of safe property veers into purifying practices of keeping the house divided from not only men and markets but blacks and immigrants.[39] The process of sentimental assimilation is forestalled by the image of a nearly endogamous race removed to another continent.

The racial and racist characterization of the servant problem exemplifies how race, like the market, operates as a (negative) defining term of self-possession. In Stowe's reenactment of the liberal theory of entitlement, the market figures as the horizon of individualism, its extent and its limit. Sentimental possession offers a way to cross the line between unprotected and protected property; entitlement inheres in the assimilation of market objects into domestic economy. As the elimination by sentimental transformation of fashion and of servants shows, the market in Stowe's imagination of individualism operates as an ever-shifting defining line of individual sovereignty. That is, the market signifies what is beyond the individual: either the freedom the disenfranchised want, or the disenfranchisement or risk the already entitled individual fears. Hostility toward the market thus represents a psychology of individuality in a market economy; in this sense the anti-market sentiments of Stowe's feminized property relation might be seen as protecting the sphere of the individual. The orbit of sympathy in which she would certify self-possession and individual rights reconstructs and fortifies the outline of the proprietorial self. *Uncle Tom's Cabin* and Stowe's subsequent writings on domesticity foreground the interiority of that figure, the milieu of individualism.

An entity conceived of as transcendent to the material conditions producing it, the individualistic self inheres in its difference from the market. The xenophobic character of market antipathy in Stowe's domestic reformations personifies the market's figuring of otherness, of the extradomestic. Just as the market is vital to the imagination of transcendent individualism, functioning as its horizon, so race performs a crucial role in representing difference and transcendence: race acts as a border that persists despite its rhetorical or actual erasure. Although some racial characteristics may be incorporated into sentimental possession—domesticated into congruence with domestic relations—color remains as the residue of Stowe's purification of possessive individualism. Stowe's attempt to extend the liberal inheritance to blacks deeds them a dubious self-possession founded on assimilation. That the legacy of *Uncle Tom's Cabin* is a history of enfranchisement, racism, and segregation is congruent with the market logic of individualism which sentimental possession both rejects and perfects.

To say this is not to say that Stowe's sentimentalism or sentimentalism in general is always racist but to point out that sentimentalism works both to alter and to emphasize dividing lines, and that in this historical instance sentimentalism has worked to institutionalize racial categories. The conditions for racism apparent in sentimental property relations are already in place in the liberal tradition Stowe amplifies, in the establishment of individualism as an extension of white, propertied men. Although the sentimental power of Stowe's domestic reconstruction of America serves to recapitulate that tradition and its biases, sentimentalism can also promote histories other than the alternative histories Stowe imagined. Different histories might begin with recognizing racism as among the varied and unpredictable affections involved in the affective life of property which sentimental possession sustains. The feminist retrieval of Stowe's great sentimental artifact has illuminated women's custodial and reformist role in the liberal tradition. The reconstructive work of disowning racism, of divesting selfhood of that possession, remains the unclaimed legacy of *Uncle Tom's Cabin*.

Part Two

Hawthorne's Gothic Revival

Chapter Three

Women's Work and Bodies in *The House of the Seven Gables*

This chapter is concerned with a division within the sexual division of labor established and maintained by domestic ideology: the division between women and their bodies. The now much-studied nineteenth-century disestablishment of women and home from the realm of production marks, not only a pivotal point in the history of capitalism and construction of gender, but also a significant moment in the representation and definition of individuality according to new forms of interiority. As domestic ideology engenders and demarcates the spaces of work and personal (as opposed to working) life, both labor and women are divested of their corporeality, defined as different from rather than extensive with the body. The Lockean association of the body with its self-expressive productivity is recast as a discontinuity. In contrast to the Enlightenment ideal, self is defined as an entity distinct from economic activity, articulated through the organizations of private life.[1]

Within these organizations—the home, the family, religion, sexuality, health—selfhood depends upon its severance from the world of work, a severance reflected in the individual's difference from her body. Idealized as independent of the vagaries of labor in the marketplace, individuality requires continual confirmation of impregnability. Self-dominion is accordingly secured in subordinating the body, the component of self all too untrustworthy for its labor history, its market service. Indeed, as *Uncle Tom's Cabin*

63

demonstrates, to be a working body is virtually to be a slave, to be labor value without personal status and potentially salable. This is why it is so crucial for Stowe that slaves be Christians, aspirants to spiritual, bodiless existence.[2] Disengagement from the body that labors (and from the labors that go to market) thus underwrites individualism.

Though women's removal from the spheres of production appears to exempt their bodies from the market exchanges which depersonalize and dehumanize bodies and labor, a concern about the body nevertheless predominates in domestic programs of women's work. In the literature of housekeeping, labor is depicted as sometimes beneficial, sometimes harmful to the body. For example, on the one hand Catharine Beecher extols housework as healthy, regenerative exercise, an ameliorative activity for women, and on the other she ponders "the secret domestic history" of housekeepers, the "terrible decay of female health all over the land."[3] The point here is not that Beecher expresses inconsistent views but that she remains consistent in defining labor as an effect *upon* women's bodies, not an effect *of* women's bodies. This formulation omits woman's agency from her own labor, disconnecting her labor from her body. Removed from her labor as well as from wage labor, woman becomes an icon of ideally invulnerable individuality.

Despite the staggering amounts and rigor of housework prescribed by Beecher and described by nineteenth-century housekeepers, despite all the evidence of physical labor and the exhaustion it entailed, domestic rhetoric expunged the corporeality of women's work.[4] Even when Beecher sought to raise the status of housekeeping to a profession, she argued for the recognition of this work as "woman's great mission," as a spiritual ministry, rather than as material labor on a par with other labors.[5] When women work, that work is characterized as spiritual, transcendental; woman is imaged as an ideal beyond her body, the selfless domestic angel.

Not only housework but female factory labor was made respectable through an appeal to a transcendent femininity; in this case, to the ladylike qualities that young women were assumed to bring to their work outside the home. Former Lowell millworker Harriet Robinson recalled that factory work became acceptable once the domestic virtues of the female workers were recognized. The primary feature of the "ladylike" or "domestic" was its evocation of a different sphere, of a labor more spiritual than mundane.[6] This thematics of disembodiment in nineteenth-century representations of women's work signals a newly emergent ideal of individual integrity identified with a double dissociation: the body's difference from its labor, and the self's difference from the laboring body.

For nineteenth-century America, dissociation of self from bodily activity assumed its most dramatic manifestation in the hysterical seizure, a condition in which the body seemed to operate under an alien force. In the 1840s, a physician specializing in *Woman and Her Diseases* reports a hysteric patient "writhing like a serpent upon the floor, rending her garments to tatters, plucking out handfuls of hair, and striking her person with a violence."[7] Such less extreme instances of loss of bodily control as headaches, nervousness, and "propensity to yield to fatigue, or exposure, or excitement" recur throughout Beecher's statistics of female health in the mid-nineteenth century.[8] Although the proliferation of hysteria has usually been regarded as a phenomenon "peculiar to the Victorian bourgeois family" and woman,[9] the victims of this disease in mid-nineteenth-century America tended to be blacks, immigrants, and miners as well as women. Beecher discovered in her survey of women that "a large portion of the worst accounts were taken from the industrial classes."[10]

Hysteria seems, then, to exemplify the pathological potential in work, the negative effects of the dissociation between self and body that makes housekeeping the transcendent activity Beecher celebrates.[11] The dynamic of disembodiment the hysteric displays, however, reduces her to nothing but a body, a mindless animal "writhing like a serpent upon the floor." For Beecher, this indicates not a problem with work per se but a symptom of insufficient or improper implementation of work. The susceptibility of the laboring classes to hysteria and nervous disease, Beecher and her sister Stowe believed, stemmed from the same source of the leisured person's "liability" to "mental disease": "imperfect exercise" of the brain and body.[12] Both lack of work and overwork are imperfect exercise, according to the sisters, because they do not develop equally all the faculties of mind and body. Variety of labor, the successful performance of the housekeeper's round of duties, is thus the best remedy for the imbalance signified by nervous disease. By this account, the housekeeping that the hysteric in effect evades through her illness would restore her to self-control. Bodily distresses would disappear along with house dust.

Beecher's formulations on women's work and health project a quite remarkable confidence in the salutary powers of housework, a vision of perfect regulation. Her prescription of the balancing activities of housekeeping assumes that the hysteric must be disembodied—distanced from her bodily behavior—in order to be cured. If the hysteric appears all too corporeal, housework will properly exercise both her brain and body so that somatic disorders will vanish. Hysteria, in this analysis, is not disembodied enough. It signifies the physical suffering of persons whose faulty relation to work has rendered them helpless to reap the rewards of work.

In the narrative of work and health Marx was concurrently developing, the alienated worker, like the hysteric, typifies a negative or unhealthy experience of work. The familiar materialist concept of alienation—the dispossession of an individual's labor power by its objectification in the market, where it is valued by exchange rather than use—represents another bodily registration of the market economy's separation of work from personal life. Tracing the fate and function of the body in Marx's exposition of capitalism, Elaine Scarry has recently demonstrated the dynamic of embodiment and disembodiment that structures the concept of human labor. In every act of human production (or making), the maker or worker projects her own sentience, which the product or artifact then reflects back upon its producer, enlarging and enhancing the scope of the worker's sentience as her consciousness encompasses this additional or new object in the world. Scarry stresses the fundamentally self-projective as well as self-referential nature of all labor, even the simple acts of subsistence so often romanticized as pure labor, as labor before its severance from the body. For Scarry, all labor assumes (and this very phrase enacts the embodiedness, the personification, of labor) both a departure from and a return to the body.[13]

Nineteenth-century images of alienated or disembodied labor foreground the departures, the divergences of body and work. In the light of Scarry's exegesis of Marx, the detachment of labor from the laborer, significantly figured as a deformation or emasculation in much nineteenth-century American literature,[14] reflects the phenomenon of an embodiment isolated from its usual dynamic relation to disembodiment. In this state, the individual is denied his own potential ease and enrichment in disembodiment. The difficulty for the worker in a capitalist organization of production, therefore, is not that his work signifies a severance from his body but that his work does not signify sufficiently: his work amplifies not his own condition in the world but that of the capitalist. Put another way, he experiences only the bodily effort of his work, and not the effect of bodily relief that work would ideally bring.

In Beecher's system of work, the hysteric figures as an alienated worker, divided from herself and her productive power and consequently overburdened with her body. The narrative of work and health Beecher unfolds recapitulates the range of experience in market culture, the continual task of surmounting the vulnerabilities to which the market exposes the individual. Like the Sisyphean chores of housekeeping, self-maintenance involves regular work, the "system and regularity" Beecher stresses.[15] It is in this project of self-protection that housework takes on its salutary and even salvific function.

Beecher's vision of domestic labor, accordingly, grants women the disembodied power that Scarry ascribes to the capitalist, a person, as she puts it, "exempted" and "absent from the production process."[16] Because the housekeeper is separated from production, from her work and from her body, she emblemizes individual integrity, the ideal of an identity impervious to contingency by virtue of its disembodiment. The housekeeping cure Beecher recommends for hysteria offers the hysteric a labor that restores as it transcends her body. Domestic ideology thus transforms the anxieties of alienability—that the self may be separated from itself as parts of the self are apportioned, as in the conditions in which one's labor is sold or one's body given over to strange paralyses and paroxysms—into achievements of identity. Housekeeping, in the idealized form domestic ideology promotes, translates and modulates experiences of severance into the conditions for individuality.[17]

In the narrative of domestic individualism I am pursuing here, the nineteenth-century protagonists of materialist and psychological history—the alienated working man and the hysterical woman—represent strategic innovations in the representation of the individual: vicissitudes of selfhood which domesticity and the market economy it thematizes can manage and regulate. I thus mean to emphasize that the disembodiment of women and of women's work shapes the notion of an interiority not so much defined against as constituted upon a self in some way divided, alienated, severed—and therefore potentially recoverable. In keeping with women's traditional service as emblems of individuality in market society, an ideally alienated female labor underpins the individual's self-integrity.[18] And it is within this structure of division, figured by woman in the nineteenth century, that the interiority of the modern individual is elaborated and continues to be debated.

I want to trace this formulation of interiority through what I take to be one of the most compelling and appropriately haunting representations of women's disembodied work in nineteenth-century American literature, Hawthorne's *The House of the Seven Gables*. As Sharon Cameron has demonstrated, much of Hawthorne's writing is concerned with the substitution of aesthetic productions for the imperfection of the human. This artificial reconstruction of human bodies, recurring in tales such as "Rappaccini's Daughter," "Ethan Brand," and "The Birthmark," is almost always figured as an operation upon the body and often as a victimization of the female body. Artifice is repeatedly advanced as an improvement on the body—for example, cosmetic surgery for the birthmark, poison for human breath—and though Hawthorne's stories often read as cautionary tales about the hubris of science and art, they also express a distrust of corporeality which is exhibited continually in efforts at disembodiment.[19] It is the feminization of this disembodiment and its supplementary restoration that *The House of the Seven Gables* details in the romantic operation of domestic ideology. Here, to engage and allay anxieties about the frailties of human bodies, domesticity appears as an act of revival, a restorative labor.

The Gothic Revival and the Cult of Domesticity

In *The House of the Seven Gables* Hawthorne tells the story of a home business: the narrative begins with Hepzibah Pyncheon "nervously" opening a cent-shop in one of the gables of her ancestral home, a venture which turns out to be a "pretty good business," as one of her neighbors says at the end of the story, when Hepzibah "rides off in her carriage with a couple of hundred thousands" to an "elegant country seat." Shopkeeping ultimately returns Hepzibah to seclusion and wealth, realizing her dream "that some harlequin-trick of fate would intervene in her favor." In Hepzibah's version of the American dream, commerce inspires and materializes "her castles in the air," her fantasy of becoming heiress to "unreckonable riches," . . . "so that instead of keeping a cent-shop" . . . "Hepzibah would build a palace."[20]

The romance spun out in this commercial success story allays nervousness about the risks of commerce with a fairy-tale ending of restored wealth and health; the trials of the market are so thoroughly overcome that the reality of free enterprise democracy seems to disappear in the closing scene of retirement to an inherited country estate. That Hawthorne's romance in this sense leaves behind or transcends commerce suggests its resemblance to another artifice of transport from (and within) market society. For this narrative of a woman's removal from commercial nervousness to the social and financial security of a comfortable home also recapitulates the development of bourgeois domesticity in the mid-nineteenth century: the removal of woman from the realm of production to an idealized home and, concomitantly, the emergence of a new individualism identified with this home.

Hawthorne's romanticization of commerce in *The House of the Seven Gables,* his representation of retail success as a return to aristocracy, reprises the revivalist gesture that domestic ideology both generates and exemplifies. In 1820, two-thirds of all the cloth

produced in this country was made by women working in their
own homes. As textile manufactures replaced household production in successive decades, the memory of household production
was retained in the new mass-produced fabric—called "domestic"—and by the ideology of domesticity, which clothed the individual with a sense of enduring value in private life. Hence, domesticity, a definition of private space articulated through intrinsic
feminine characteristics, emerged as an imaginative reconstruction
of a past life recalled as continuous and sustaining.[21] Forwarding
and fostering the succession of one economic mode by another,
the rise of domestic ideology in nineteenth-century America thematizes as it sanctions a progressive convertibility. The tautological turn by which the domestic encapsulates nostalgia for itself
works as the mainspring of a fable of continuity. And the fuel of
this romantic machine is a seemingly inexhaustible one: change
itself. From the phenomenon of economic change, domesticity
mines a transformative power by which the past may be reanimated even as it is superseded. It is within this domestic circularity
that Hawthorne discovers a new life for the "circle of gentility"
(44), the possibilities for aristocracy within democracy.

It is in reference to this aristocratic potential of the domestic
domain that Emma Hewitt later in the century called her popular
household manual *Queen of the Home*. Hewitt declares: "In this
glorious land where none are royal, all [women] are queens, governing by the God-given right of womanhood."[22] The aristocratic
associations prominent in middle-class domestic ideology signal,
not merely the persistence of aristocratic ideals and middle-class
aspirations, but the nostalgic function domesticity serves: its representation of the present in the terms of the past. Thus the transformation of the House of the Seven Gables from aristocratic estate
to petty shop, described in Hepzibah's descent from "her pedestal
of imaginary rank" to "hucksteress of a cent-shop" (38), is a vision
of market progress already antiquated in 1851. Hepzibah knows she
cannot compete with the "magnificent shops in the cities": "Gro-
ceries, toy-shops, dry-goods stores, with their immense panes of
plate-glass, their vast and complete assortments of merchandize, in
which fortunes had been invested; and those noble mirrors at the

farther end of each establishment, doubling all this wealth by a brightly burnished vista of unrealities!" (48). The large retail and department stores which appeared in the 1850s, with their great resources of capital, display, and advertising, eventually replaced both small-town general stores and urban specialty shops.[23] So even the transformation of the House of the Seven Gables is already an anachronism; the belatedness of this accomplishment is underscored by Hawthorne's citation of a precedent for Hepzibah's enterprise in the "petty huckster" Pyncheon ancestor who "bethought himself of no better avenue to wealth than by cutting a shop-door through the side of his ancestral residence" (29).

Hepzibah's shopkeeping thus follows the tradition of the house, a tradition that encompasses the transformation of the "patrician" into the "plebeian" (38), and the rise of the plebeian to proprietor of a "country-seat" (317). In this cyclic narrative, as in the domestic institution of continuity, the past returns. The revivalist energies and effects of domesticity elaborated in *The House of the Seven Gables* are articulated more explicitly in the 1840s and 1850s Gothic Revival vogue in home architecture, popularized in America by the domestic architect and landscape designer Andrew Jackson Downing. Sharing with the cult of domesticity a belief, "above all things under heaven, in the power and influence of the *Individual Home*,"[24] Downing sought to translate domestic rhetoric into a style evocative of home values. Downing believed that the rural Gothic style implemented in England during the 1830s and 1840s, "characterized mainly by pointed gables," "best manifested . . . in every part the presence of cultivated and deep domestic sympathies."[25] Features crucial to the domestic quality of a house included "the chimneys, the windows, and the porch, veranda, or piazza." The identification of these architectural voids as spatial elements of domesticity—"a broad shady veranda suggests ideas of comfort" and bay windows, balconies, and terraces denote "those elegant enjoyments which belong to the habitation of man in a cultivated and refined state of society"—links the space of interiority with an ideal of leisure and privacy, an ideal of private views and protected access.[26] (See figures 2–4.) The American Gothic Revival home retreats from or, like Hepzibah Pyncheon, transcends the nine-

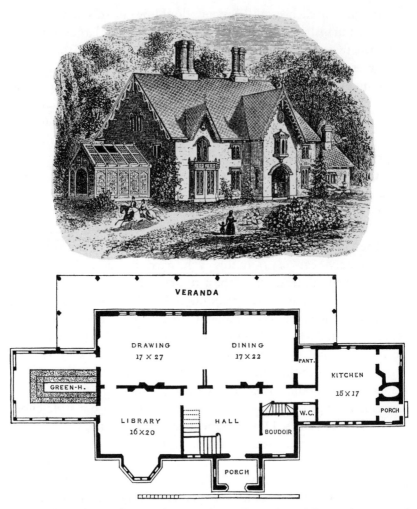

2. Rural Gothic Villa. Andrew Jackson Downing, *The Architecture of Country Houses*, 1850.

teenth-century marketplace, the public realm where "strange and unloving eyes . . . have the privilege of gazing" (46). Downing conjoined this removal of individuality from the present with the Gothic's romantic suggestions of the past.

The English Gothic Revivalists who influenced Downing's designs admired the detail work on the Gothic cathedral, identifying in the irregular components and intricate decorations the mark of

3. Drawing Room at Kenwood, Gothic Style. Andrew Jackson Downing, *The Architecture of Country Houses*, 1850.

unique artisanship, the lasting effects of the individual. They accordingly developed a domestic architecture that stressed asymmetrical designs to emphasize human artisanship and thus to suggest through picturesque and romantic effects a domain of individuality in the home. Following Ruskin's view that the Gothic "admits of a richness of record altogether unlimited," Revivalists sought to preserve a sense of the past, defining home as "a kind of monument" to human life, work, and experience.[27]

For Ruskin, whose stress on preserving the past dominated the values of the Gothic Revival in domestic architecture, "there is sanctity in a good man's house which cannot be renewed in every tenement that rises on its ruins." Durability and stability in houses are urged as remedies against "loosely struck" roots in the contemporary landscape—the "pitiful concretions of lime and clay" recently built "upon those thin, tottering, foundationless shells of splintered wood and imitated stone." Ruskin takes it as "an evil sign of a people when their houses are built to last for one generation only." To celebrate a "spirit of honorable, proud, peaceful self-possession," Ruskin "would have, then, our ordinary dwell-

ing-houses built to last." And such houses would be monuments
to their builders, museums of their lasting ownership. "This right
over the house, I conceive, belongs to its first builder, and is to be
respected by his children; and it would be well that blank stones
should be left in places, to be inscribed with a summary of his life
and its experiences."[28]

It is just this endurance of the past and Gothic-romance exposition of paternal power that both Holgrave and Clifford, the last
male descendants of the Maules and Pyncheon, oppose in their
critiques of family estates. "There is no such unwholesome atmosphere as that of an old home, rendered poisonous by one's de-
funct forefathers and relatives," Clifford contends (261). Holgrave welcomes the day "when no man shall build his house for
posterity." "If each generation were allowed and expected to build
its own houses," he speculates, "that single change, comparatively
unimportant in itself, would imply almost every reform which
society is now suffering for" (183–84). Observing "the ease of
obtaining a house and land, and the ability of almost every indus-
trious citizen to build his own house" in America, Downing advanced an architecture in keeping with Holgrave's ideal.[29] Rejecting Ruskin's preference for the past over the present, Downing
appropriated the individualism of English Gothic Revival styles
for American values—for the construction of a democratic home
as a locus of value and continuity not founded in inheritance.
"Placing national feeling and national taste above all others,"
Downing's "true home" was "not, indeed, the feudal castle, not
the baronial hall, but the home of the individual man—the home
of that family of equal rights, which continually separates and
continually reforms itself in the new world." Like Hawthorne,
Downing noted the failure and unsuitability of ancestral estates in
America, which were "contrary to the spirit of republican
institutions. . . . The just pride of a true American is not in a great
hereditary home, but in greater hereditary institutions."[30]

---

4. A Cottage in the English or Rural Gothic Style. Andrew Jackson
Downing, *Victorian Cottage Residences*, 1842.

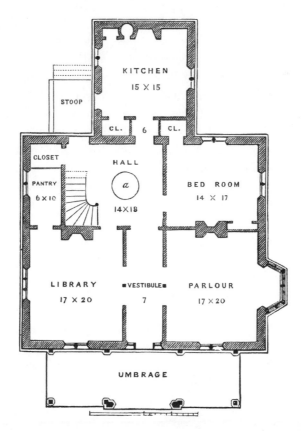

KITCHEN
15 X 15

STOOP

CL. 6 CL.

CLOSET

HALL

PANTRY
6 X 10

a

14 X 18

BED ROOM
14 X 17

LIBRARY
17 X 20

VESTIBULE
7

PARLOUR
17 X 20

UMBRAGE

Yet even though Downing inveighed against Pyncheonesque hereditary homes built by the "robbery of the property of another class," he admitted that there was "something wonderfully captivating in the idea of a battlemented castle." The home Downing proposed in place of the castle was "the beautiful, rural, unostentatious, moderate home of the country gentleman." Downing desired "something of the castle in the man," a distinction in individuality.[31] For Downing, aristocratic attributes and democratic values were not incompatible. Democracy offered every individual castles in the air, the opportunity of a kingdom in the domestic domain, apart from democratic struggles. Downing's accommodation for aristocracy within democracy suggests the continuity between Holgrave's radical democratic views and his domestication by Phoebe, who "made the House of the Seven Gables like a home to him" (182). Holgrave's conversion to conservative respect for the "permanence" of a "domestic architecture in stone" reiterates the nostalgic narrative of domestic ideology in which the past is invoked as the rationalization for a new order.[32] The fact that Holgrave can, as it were, have his house and hate it, too, demonstrates the convertibility to continuity that change generates. In other words, the flux of the present, to which Holgrave weds his democratic enthusiasms, is precisely what empowers domestic conversions. The attainment of a democratic home—the property available to the American individual—signifies the establishment of a new system of individual private property. That this new distribution of property entails new forms of inequality is not the point here. What Hawthorne and Downing exhibit is the mechanics of continuity whereby such innovations (and their imbalances) are implemented.

The persistence of aristocratic associations in Downing's American Gothic thus reprises domestic ideology's revivalist performance: the sleight-of-hand whereby progress appears as the reanimated and regenerate past. Downing takes this logic of revivalism even further, to make even the creative processes of domestication disappear. His ethos of retreat and privacy involves not only the removal of the individual from the present world but also the removal of domestic processes, of housework, from the sight of the individual. In order to distinguish the domestic from the economic realm, to create a "counterpoise to the great tendency toward constant changes" in American economic and social life, Downing's house plans obscured every sign of work.[33] He placed the kitchen as far as possible from the parlor, usually in the rear of the house and often in the basement. He designed screens and walls to keep kitchen gardens out of sight. Instead of considering the house as women's workplace, Downing emphasized the primacy of the house's "pleasing effect." In his "ideal of domestic accommodation," he envisions "[e]ach department of the house [as] being complete in itself, and intruding itself but little on the attention of family or guests when it is not required to be visible."[34] This compartmentalization removes labor from the pleasures of domesticity and, more important, from the perspective of domesticity. In Downing's philosophy of domestic architecture, domestic economies recede; the symbolic agency of the home supersedes its work processes. Domesticity in Downing's treatment becomes a nostalgic romance that eliminates any form of industry altogether, imagining an aristocratic republic without the labor that underpins it.

Woman's Work and Ladies' Leisure

The House of the Seven Gables unfolds a similar domestic romance of transformative, invisible labor. In the fulfillment of Hepzibah's fantasy, a family inheritance from the commercial fortune of her cousin Jaffrey eventually transports her to her castle. An incorporation of commercial success into a scenario of restored aristocratic order, this happy ending is assured by a "harlequin-trick" (64), the appearance of the young cousin Phoebe Pyncheon with her "natural magic" (71). Announcing "I am as nice a little saleswoman, as I am a housewife" (78), Phoebe transforms the "squalid and ugly aspect" of trade. Her "homely witchcraft" (72) brings to the labors of shopkeeping and housekeeping "the easy and flexible charm of play" (82). This representation, or disguise, of labor as magic and play spiritualizes housekeeping and shopkeeping, distinguishing them from ordinary human work by their Godlike creative power and ease. The "spiritual quality in Phoe-

be's activity" effectively eliminates the mundaneness of work,
linking her process to that of "God's angels" who "do not toil,"
"but let their good works grow out of them" (82). So the entry
into the House of the Seven Gables of this domestic angel with
"her vastly superior gifts as a shop-keeper" (79) proves to be the
harbinger of Hepzibah's success. Commutation of commerce into
its own antithesis of domestic comfort restores "the aristocratic
hucksteress" (79) to her "circle of gentility" (44). This fairy-tale
rescue of Hepzibah from "the business of setting up a petty shop"
to "earn her own food" (38) images the rise of domesticity and
commercial culture as a return to aristocracy. The formation of
culture later characterized by Veblen as the culture of conspicuous
leisure and consumption is anticipated here in a legend of magical
achievement.[35]

The arrival of Phoebe "at the instant of time when the patrician
lady is to be transformed into the plebeian woman" signals the
preservation of the lady by domestic fiat, the incorporation of
ladyship into the domestic domain. "In this republican country,
amid the fluctuating waves of our social life, somebody is always
at the drowning-point" (38), explains the narrator of *The House of
the Seven Gables*. To counter such flux and resuscitate such victims
as Hepzibah, one contemporary etiquette guide declared that
Americans needed "some standard that knows no fluctuation, no
caprice."[36] Barbara Welter echoes Hawthorne's description of
fluctuations in a free enterprise society: "In a society where values
changed frequently, where fortunes rose and fell with frightening
rapidity, where social and economic mobility provided instability
as well as hope, one thing at least remained the same—a true
woman was a true woman, wherever she was found."[37] The domestic cult of true womanhood that flourished in popular literature from 1820 to 1860 thus functioned to define a stable identity,
a fixity of class through a character transcending class changes.
Domestic femininity served as a fluctuating society's imagination
of itself, its ideal of value and inviolability. This is why Hepzibah's
boarder, the daguerreotypist Holgrave (whose presence and occupation themselves indicate the incursion of the social stream of
novelties into Hepzibah's long-secluded existence), assures her that

it is "better to be a true woman than a lady" (45). The prerogatives of identity and continuity once identified with an aristocratic class are now located in the democratic cult of domesticity: the lady survives in the true woman.

The aristocratic definitions of the lady and the estate provide self-insurance: one always has one's place. It is this assurance that makes the aristocratic fantasy so powerful and so necessary to Hepzibah, that causes her to take such pride in her family's defects and infirmities. For her, the "native inapplicability . . . of the Pyncheons to any useful purpose" (77) confirms their particularity and distinction. With her practical skills and gifts, "Phoebe is no Pyncheon," in Hepzibah's view, and the older woman cannot help thinking, "[I]f only she could be a lady, too!" (79). But Phoebe's "patrimony, the gift of practical arrangement" (71), grants her the faculty of being "admirably in keeping with herself" (80), the quality of the lady subsumed under the definition of true womanhood. "Instead of discussing her claim to rank among ladies," the narrator recommends, "it would be preferable to regard Phoebe as the example of feminine grace and availability combined, in a state of society, if there were any such, where ladies did not exist. There, it should be woman's office to move in the midst of practical affairs, and to gild them all, were it even the scouring of pots and kettles—with an atmosphere of loveliness and joy" (80). This is the romantic ideal of true womanhood and "the sphere of Phoebe" (80). Phoebe's sphere, like her angelic assistance in Hepzibah's shop, offers "the decayed gentlewoman" a more secure ladyship.

In Hepzibah and Phoebe, Hawthorne figures the installation of the domestic ideal as a reenactment of a fantasized prior order. Not only do housekeepers appear as ladies in this romance, but housework appears as leisure. The ascension of the Angel in the House romanticizes market history by spiritualizing women's work so that it is dissociated from the physical efforts that signify the human imprint on history. Change itself is thus domesticated in the disembodiment of women's work, in the imagery of women not working. Neither Phoebe nor Hepzibah seems to work: "what precisely was Phoebe's process, we find it impossible to say," the narrator says of her housekeeping (72); the nervous lady "with her habitual sluggishness" (77) cannot work. This appearance of no connection to labor is also characteristic of the domestic ideal of housework, despite its emphasis on prodigious industry. Stowe stressed this facility in her many portraits of successful housekeepers such as Katy Scudder in *The Minister's Wooing.* For such a housekeeper, the more she does, the more ladylike and leisurely she appears:

She shall scrub floors, wash, bake, and brew, and yet her hands shall be small and white; she shall have no perceptible income, yet always be handsomely dressed; she shall have not a servant in her house, with a dairy to manage, hired man to feed, a boarder or two to care for, un-heard-of pickling and preserving to do,—and yet you commonly see her every afternoon sitting at her shady parlor-window behind the lilacs, cool and easy, hemming muslin capstrings, or reading the latest new book.[38]

In this sense the cult of true womanhood (re)produces the lady of leisure by denying the corporeality of women's work.

In this light, Hawthorne's infamous remark on the literary monopoly of "the damned mob of scribbling women" articulates not simply professional jealousy but also his sense of an aesthetic violation: the conspicuousness of exertion, the public sight of women's productivity and corporeality. A mob of scribbling women poses for Hawthorne the question of whether there can be aesthetic creations in the marketplace—not because women cannot write but because they should not *appear* to write. This may be why Hawthorne cast his admiration of Fanny Fern, the author of *Ruth Hall,* in (albeit negative) supernatural terms: "the woman writes as if the Devil were in her."[39] For Hawthorne, a woman's work is ideally never *done.*

The goal of housekeeping is thus its own erasure in leisure. In *The House of the Seven Gables,* this appearance of leisure in house or shop assumes on the one hand a superhuman feminine labor, and on the other a feminine incapacitation. The disappearance or, more precisely, the elision of women's agency in their work facilitates the romanticization of change by denying the connection between women and labor and thus eliminating the process and change that are labor's office. What haunts the House of the Seven Gables, then, is not only the sins of the fathers but also the disembodiments of the present, the ghosts of feminine labor.

The Mesmerized Working Body

Hawthorne's tale is a fable of market labor in which the individual's work, whether shopkeeping or housekeeping or the imaginative labor of story-telling, forms a sphere secure from the processes work signified in the nineteenth century. As I have indicated in the opening pages of this chapter, the idea of work as damaging to the individual pervades nineteenth-century thought; it recurs not only in Marx's exposition of the alienated worker but also in Beecher's worries about the health of housekeepers, in factory novels' descriptions of injured and deformed laborers, and in medical admonitions about the perils of overwork.[40] In *The House of the Seven Gables,* Hawthorne contributes to this colloquy a fiction of safe (protected and protective) labor. The erasures of labor and escapes from commerce performed in Hawthorne's romance and Downing's architecture effectively rescue the body from the publicity of economic processes.

If, for Hawthorne, Phoebe's providential housekeeping serves as a model of imaginative practice and production in which the individual is immunized from the effects of labor (that is, from the vulnerability of her body), then Hepzibah's shopkeeping demonstrates the bodily risks in labor, the ways labor continually exposes and emphasizes the body. For an elderly, poor, genteel spinster in the mid-nineteenth century the economic opportunities were few: sewing, teaching, petty shopkeeping. All of these, in Hawthorne's representation, refer to facts and frailties of Hepzibah's body: "she could not be a seamstress" because of her nearsightedness and "those tremulous fingers of hers," she could not teach school because of the "torpid" state of her heart toward children and the limitations of her memory and learning (38–39). Shopkeeping entails the greatest exposure, the display of herself to the world. What Hepzibah dreads most in opening her shop is the fact "that she must ultimately come forward, and stand revealed in her proper individuality" (40). This is why she tries to imagine a way of performing her transactions unseen: "to minister to the wants of the community, unseen, like a disembodied divinity, or enchantress, holding forth her bargains to the reverential and awe-stricken purchaser, in an invisible hand" (40).

Hawthorne underscores labor's foregrounding of the corporeal in making us "spectators to [Hepzibah's] fate," in dwelling on her "strange contortion of the brow"—"the innocent result of her near-sightedness" mistaken by the world for a scowl—and on the nervous frenzy of "her rigid and rusty frame" "upon its hands and knees" trying to set "her shop in order for the public eye" (33–39). It is as though the conspicuousness to which commerce subjects the woman literally subjects her to the eye, bringing her to her knees.

The subjection to sight enacted and thematized in this cruel scene recalls another public display and humiliation of an aristocratic woman: Alice Pyncheon's mesmeric subjugation by Matthew Maule. Under Maule's power, "a will, most unlike her own, constrained her to do its grotesque and fantastic bidding" (208); upon his command "her spirit passed from beneath her own control," and the proud Alice would suddenly "break into wild laughter" or into tears, or dance "some high-paced jig" more "befitting the brisk lasses at a rustic merry-making" (209). This induced hysteria—the dissociation of will and body accomplished by the mesmerist—exposes the woman in uncharacteristic behaviors, "lost from self-control" (209). The ultimate alien act she performs is a labor for a laborer: she is summoned to wait upon Maule's bride, a laborer's daughter.

In both cases the aristocratic lady is subjugated, but these are not fables of democratic progress or egalitarian justice. Rather, they are horror stories of labor from the aristocrat's point of view. In Hawthorne's horrific imagination and in the aristocrat's horror of the rise of trading and working classes, labor means subjection to a mesmeric power that hystericizes the individual body, undermining the will and compelling certain performances by the individual. Thus Hepzibah's "heart seemed to be attached to the same steel-spring" (49) as the shop-bell that summons her to work. At the sound of the bell, "[t]he maiden lady arose upon her feet, as pale as a ghost at cock-crow; for she was an enslaved spirit, and this the talisman to which she owed obedience" (42). The labor enslaving these ladies reduces their pretensions to aristocratic individuality by accentuating their corporeality and the usages to which it can be put.[41]

Although selling may seem a highly abstract form of labor, removed from the actual bodily endangerment of mill or factory machinery and exempt from the physical and mental exertions of sewing or teaching, in Hawthorne's depiction acts of selling crucially reflect and even magnify the role of the body in commerce. The exchange of goods for money involves an intensification of corporeality: not only is the merchant on display with her goods, her materiality subject to public perusal and indeed a factor in her selling, but she is in touch with each transaction, a contiguity dramatized in Hepzibah's fantasy of making her hand invisible in her transactions and in her practice of drawing on silk gloves before counting her money. But her hand is both visible and available in her shopkeeping; when she takes money, she feels as if "[t]he sordid stain of that copper-coin could never be washed away from her palm" (51). The soiling effect of money is also the theme of stories about Hepzibah's shopkeeping ancestor circulating the fact "that, with his own hands, all beruffled as they were, he used to give change for a shilling, and would turn a half-penny twice over, to make sure that it was a good one" (29). Miserliness, the preoccupation with hoarding and holding money, highlights the role of the hands in trade, the fact of brute physicality in the touch and love of money, and this is also emphasized in Hawthorne's depiction of the grasping hand of the organ-grinder's monkey, noted as well for its "too enormous tail" and "excessive desire."

Though Hawthorne seems to register a revulsion from the corporeal and the commercial in these examples, the real horror lies in the vision of corporeality as subjugation: like Hepzibah's scowl, the body parts appear to move without volition. The scandalous character of hands in commercial operations derives from their automation, their mechanical and repetitive performances. The monkey, "holding out his small black palm" for money, takes it "with joyless eagerness" and "immediately re-commence[s] a series of pantomimic petitions for more" (164). Similarly, the "petty huckster" Pyncheon is imaged as continually calculating:

It used to be affirmed, that the dead shopkeeper, in a white wig, a faded velvet coat, an apron at his waist, and his ruffles carefully turned back from his wrists, might be seen through the chinks of the shutters, any night of the year, ransacking his till, or poring over the dingy pages of his day-book. From the look of unutterable woe upon his face, it appeared to be his doom to spend eternity in a vain effort to make his accounts balance. (29)

This story of the shopkeeper's ghost recapitulates another scenario of automatism, the story about a looking glass in the House of the Seven Gables which "was fabled to contain within its depths all the shapes that had ever been reflected there." The story runs "that the posterity of Matthew Maule had some connection with the mystery of the looking-glass, and that—by what appears to have been a sort of mesmeric process—they could make its inner region all alive with the departed Pyncheons; not as they had shown themselves to the world, nor in their better and happier hours, but as doing over and over again some deed of sin, or in the crisis of life's bitterest sorrow" (20–21). The woeful shopkeeper seen at his Sisyphean accounts appears to be under the mesmeric power of the Maules. This power over the Pyncheons seems to operate as a punitive exposure and repetition compulsion; more than an allegory of the psychology of guilt, these stories work to manifest the operations of commerce. What seems crucial in the scenes of repetition the Maules conjure up is not only Hawthorne's moral "that the wrong-doing of one generation lives into the successive ones, and divesting itself of every temporary advantage, becomes a pure and uncontrollable mischief" (2) but the fact that unlawful commerce subjects the Pyncheons to the loss of privacy and self-control all commerce entails. In *The House of the Seven Gables,* it is the poetic justice of commerce to reverse as well as restore fortunes, to undermine as well as underpin self-possession. Thus the shame of the Pyncheons is epitomized in the spectacle of the shopkeeper's subjection to commerce. The manifestation of the dead shopkeeper "ransacking his till" or "poring over" his accounts figures the commercial mechanics of disembodiment and automation, the same mesmerization to which Hepzibah is subjected.

The subjection of body to commerce is foregrounded in still another example of automation, the organ-grinder's "company of little figures, whose sphere and habitation was in the mahogany case of his organ, and whose principle of life was the music, which the Italian made it his business to grind out":

In all their variety of occupation—the cobbler, the blacksmith, the soldier, the lady with her fan, the toper with his bottle, the milk-maid sitting by her cow—this fortunate little society might truly be said to enjoy a harmonious existence, and to make life literally a dance. The Italian turned a crank; and, behold! every one of these small individuals started into the most curious vivacity. The cobbler wrought upon a shoe; the blacksmith hammered his iron; the soldier waved his glittering blade; the lady raised a tiny breeze with her fan; the jolly toper swigged lustily at his bottle; a scholar opened his book, with eager thirst for knowledge, and turned his head to-and-fro along the page; the milk-maid energetically drained her cow; and a miser counted gold into his strong-box;—all at the same turning of the crank. Yes; and moved by the self-same impulse, a lover saluted his mistress on her lips! (163)

Yet "the most remarkable aspect" of all this activity "was, that, at the cessation of the music, everybody was petrified at once, from the most extravagant life into a dead torpor" (163). Commerce stills as well as animates process, subjecting human labor to the same conditions to which labor subjects the body. Its intensification of corporeality consists in its power to manipulate the activities through which persons appear more or less in control of their bodies, more or less in possession of their bodies. Like the mesmeric pass, the wave of the hand by which mesmerists directed their subjects, this manipulation displays persons as simultaneously most bodylike, that is, as doing what bodies can usually do—working, hammering, waving, drinking, reading, counting, kissing—and most bodiless, in the sense of being disconnected from the direction of the body. The automated working figures register the double experience of embodiment and disembodiment that commerce generates.

The Interior Exposed

The state of the mesmerized body has become more familiarly associated with hysteria, where the bodily exhibitionism of mesmeric performances becomes more explicit. The spectrum of mesmeric effects Hawthorne describes, running from animation to petrification, reappears in later nineteenth-century classifications of hysterical symptomology. Charcot's famous taxonomy of hysteria detailed the range of hysteric presentations from the seizure—in all its forms, including epileptic fits, acrobatic movements, passionate attitudes, and deliria—to paralysis. Within the seizure itself the static pole of hysteric behavior also recurs in the tableaux of hysteric postures that were photographed and in the momentarily held "grand movements" such as the "arc-en-cercle," a back-bend into which hysterics spontaneously propelled themselves.[42] In the well-known André Pierre Brouillet painting "A Clinical Lesson of Dr. Charcot at the Salpêtrière" (1887), a sketch or engraving of a hysteric in this arched pose occupies the left background. Diagonally opposite from this figure of arrested commotion, the female hysteric supported by Charcot in the right foreground of the painting appears limp and enervated, passively arched backward. This figure was drawn from a fifteen-year-old working-class girl named Blanche Wittman who came to the Salpêtrière in 1877 as a nurse and patient. There she became known as the Queen of Hysterics because of "her facility as a hypnotic subject." Noting Wittman's hypnotic state in the painting, Catherine Clément and other feminists have emphasized the theatricality of this clinical exploration, its exhibition of female acrobatics and trances.[43] The resemblance between mesmeric and hysteric performances had led physicians to look for the roots of hysteria in auto-suggestion and to hypnotize hysterics in order to discover and change the influence under which they were acting.[44] Hypnosis, once having illuminated the hysteric's subjection (to her unconscious) by reproducing and objectifying it, became not only a treatment for hysteria but a means of staging it in the clinic or classroom. It is the same ethos of showmanship and publicity that Hawthorne finds unseemly in mesmeric practices.

For Hawthorne, the horror of mesmerism consists in its power to intrude into the "holy of holies," as he wrote to Sophia Peabody before their marriage. Alarmed that Sophia was seeking relief from headaches through mesmeric treatment, Hawthorne urgently protested "that the sacredness of the individual is violated by it." In addition to his fear of this violation by an "intruder" who "would not be thy husband," Hawthorne confides his "repugnance" at the idea of Sophia's "holy name being bruited abroad in connection with these magnetic phenomena."[45] It is the fact that Matthew Maule's rapelike possession of Alice Pyncheon must display itself—the reenactment of the initial violation which publicity entails—that constitutes the horror of mesmerism in *The House of the Seven Gables.* Such crimes against Pyncheon women rehearse the exposure of Pyncheon criminality, dramatizing that crime will out because of the penetrability of secrecy, the availability of human interiority and motivations. Hawthorne's feminization of the Pyncheon subjection to public sight, showing the individual as a body without a will of her own, underscores this vulnerability of the interior; putting Pyncheon women on exhibition makes clear that no privacy is inviolate. In *The House of the Seven Gables,* hysterics suffer mainly from public exposure.

Revealed in this exposure is not only "the sacredness of an individual" but the fact of the accessibility of individual interiority. For, as Hawthorne warned Sophia, it is more than her "own moral and spiritual being" that she surrenders to "the magnetic lady" (her mesmerist, Cornelia Park). He objects to "being brought, through [Sophia's] medium, into such an intimate relation" with the mesmerist. Because Sophia is "part of" Hawthorne, access to her is access to himself.[46] Like the scientific inquiry and experimentation imaged so threateningly in stories such as "The Birthmark" (1843), "Rappaccini's Daughter" (1844), and "Ethan Brand" (1851), mesmerism magnifies individual penetrability. Individuality, of course, is always showing itself; interior states register themselves in objective correlatives. This is another great theme in Hawthorne's writing: the external manifestations of interior conditions shaping such tales as "The Minister's Black Veil" (1836), "The Prophetic Pictures" (1837), "The Great Stone Face" (1850), and, obviously, *The Scarlet Letter*. Not content with allegorical and representational practices whereby individuality is expressed, Hawthorne's mad scientists and doctors seek to take apart or alter the machinery of mental or physical processes; they would intervene in the body's artifactual processes. Mesmerism similarly images the revelation of how the interior of an individual body works. Even more than erotic entries and intimacies can be laid bare: the very physiology of interiority becomes manifest in mesmerism.

Mesmerism, in fact, contributed to the nineteenth-century understanding of mental physiology. Clinical exploration of the mind often engaged with the claims and methods of mesmerism, called variously mental alchemy, electrical psychology, animal or vital magnetism, supernal theology, somnolism, somnambulism, psycheism, the science of the soul, spiritual physiology, or simply psychology.[47] For the mid-nineteenth century, psychology meant mental processes, which were understood or hypothesized as fundamentally physiological. Thus while on the one hand mesmerism inspired interest in spiritualism, on the other hand it helped illuminate the physiology of the brain and function of the nervous system. Though some medical examinations sought to debunk the metaphysical claims of enthusiasts of mesmerism, the impetus to explain mesmerism was guided more by a spirit of scientific inquiry than one of materialist skepticism. Rationalizing mesmerism illuminated physiological knowledge. Mesmeric phenomena, Dr. Joseph Haddock wrote in 1849, "afford us the means of acquiring a knowledge of the laws and nature of the psychical, or mental, part of our being" and "the means of becoming better acquainted with the more abstruse points in our bodily organization." The knowledge mesmerism makes available is "that every individual has two distinct brains," the cerebrum and the cerebellum. Voluntary nerves and actions arise in the former; involuntary nerves and actions arise in the latter. This standard nineteenth-century account of the nervous system, according to Haddock, explains mesmerism as a variation on the fact "that the brain has an automatic movement of its own." Under a mesmerically induced somnolent state, the cerebral actions of the operator and the subject or subjects are one: "In each person the cerebellum and its system of nerves is in the normal [that is, involuntary] condition, but there is only *one* normal and active cerebrum, namely, that of the mesmeriser or operator." The subjects of the operator "are so intimately, interiorly blended with him, that the absence of their own external cerebral consciousness causes them to feel his cerebral consciousness as their own." Thus, "the idea existing externally in the cerebrum of the mesmeriser, is, when willed by him, perceived by the subject as if existing in his or her own cerebrum."[48] The subject does not even experience his or her own subjection. By this account, the state of normalcy which mesmerism exacerbates is a fluctuation between the voluntary and the involuntary. Mesmerism makes us see the inner workings of the mind—and the vulnerability these internal processes, like other labors, entail.

The interiority Hawthorne, Downing, and Stowe imagine as transcendent to economic processes appears in the physiology of mesmerism as both similar and sensitive to external events, as a site of engagement with the world. Though Haddock insisted on "the internal operations of the body" as unique, he also characterized them as, "in fact, the anti-types of which the types are found in outward nature."[49] This correspondence between the interior and the exterior predominates in the formulations about mesmerism and the nervous system that emerged in the wake of the invention of the telegraph in 1837. The founder of "the science of magnetism," Franz Mesmer, had in the late eighteenth century postulated the presence of a fluid he called animal magnetism running through the body. In the mid-nineteenth century medical theorists often explained mesmerism by appearing to a more sophisticated paradigm of the nerves as an electrical system. Dr. John Bovee Dods, in the series of lectures he was invited to deliver at the United States Capitol in 1850, declared electricity to be "the connecting link between mind and inert matter." In Dods's view, mesmerism is only a special case of mental functions that work by "electricity, which passes from the brain through the nerves, as so many telegraphic wires, to give motion to the extremities." Disease occurs when "the electricity of the system [is] thrown out of balance," either by "mental impressions" or "physical impression from external nature."[50] It is the force of such impressions, Dods argues, that explains why persons confessed to witchcraft at the Salem trials. On the basis of this model of sympathy between interior and exterior life, physicians introduced electrotherapy as a cure for nervous diseases, including hysteria. It is this link, the potentially oppressive intimacy between the mind and the world, that Hawthorne emphasizes in the Maules' mesmeric manipulation of the Pyncheons and excoriates in Clifford's denunciation of the telegraph as an infringement of "natural rights" to "refuge" (265). Like the other mesmeric powers of commerce, the telegraph threatens an "infinite wrong": no privacy, no relief from whatever we have "fled so far to avoid the sight and thought of" (265).

The Domestic Revival: Phoebe's Magic

In *The House of the Seven Gables,* commerce may hold the mesmeric dangers the Pyncheons encounter, but it is also imaged as a revivifying and productive force.[51] Censuring the investigative instrumentality of the telegraph "as regards the detection of bank-robbers and murderers," Clifford alternatively envisions it as a beneficent agent of intimacy:

An almost spiritual medium, like the electric telegraph, should be consecrated to high, deep, joyful, and holy missions. Lovers, day by day—hour by hour, if so often moved to do it—might send their heart-throbs from Maine to Florida, with some such words as these—"I love you forever!"—"My heart runs over with love!"—"I love you more than I can!"—and, again, at the next message—"I have lived an hour longer, and love you twice as much!" Or, when a good man has departed, his distant friend should be conscious of an electric thrill, as from the world of happy spirits, telling him—"Your dear friend is in bliss!" Or, to an absent husband, should come tidings thus—"An immortal being, of whom you are the father, has this moment come from God!"—and immediately its little voice would seem to have reached so far, and to be echoing his heart. (264–65)

Seen this way, telegraphic communications extend and amplify the body. It is thus the mesmeric force of commerce to reanimate as well as automate the body. The conspicuousness and contiguity to which trade exposes the individual can be gratifying as well as threatening, as Hepzibah discovers in her shopkeeping: she experiences "a thrill of almost youthful enjoyment" in having "put forward her hand to help herself." The coin she touched "had proved a talisman, fragrant with good, and deserving to be set in gold and be worn close to her heart." So much was she affected "both in body and spirit" by its "potent" "efficacy" that "she allowed herself an extra spoonful in her infusion of black tea" (51–52). The new "solidity" (51) Hepzibah experiences expresses a recovery of body effected by commerce.

This possibility of the restoration of body through the magical transformations of commerce is epitomized in the "nice little body" (79) of Phoebe, whose "homely witchcraft" brings out "the hidden capabilities of things" (71) and whose "facile adaptation was at once the symptom of perfect health, and its best preservative" (135). Her true womanhood inheres in this adaptability that does not touch or temper human essence; a perfect individuality is characterized by a sound body in any circumstance. So sound is Phoebe's body that her "homely duties seemed to bloom out of her character; so that labor, while she dealt with it, had the easy and flexible charm of play" (82). Her relation to labor reverses its mesmeric power so that she seems to attract housework "to herself, by the magnetism of innate fitness" (76). The "potency" of Phoebe's "purifying influence" not only exorcises the gloom and "grime and sordidness of the House of the Seven Gables" (136–37) but also revives her elderly companions: Clifford "grew youthful, while she sat beside him" (139). "They both exist by you!" Holgrave tells her. "Whatever health, comfort, and natural life, exists in the house, is embodied in your person" (216).

Phoebe's beneficent mesmerism images a safe model of labor within a market economy: the conversionary capacity of commerce to aid and amplify the individual. Women's work, disembodied, is reembodied as a rescue mission, and it is in this mission that Phoebe's housework (like Holgrave's photography, a method of letting the sunshine in) preserves the old order of Hepzibah by grafting it onto the new. Rescue entails repairing imperfections in work, enabling escapes or recuperations from the accidents of labor. The reembodiment of women in rescue work explains how "Phoebe's presence made a home about her" (141). Work itself is repaired in Hawthorne's romance so that perfect homes can be made by true women. In keeping with the logic of this reparative labor and reconstructed life, Hawthorne attributes to Phoebe, the "little figure of the cheeriest household life" (140), a palpability and physical presence unique for both its integrity and its reassuring effect. "Holding her hand, you felt something, a tender something; a substance, and a warm one; and so long as you should feel its grasp, soft as it was, you might be certain that your place was good in the whole sympathetic chain of human nature" (141). Whereas the hands of Hepzibah and her shopkeeping ancestor manifest the operations of capitalist desire—that is, they are the medium through which trade passes, the automated expressions of a market economy—Phoebe's hand imparts a "natural magic" (71) that animates objects and revives humanity. "Look where she would, lay her hand on what she might, the object responded to her consciousness, as if a moist human heart were in it" (219).

As Phoebe revives the lady, she also reanimates the laborer. As she restores Hepzibah and Clifford, her marriage restores the family estate to the dispossessed Maules. In Hawthorne's romance of labor, domestic revivalism amends Ruskin's proposal that we honor houses as monuments to their founders to suggest that houses memorialize the original housebuilder as well—the carpenter. So it is especially fitting that the Pyncheon estate passes to a Maule when Phoebe marries the last Maule, Holgrave, who, like herself, "gave a warmth to everything he laid his hand on" (181). In the ideal housekeeper, "admirably in keeping with herself" (80), Hawthorne figures a labor so perfect it *can* be embodied, because it is perfectly consonant with and thus immune from contingency. Like Phoebe's display of dual talents in house and shop, her marriage highlights the identity of housekeeping with commerce; for in the ability "to bring out the hidden capabilities of things around them" (71), women like Phoebe and artists like

Holgrave (he is a photographer, a writer, and a mesmerist) perform transformations and illusions akin to the seemingly magical ways of commerce. It is therefore finally commerce that makes possible a restoration or reconstruction of the body. And it is the commercial production of domestic romance that generates such new forms of individuality as the integrity and interiority of private life exemplified in Downing's homes and Hawthorne's housekeepers. That Hepzibah's "return" to a fantasized prior order is itself a feat of capitalism is made clear in the composition of the country seat to which she removes: it is, as Holgrave somewhat disappointedly notes, a house built of wood, the favored material and construction innovation of Downing in his Americanization of the Gothic Revival. While the ancestral home "belongs to the past, . . . no more to be reanimated in the republic of the new world than the simple faith in the Virgin, which built the mighty cathedrals of the middle ages," Downing maintains that "the true home still remains to us."[52] It remains to us as a result of what Hawthorne calls "pretty good business" (319).

This is not to say that *The House of the Seven Gables* is a manifesto for capitalism and its ethos of changeability, but that it is an imaginative exposition of the beneficent mesmeric potential this transformative economy offers. The romantic architectures of interiority Hawthorne and Downing designed serve to shelter the self from the less attractive effects of this same economy. For Hawthorne, Walter Michaels has recently written, the point of romance, and specifically the point of this novel, is "to domesticate the social dislocation of the 1840s and 1850s in a literary form that imagines the past and present as utterly continuous, even identical, and in doing so, attempts to repress the possibility of any change at all."[53] Yet what gets "repressed" or, more precisely, elided in the institution of continuity depicted in Hawthorne's narrative is not change—indeed, change facilitates the restoration of Hepzibah's aristocratic lifestyle—but the labor of accommodating and incorporating change, the process of domestication.

The modernization of the Pyncheons and the Maules into a nineteenth-century middle-class family living in a wooden country home depends on and reflects the rise of American bourgeois domesticity. It is the invisible operations of homemaking, what might be called the interior dynamics of romance, that this discussion of *The House of the Seven Gables* has attempted to substantiate. If housekeeping is Hawthorne's analogue for romance, this homely magic thematizes and exemplifies the ethos of changeability which I am arguing that romance reproduces. As we have seen, the appearance of magical housework in *The House of the Seven Gables* replaces and transforms another type of women's work: the mesmerized labors of the Pyncheon ladies. Labor induced by mesmeric fiat, like the labors compelled by economic reverses and social dislocations, takes the form of hysteria in Hawthorne's romance. This all too visible subjection of women is superseded by the elevation of the healthy and healthful housekeeper, whose work is imagined as unseen and incorporeal, and hence immune from any somatic impressions of social disorders. The replacement of the hysterical lady by the true woman represents domesticity as a welcome change that relieves the effects of other changes.

Prior to this replacement, Alice Pyncheon's hysteria reflected the malevolent manipulations through which "the old Pyncheon-house" was attained and maintained (5). In accordance with the mutability of ownership and control that the house epitomizes, hysterical movements and gestures signify a continual subjection to change. The house itself bears the marks of change: the House of the Seven Gables has become in the nineteenth century "a rusty wooden house," the aged and "weather-beaten edifice" from which the Pyncheons finally remove themselves (5). If this image projects the temporality of the newly inherited estate to which the Pyncheons and Holgrave retire, it also implies that the wooden house in which the healthy housekeeper resides may persist as another, more legitimate, long-standing family landmark—stable and solid like "the great elm-tree" known as "the Pyncheon-elm" (5). Indeed, the seven-gabled wooden house upon which Hawthorne based his romance still stands. (See figure 5.) Tradition thus endures through transmutation, through the innovations that rehabilitate it.

To further refine Michaels's account: romance, as Hawthorne

5. The House of the Seven Gables, as it stands today. Photograph courtesy of the House of the Seven Gables Settlement Association, Salem, Massachusetts.

expounds it, consists in convertibility—the capacity to convert change itself into tradition. That Hawthorne recognized the perfect romance in the rise of the middle-class domestic woman and the individual home she tended is underscored in the novel's final image of Alice Pyncheon "as she floated heavenward from the HOUSE OF THE SEVEN GABLES!" (319). Just as Catharine Beecher envisioned housework as the cure for hysteria, so Hawthorne's romance of Phoebe's magical restoration of Hepzibah restores "joy" (319) to the "mournful" mesmerized lady who "was supposed to haunt the House of the Seven Gables" (83). Under the presiding spirit of domesticity even the ills of the past can be transformed.

Chapter Four

The Mesmerized Spectator

The symbolic function of women for individualism dominates *The Blithedale Romance* as it did *The House of the Seven Gables,* its companion piece in Hawthorne's Gothic Revival. We have seen in the earlier novel the transformation of women's work into a trans- formative homely magic. Women's work recedes from sight in a different way in *The Blithedale Romance,* where Hawthorne fore- grounds women's bodies and the act of viewing of them. From Miles Coverdale's first visit to "the wonderful exhibition of the Veiled Lady" to his witnessing of the dredging of Zenobia's corpse, the novel follows its narrator as he watches women.[1] In this novel the displays of woman that motivated the romantic rescues and restorations in *The House of the Seven Gables* are a point of individual interest. And it is this interest, with its implications for individuality, that *The Blithedale Romance* tracks. While the former romance describes and ultimately modulates the exposure of the individual in labor, the latter develops the pleasure and perils of such exposures for the spectator of them. Having imaged in *The House of the Seven Gables* the vulnerability of the mesmer- ized or hystericized woman, Hawthorne then investigates how the voyeurism of the individual who views such a "phenomenon in the mesmeric line" entails his own mesmerization.

The Blithedale Romance spotlights narrative subjectivity, putting Coverdale on exhibit along with the objects he watches. Under this light, his perceptual and ocular acts—the watching, witnessing, spying, speculating, fantasizing, and imagining that fashion his story—appear as "slippery" as the Veiled Lady's "Sibylline" pronouncements: "nonsensical," and "yet, on closer study, unfolding a variety of interpretations" (6). From these acts Coverdale gleans the events of the story he relates. The information Coverdale relays—often his conjectures, sometimes his reports of others' narrations such as Zenobia's legend of "The Silvery Veil" or Moodie's disclosure of the "Fauntleroy" story—conveys an ambiguity about both the intrigues at Blithedale (Are they imagined? or distorted?) and Coverdale's interest in them (Is it genuine? or self-serving?).[2]

The question of Coverdale's reliability redacts the problems of identification the Veiled Lady poses: the "enigma of her identity" and the status of her mesmeric power as "science" or "humbug" (6, 5). Both the narrator and the medium invite speculations about their individuality and about the truth of their representations. They thus give rise to a certain suspense not only about their veracity but also about the limits of their representative powers, powers which themselves are "enshrouded" (6) in the contrivances of their exhibitors.

Focusing on the medium through which the Blithedale events are imparted, Hawthorne establishes the quintessentially American theme of the simultaneously manipulative and manipulated spectator, a theme that Hitchcock's films *Rear Window* and *Vertigo* would so memorably embody in the James Stewart voyeuristic characters.[3] The drama of spectatorship in *The Blithedale Romance* concerns the pitfalls of watching that nineteenth-century consumer culture creates. Mesmeric performances like that of the Veiled Lady in Hawthorne's account are paradigmatic of consumerist attractions and the anxieties about commodification they provoke.[4] An infinite chain of spectatorship and consumption is forged in the activity of looking, as viewers continually become objects for other viewers. It is this convertibility of viewers into objects that the Veiled Lady symbolizes, as she herself is displayed in the act of gazing into "the Absolute" (201).

Thus the story about the Veiled Lady developed by Coverdale quickly changes from an epistemological riddle and identity puzzle to a Gothic tale in which she appears "enthralled in an intolerable bondage" (190). The magnetic force she exerts is encompassed by the mesmeric force that controls and displays her. For Coverdale, the salient aspect of the Veiled Lady is her subjection to her exhibitor, who profits from the epistemological interest generated by mediums. Her viewers face this same fate, the loss of personal control and privacy epitomized by the commodification of individual "peculiarities" such as the Veiled Lady's "gift of second-sight and prophecy" (187). In figuring narration as a form of mediumship and the narrator as also a potential victim of mesmerizing forces, *The Blithedale Romance* explicates the commercial ethos of spectatorship in which individuality is threatened—and, in Coverdale's case, also insulated—in the act of looking.

Looking, Leisure, and Labor

Just as conspicuous as the veiled and unveiled ladies that appear through this novel is the leisure of looking at them. The visionary labor program of Blithedale Farm all but vanishes from the narrative as it traces Coverdale's voyeuristic adventures. His pleasures of looking arise in the replacement of labor by leisure. Yet leisure is not simply the material condition of spectatorial activity but is itself a process: the aesthetic practices of transcending labor that we have just seen detailed in Downing's Gothic Revival and Hawthorne's own Gothic Revival design in *The House of the Seven Gables*. Hawthorne presents Coverdale's aestheticism as another romanticization of labor through which individuality is insulated from contingency. It is thus apposite that this look at looking in *The Blithdale Romance* begins with a similar removal of labor: the censure of kitchens and housework.[5]

Early in Hawthorne's "fancy-sketch" of the Brook Farm utopian socialist experiment, Coverdale laments, "What a pity . . . that the kitchen, and the housework generally, cannot be left out of our system altogether." What Coverdale dislikes about kitchens and housework is the degeneracy of labor they epitomize: "[T]he kind of labor which falls to the lot of women is just that which chiefly distinguishes artificial life—the life of degenerated mortals—from the life of Paradise!" In Eden "Eve had no dinner-pot, and no clothes to mend, and no washing-day" (16). Hence the tradition of housework marks the loss of paradise, signifying need and temporality. Against this tradition, Coverdale fantasizes a utopian economy that revives the Edenic housekeeping arrangement of no housekeeping at all.

Zenobia, a more pragmatic participant in Blithedale's utopian plan "for beginning the life of Paradise anew" (9), points out that the "Paradisiacal system" (16) Coverdale desires depended upon a benevolent nature which amply supplied human needs with figs, pine nuts, breadfruit, and coconuts. This Edenic provision for human consumption evoked in Zenobia's catalogue of the fruits of paradise unavailable to wintry New England constitutes Coverdale's ideal economy. Coverdale sees the prospect of this bountiful paradise regained in the Blithedale community's "beautiful scheme of a noble and unselfish life" (245). In Coverdale's vision of Blithedale at its best, "man looked strong and stately! and woman, oh, how beautiful! and the earth, a green garden, blossoming with many-colored delights!" (62).

Contrary to this scene of beauty and plenitude, domestic labor evokes man's alienation from nature and fall from Edenic balance. Domestic economy, concerned with the post-Edenic exigencies of shelter, clothing, and food, epitomizes degenerate labor and the economy of scarcity and struggle utopian socialism was to replace.[6] Domestic practices, mundane exigencies always marking the necessity of labor, therefore impede the formation of Coverdale's "modern Arcadia" based upon "delectable visions of the spiritualization of labor" (65). What appears most prominently in Coverdale's delectable visions is the female body. While housework, the responsibility "to bake, to boil, to roast, to fry, to stew . . . to wash, and iron, and scrub, and sweep" (16), seems to Coverdale decidedly unutopian, the female bodies performing those labors fascinate him. As soon as he pictures Zenobia in Eden, he imagines her naked, "that fine, perfectly developed figure, in Eve's earliest garment" (17). He has already remarked "the good fortune" that Zenobia's dress neckline offers a "glimpse of a white shoulder" (15).

Looking at women appears to be Coverdale's primary occupation at Blithedale Farm. For Coverdale, the aesthetic pleasure of this activity consists in its commercial possibilities. He wants to convert what he sees and imagines into aesthetic productions available to others. Coverdale envisions even his own work in the fields as a subject for "a romantic story," or perhaps "an epic Poem," imagining the Blithedale project as a romance of heroism in which he and his companions figure as "mythical personages" (129). Fleshing out this fantasy, Coverdale relishes the picture in which he might appear for posterity: "I will be painted in my shirt-sleeves, and with the sleeves rolled up, to show my muscular development" (129). Future generations, Coverdale continues, will pass on stories of the Blithedale men's "mighty strength" and "legends of Zenobia's beauty, and Priscilla's slender and shadowy grace" (129). Blithedale's "beautiful scheme" is thus realized in the production of a series of pleasing portraits (245).

Coverdale's preoccupation with "aimless beauty" causes his fellow communitarian Hollingsworth to diagnose him as suffering "the languor" "of an indolent or half-occupied man" (133). As the man who "might be bold to offer up" his life for a cause, provided "the effort did not involve an unreasonable amount of trouble" and the battle took place on "a mild, sunny morning, after breakfast" (246–47), Coverdale epitomizes an individualistic aestheticism.[7] His languor, contrary to Hollingsworth's assessment, has its purposes. Against Hollingsworth's reformist imperative, Coverdale asserts the primacy of personal preference: the consumer's right to see and choose his objects. Coverdale's aestheticism or, more accurately, his dilettantism, which Richard Poirier aptly characterizes as his dandyism, thus signifies not only the consumerist values that conspicuous leisure projects but the individualistic ideals that these values subtend.[8] His lifestyle accordingly typifies the private retreat from work and worldly strife which Downing's Gothic Revival domestic architecture promoted: the "dignified love of leisure and repose."[9]

Coverdale indeed leads the life of a man of leisure and of leisurely consumption, going from his "writing-table with a half-finished poem" in his "pleasant bachelor parlor" to his "morning lounge at the reading-room or picture-gallery" to his "noontide walk" to his "dinner at the Albion" and "evening at the billiard-club, the concert, theatre or at somebody's party" (40). Sharing Downing's advocacy of the invisibility of labor and the cultivation of leisure, Coverdale values "the luxurious life" (40) of his "cosey pair of bachelor-rooms" and such domestic comforts as "a good fire burning in the grate" (10). Since it is the fact of domestic labor and not domesticity that displeases him, his bachelor rooms without a woman's touch or the trace of her work are an appropriate home for him. He finds his utopian fantasy in a Downingesque domesticity in which housework disappears.

The conspicuous leisure Coverdale enjoys figures in *The Blithedale Romance* as more than the sign of class distinction Veblen would identify at the end of the century.[10] For Coverdale, conspicuous leisure represents his right to class distinction; it signifies the exercise of the tastes by which a person distinguishes himself. The expression of class distinction, in this radically individualistic view, is a democratic right. Like Downing's domestic romance, Coverdale's leisure embellishes the democratic principle "of individual expression."[11] And like the seclusion provided in Downing's homes, Coverdale's "occasional retirements" renew "the better part of [his] individuality" (89).

During his residence at communal Blithedale, Coverdale maintains a refuge, "a little hermitage" in a natural tree-house, his "one exclusive possession" which "symbolized [his] individuality, and aided [him] in keeping it inviolate" (98–99). This shelter "of rare seclusion," like Downing's model country home, ensures the sanctity and satisfaction of the individual. "It was an admirable place to make verses . . . it was just the nook, too, for the enjoyment of a cigar" (99). In Downing and Coverdale's romantic domesticity, pleasure and satisfaction replace the domestic virtue of self-sacrifice. Domestic sites offer escape not only from commerce but from labor as well, providing an easeful environment in which the self can be imagined as inviolate and in which it can be free to imagine anything at all, including utopias.[12] In addition to affording sensual satisfactions, leisure facilitates the imaginative processes by which the self is sustained in its relation to society (whether in an oppositional or affirmative mode).

This formulation of the subjective position as itself a product of the economic order is now perhaps most familiar to us as what

Lukács termed reified subjectivity. What Coverdale's hermitage exemplifies, however, is not the falsity of subjectivity or the hegemony of consumerist society which engages Marxist critics, but the way subjectivity inheres in consumerist values such as leisure.[13] That is, in Hawthorne's presentation, far from consumerism producing a false consciousness, it projects and protects the very concept of interiority. As *The House of the Seven Gables* demonstrates, even though commerce threatens individuality, commerce is also imagined as rescuing the individual from its own negative effects. For Coverdale, the consumerist pleasures of domesticity operate as democratic rights.

In the light of such individualistic values, the philanthropist Hollingsworth appears villainous in Coverdale's eyes: his "inflexible severity of purpose" (43) constrains individuality. If Coverdale lacks purpose, Hollingsworth has "a surplus of the very same ingredient" (246). His "tremendous concentrativeness and indomitable will" overthrow the democratic principle that Coverdale holds dear: "his right as an individual [to look] at matters through his own optics" (135). Hollingsworth imagines Blithedale as the site of his "one castle in the air" (56), but his aspirations disclose no democratic aims. Coverdale reports seeing Hollingsworth "a hundred times" "sketching the facade, the side-view, or the rear of the structure, or planning the internal arrangements, as lovingly as another man might plan those of the projected home, where he meant to be happy with his wife and children" (56). Hollingsworth, however, is not working on blueprints for a domestic residence; his "visionary edifice" (56) is a criminal reformatory, not a romantic retreat.

For the site and landscape of his edifice, Hollingsworth chooses "a certain point on the slope of a pasture" of the Blithedale Farm, a point commanding a view of the entire "domain, besides a view of the river and an airy prospect of many distant hills" (79–80). Coverdale, mistaking Hollingsworth's architectural interests for domestic plans, objects to the openness of the site. The ensuing debate on visible versus secluded locations reveals the two men's conflicting conceptions of utopian enterprise at Blithedale. Coverdale, adhering to Downing's advice on domestic architecture, proposes a spot "just a little withdrawn into the wood, with two or three peeps at the prospect" (80). Following the American utopian tradition, Hollingsworth wants his edifice "on the open hillside" to be "a spectacle to the world, . . . that it may take example and build many another like it" (80).

Many nineteenth-century reformers celebrated domesticity as just such an exemplary utopian site. They assumed that American progress, guided by the example of women, would logically proceed toward the millennium, the Christian utopian moment of heaven on earth. Catharine Beecher, perhaps the most vocal advocate for a Christian domestic utopia, characterized housekeepers as "agents in accomplishing the greatest work that was ever committed to human responsibility": "the building of a glorious temple, whose base shall be co-extensive with the bounds of the earth, whose summit shall pierce the skies, whose splendor shall beam on all lands." To Americans "is committed the grand, the responsible privilege, of exhibiting to the world, the beneficent influences of Christianity, when carried into every social, civil, and political institution"; and "then to American women, more than any others on earth, is committed the exalted privilege of extending over the world those blessed influences, that are to renovate degraded man, and clothe all climes with beauty." Women working in the home were performing "those labors that are to be made effectual in the regeneration of the Earth."[14]

Embracing and altering the imperialism of Beecher's manifest domesticity, Hollingsworth's obsession with his "philanthropic theory" (55) transforms utopian pursuits and domestic idealism into "a stern and dreadful peculiarity" (70). In Hollingsworth, "god-like benevolence has been debased into all-devouring egotism" (71); a mad version of Beecher's messianic, beneficent, and hard-working housekeeper, he is "the bond-slave" "to the terrible egotism which he mistook for an angel of God" (55). Surrendered to his antiseptic "over-ruling purpose" (70), Hollingsworth deviates so thoroughly from the nineteenth-century investment in the ideal of a utopian home that he upsets the logic of haunted houses: "Unlike all other ghosts, his spirit haunted an edifice which, . . . had never yet come into existence" (56). He is finally haunted by

his own criminality; his history at Blithedale is a Gothic tale without houses, a horror story of utopian exploits.

Like Beecher's vision of the golden temple domestic economy
would create, Hollingsworth's dream is of an institution to serve
as the ideal type for the reform of degenerate men. Hollingsworth
also shares Beecher's belief in noble labor as continuous with what
Zenobia calls "a strong and noble nature" (68). "I have hammered
thought out of iron, after heating the iron in my heart," Hollingsworth declares, asserting that the "earnest" character natu-
ralizes and elevates any labor (68). He intends to excise criminality, the unnatural in character and actions—"whatever vile, petty,
sordid, filthy, bestial and abominable corruptions have cankered
into our nature" (53); he would also banish romanticizations of
labor like Coverdale's. The "good in a life of toil," Hollingsworth
avers, is "that it takes the nonsense and fancy-work out of a man,
and leaves nothing but what truly belongs to him" (68).

For Hollingsworth, work functions as a kind of regenerative
diet, reducing individuals to their essence. This anti-consumerist,
or counter-consumerist, model of individuality as inhering in self-
winnowing labor figured importantly in actual antebellum reform
efforts. At the same time, it is worth noting, communitarian socialists regularly advertised as attractive features of their reorganized economies their labor-saving inventions and kitchen
utensils.[15] Work might redeem individuals, but work itself could
be refined. The stakes of Coverdale's leisure project, and his fundamental difference from Hollingsworth, will become yet clearer
after seeing how mid-nineteenth-century reformers and utopians
freighted labor and leisure with human destiny and individual
welfare.

Work Ethics: Spiritualizing Labor,
Erasing Desire

The vision of work as the means of transcending itself and elevat-
ing humanity reflects the crosscurrents in the meaning of work in
nineteenth-century American life. On the one hand, in the Lockean and Puritan traditions, work signified individual worth and

virtues. On the other hand, as wage labor, mechanization, and specialization changed the experience of labor, work increasingly represented a condition of immediate necessity to be overcome, an impediment to the pursuit of higher occupations. In the former model of work, labor signifies human property, power, and potential, and therefore the means to regeneration. Antebellum reformers sought to alter the latter model, in which the self is alienated from labor and prevented by labor from achieving realization through meaningful activity. Coverdale's objection to housework and its degenerate nature parodies and echoes the argument against alienated labor that romantic reformers advanced in their proposals and programs for alternative economic arrangements by which the individual might best express himself or herself. According to economic reformers and communitarian experimentalists, capitalism threatened the positive relation between the individual and his work. As market capitalism expanded, alienation intensified. Reformers therefore attempted to reinstate the intimacy between worker and work, to reassert the principle of redemptive, self-improving, and self-realizing labor.[16]

Situated on the fringes of society, in the woods, in vanishing rural America, or in the imagination, utopian projects shared domesticity's ideal of creating a sphere apart from the marketplace;[17] their plans, however, involved a less accommodating stance toward the political economy domesticity accompanied and effectively rationalized. Transcendentalists and experimentalists such as Henry David Thoreau at Walden, George Ripley at Brook Farm, and Bronson Alcott at Fruitlands sought alternative lifestyles that radically reformed the relation of the individual to society, preferring either "higher laws" or communal values to the ethic of economic self-seeking. Their ventures maintained, in rhetoric at least, an opposition to competitive self-interest; and they pursued their goal of eliminating capitalist individualism in self-contained communities apart from society, utopian spheres like Stowe's anti-market matriarchy, perfecting domestic refuge and regenerative promise.[18]

In service to such environments, whether Thoreau's woods or Ripley's socialist farm or Alcott's consociate family, the individual could secure a place apart from market conditions and competition: he or she could find sustenance in the perfect community rather than being subjected to the trials of American society. English industrial reformer Robert Owen established his New Harmony, Indiana, community "to introduce an entire new system of society; to change it from an ignorant, selfish system to an enlightened social system which shall gradually unite all interests in one, and remove all causes for contests between individuals."[19] In fixing society in this manner, socialist communitarians were in effect removing domestic individualistic ideals from the superstructure these values underpinned.

To escape from the "selfish competition" through which "every son of woman both perpetrates and suffers his share of the common evil," the "knot of dreamers" at Blithedale seek "profit by mutual aid" and "familiar love." In place of "the established system" based on "false and cruel principles," the Blithedale communitarians base their institution on "the earnest toil of [their] bodies, as a prayer, no less than an effort, for the advancement of [the] race" (19). The "advancement of the race" was to be effected by lessening "the laboring man's great burthen of toil" and by the experience of physical labor itself: "Each stroke of the hoe was to uncover some aromatic root of wisdom" (65). Through the eradication of the market mediating between producers and consumers, labor itself would become a transcendent activity, a situation affording "glimpses into the far-off soul of truth." Coverdale soon concludes that instead of "clods of earth [being] etherealized into thought, . . . thoughts, on the contrary, were fast becoming cloddish" (66).

At Brook Farm, where Hawthorne lived in the spring and summer of 1841, "the spiritualization of labor" meant the attainment of leisure for self-improvement. Not going quite so far as the Blithedale participants who envisioned labor as their "ceremonial of worship" (65), Brook Farm's founder, George Ripley, understood the reform of labor as the freeing of the spirit through the erasure of working hierarchies. He proposed "to insure a more natural union between intellectual and manual labor than now exists."[20] The aims of the Brook Farm Institute for Agriculture and Education were "to guarantee the highest mental freedom, by providing all with labor, adapted to their tastes and talents, and securing to them the fruits of their industry," and "to do away with the necessity of menial services, by opening the benefits of education and the profits of labor to all." The collective undertaking of agriculture, an ideally extra-market, subsistence occupation, would create the leisure for moral progress and "prepare a society of liberal, intelligent, and cultivated persons, whose relations with each other would permit a more simple and wholesome life, than can be led amidst the pressure of our competitive system."[21]

Hawthorne himself found the effects of physical labor at Brook Farm not at all enlightening or regenerating. "Labor is the curse of this world," he wrote his future wife, Sophia, "and nobody can meddle with it, without becoming proportionately brutified."[22] Coverdale's rhapsodic transmutation of farm labor into a Blithedale mythology, which he himself admits is "nine-tenths of nonsense," parodies Ripley's idealization of agriculture. If huswifery in the kitchen seems mundane and degenerate, husbandry in the field is equally uninspiring. Coverdale's arbitrary romanticization of labor exhibits Hawthorne's sense of the absurdity of transcendentalist efforts to spiritualize labor. Labor stubbornly remains labor.

Ripley's ideal economy required the redemption of labor, but even reorganized labor resisted spiritualization and persisted in manifesting the "competitive system" rather than the "more simple and wholesome life" imagined by Ripley. Brook Farm increasingly resembled the system it opposed. In 1844, the enterprise, renamed the Brook Farm Institute for Industry and Education, adapted the Fourieristic design for economic reform. Charles Fourier, whose theories Coverdale reads and finds "horribly tedious" (53), conceived of the ideal society as harmonious associations of simultaneously competitive and cooperative individuals. Fourier's assumption of the human proclivity for competition offends Coverdale's fellow communitarian Hollingsworth, who condemns Fourier's system for its promotion of "the selfish principle—the principle of all human wrong . . . which it is the whole aim of spiritual discipline to eradicate" (53). What happened at Brook

Farm bears out Hollingsworth's charge that Fourierism is "an infernal regeneration" (53), reproducing market capitalism in paradisiacal guise. Brook Farm's implementation of Fourier's design meant incorporating manufacturing into its labor system; the community's expansion of industry entailed replacing its subsistence economy with a system of diversified labor and exchange reminiscent of the market capitalism Ripley opposed.[23] Instead of offering refuge and seclusion from competitive American society, Brook Farm became another version of that society.

In order to forestall the eventuality of the market impinging upon alternative economic systems, the reform of labor logically demanded the eradication of the human desires upon which the competitive market both preyed and depended. The closest approximation to the erasure of desire, and perhaps also to Coverdale's vision of a community without mundane labor, was Bronson Alcott and John Lane's utopian experiment at Fruitlands. In a radical effort to expunge all traces of competition, Alcott and Lane established their "consociate family" at Fruitlands upon the rule of "aesthetic labor."[24] Alcott and Lane believed market tendencies to be so prevalent and pervasive that even animal labor was paradigmatic of market hierarchies and exchanges, and therefore immoral. A purified economy must banish all signs of the low human tendencies encouraged by capitalism, and farm animals embodied brute instincts and signified in their labor the brutishness of human usage for profit. For the leisure to think and improve, the Fruitlands organizers advocated what amounted to the elimination of labor altogether; aesthetic labor proved to be the spiritualization of labor through the denial of desires. Elaborating abstinence as the means to an ideal, minimalist economy, Alcott and Lane focused on diet more than any other practice, instituting an economy of containment in the body. Alcott's pursuit of the pure life did not follow the principles of abstinence as far as Lane's, for Lane thought celibacy necessary to the containment of desire. When Fruitlands dissolved, Lane joined the Shakers, who celebrated and practiced celibacy as the cornerstone of an alternative, spiritual community.[25]

Lane's commitment to abstinence for the aestheticization of labor in some ways resembles domestic doctrine's program for reform. In her *Treatise,* Beecher advised that for "the happiness of our race . . . the submission of the will . . . is the best preparative" (*Treatise,* 225). Housekeepers exemplified the self-sacrifice necessary to the realization of America's utopian potential. The most utopian of reformist exploits, Fruitlands represents the purest form of domestic virtue: self-denial as a way of life. In fact, Fruitlands not only adopted Beecher's domestic-economy triad of "the three most important habits"—"submission of the will, self-denial, and benevolence"—but very much depended upon the womanly self-denial and physical labor of Alcott's wife, Abigail, and their daughters. Alcott and Lane's experiment in abstinence involved the Alcott children, who subsisted on apples and little else, and required Abigail's self-sacrifice to mundane labor. In order to sustain the family and finance necessities, Abigail took in sewing.[26]

Ironically, the self-sacrifice of women and the spiritualization of labor which were to redeem life from the degenerate conditions of market economy effected the reverse: Abigail's labor reconnected Fruitlands to the society Alcott and Lane had tried to escape. In Alcott and Lane's redefinition and redistribution of labor, women engage in labor and exchange while men virtually take the housekeeper's position. Though this gender reversal followed from the impracticalities of the Fruitlands system, it was the ideal of this experiment to achieve only one change in identification, that of removing men from markets, linking man with domestic self-discipline and repose. An ethic of abstinence—and, in Alcott's case, an ethical refusal of employment—perfects the domestic escape from the market by translating self-sacrifice into the ultimate labor reform, into leisure. Literalizing and extending Hollingsworth's conception of work as regenerative diet, the Fruitlands experiment winnowed both desire and labor, making leisure an ascetic pursuit.

Leisure Ethics and Erotics

One permutation of work ethics in utopianist and reformist thought is thus the alignment of true self-expression with leisure, a principle following from the redefinition of leisure as a nonconsumerist activity and value. Coverdale's aesthetic pursuit of leisure, however, in contrast to the Fruitlands dietetic imagination of self, minimizes labor and maximizes desire. Whereas utopianists like Alcott minimized both labor and desire in order to eliminate market relations, Coverdale maximizes desire and leisure in order to eliminate the dangers desire entails. In other words, Coverdale might be said to typify a utopian consumerism, the pleasures of consumerism without the problems. These problems, *The Blithedale Romance* makes clear, arise from the power objects of desire exert. Unlike Stowe, who ascribes to objects a self-ratifying power, Hawthorne attributes to them a magnetic force in which the individual may be caught. And this threat, we will see, is met with a renewal of the consumerist practice of just looking.[27]

The experiences in Coverdale's sick-chamber disclose and amplify the danger in his usual consumerist pleasure: the risk of subjection to desire. Bedridden with a "fit of sickness" and "fed on water-gruel," Coverdale reports that he "speedily became a skeleton above ground" (41). In this "reduced state of the corporeal system" (46) Coverdale begins to entertain "a great many conjectures" about "the mystery" of Zenobia (47) and to wonder "whether Zenobia had ever been married" (46). Coverdale attributes his obsessive speculation to the effect of his "wasting illness" in which "the soul gets the better of the body" (46). According to this etiology of prurience, "vapors then rise up to the brain, and take shapes that often image falsehood, but sometimes truth" (46). The susceptibility to visions of all kinds increases in his bodily "weakness," Coverdale reports, transforming him "into something like a mesmerical clairvoyant" (47). Apart from affording potential access to "truth" and insight, a "reduced state of the corporeal system" (46) makes the individual a channel of the self-expression of others. "The sphere of our companions have, at such periods, a vastly greater influence upon our own, than when robust health gives a repellent and self-defensive energy" (46). An invalid's diet increases Coverdale's desire to look and speculate, but does not grant the self-defensiveness of healthy leisure. In his "sensitive condition of mind and body" (48) "Zenobia's sphere" seems to impress itself so "powerfully" upon Coverdale he begins "to wish that she would let [him] alone" (46, 48). The mediumistic state to which illness reduces Coverdale thus makes him subject to the objects of his observation. A safer—or more controllable—consumerist relation obtains in his hermitage or bachelor rooms, where he indulges all his tastes and enjoys the privacy that others cannot penetrate.

The leisure of Coverdale's convalescence, then, takes on a defensive consumerist style. His variable attitude toward Zenobia, alternating between the wish to see more of her and the wish to banish her from sight, leads him to wish for her mass production. "The image of her form and face should have been multiplied all over the earth. It was wronging the rest of mankind, to retain her as the spectacle of only a few" (44). Public access to Zenobia's beauty—"the stage would have been her proper sphere"—would seem to mitigate and diffuse her power over the individual (44). He advocates this democratic consumer right to see Zenobia while confiding that her sight makes him "morbidly sensitive" (44). "I know not well how to express, that the native glow of coloring in her cheeks, and even the flesh-warmth over her round arms, and what was visible of her full bust—in a word, her womanliness incarnated—compelled me sometimes to close my eyes," Coverdale confesses (44). It is against this compulsion that a wider marketing and consumption of Zenobia would operate. The commercial solution generalizes and depersonalizes desire. Imagining Zenobia as a public beauty, a pin-up of sorts, limits her personal effect.

While Zenobia makes the invalid Coverdale both curious and "nervous" (48), "Hollingsworth's more than brotherly attendance" gives him "inexpressible comfort" (41). In the intimacy of this nursing Coverdale perceives that "there was something of the woman molded into the great, stalwart frame of Hollingsworth" (42). Hollingsworth's "tenderness" makes him better than even Coverdale's bachelor domestic comforts. "There was never any blaze of a fireside that warmed and cheered me," Coverdale professes, "so effectually as did the light out of those eyes, which lay so deep and dark under his shaggy brows" (42). Passivity under

Hollingsworth's care has rendered Coverdale susceptible to those "deep eyes" (71). While Zenobia's overwhelming sexual presence causes him to insist rather testily that he "should not, under any circumstances, have fallen in love with" her (48), he readily discloses that he "loved Hollingsworth" (70).[28]

Nowhere are the issues of self-definition and self-protection more crucial than in erotic relations. In the case of Coverdale's relation to Hollingsworth, the imperatives of individuality make their intimacy impossible. There is, then, a certain relief for Coverdale in the fact that "the tenderest man" who is his "truest friend on earth . . . had a closer friend than ever [he] could be. And this friend was the cold, spectral monster which he had himself conjured up, and on which he was wasting all the warmth of his heart. . . . It was his philanthropic theory!" (55). More than a rival for Hollingsworth's alliance, this theory keeps the philanthropist its "bond-slave" and threatens to enslave others (55). Although, as Coverdale confides to Hollingsworth, "I heartily wish that I could make your schemes my schemes, because it would be so great a happiness to find myself treading the same path with you" (56), he finally cannot join in "this great scheme" (133) because he fears Hollingsworth's "all-devouring egotism" (71). It is Hollingsworth's self-denying (in all senses of the phrase) "purpose" that alerts Coverdale to the peril of his own submission to a man whose single-mindedness must prove "pernicious to the happiness of those who should be drawn into too intimate a connection with him" (70).

At the same time, so great is Hollingsworth's "hold of [Coverdale's] heart" (134) that refusing his "proposal" (135) is like withstanding "an almost irresistible force" (134). Saying no induces a "heart-pang . . . not merely figurative, but an absolute torture of the breast" (135). The cost of this refusal is explicitly erotic. Crying and holding out his hands to Coverdale, Hollingsworth pleads with him that "there is not the man in this wide world, whom I can love, as I could you" (133). In order to keep "aloof" from this appeal, Coverdale fortifies himself with "doubts" about Hollingsworth's "integrity" (134). This speculative self-fortification against his own sense that, "[h]ad I but touched his extended hand,

Hollingsworth's magnetism would perhaps have penetrated me with his own conceptions of all these matters" (134) is a process Coverdale has earlier adapted, almost as if in anticipation of this crisis of will.

To avert Hollingsworth's power over him, Coverdale has already taken to making the philanthropist a "mental occupation" (69). "Had I loved him less, I might have used him better," Coverdale relates, "but I could not help it" (69). He cannot help his "prying" (69) because it helps him distance himself from Hollingsworth. This self-protective habit succeeds to such an extent that Hollingsworth becomes unattractive to Coverdale. Just as Coverdale's speculations about Zenobia eventually diminish his erotic interest in her, his "mode of observation" leads him to shudder at his friend, now monstrous in appearance. "In my recollection of his dark and impressive countenance," Coverdale explains, "the features grew more sternly prominent than the reality, duskier in their depth and shadow, and more lurid in their light; the frown, that had merely flitted across his brow, seemed to have contorted it with an adamantine wrinkle" (71). The man whose "expression of tender, human care, and gentlest sympathy" Coverdale has "often thought . . . beautiful" (72) becomes a repulsive object.

Coverdale resists Hollingsworth's magnetism by making the object of his desire unattractive. This defensive transfiguration of persons, besides distancing the viewer from his objects, reasserts the mediumistic character of persons and hence their subjection. Imagining Hollingsworth as monstrous exemplifies Coverdale's speculative practice of making persons into mediums, into sites for other sights. When he looks at Priscilla, he seems to see Margaret Fuller. Such transfiguration of persons into mediums is also a transfiguration of persons into spectacle, available to general view. The public dimension of mediumship Hawthorne excoriates in *The House of the Seven Gables* here affords a critical protective distance. The object viewed can be viewed by others; the danger of subjection to that object dissolves as desire for it is dispersed over a field of viewers.[29]

It is this structure of spectatorship I am calling self-protective

consumerism that shapes Coverdale's story of Blithedale as a report of his watching the women who want Hollingsworth. Displacing and dispersing his own desire, Coverdale's relation to
Hollingsworth and to Zenobia and Priscilla resembles "that of the
Chorus in a classic play, which seems to be set aloof from the
possibility of personal concernment, and bestows the whole measure of its hope or fear, its exultation or sorrow, on the fortunes
of others, between whom and itself this sympathy is the only
bond" (97). Rationalizing his "vocation" as "calm observer" (97)
as merely sympathetic, Coverdale can indulge himself in prying,
peeping, and eavesdropping into Hollingsworth's affairs. This interest focuses on those who replace Coverdale as Hollingsworth's
intimates. For what fascinates Coverdale about the other man is
less the psychology of the philanthropist (or the Emersonian dictum that the reformer should first reform himself),[30] than the
women he attracts—"what Hollingsworth meant to do with
them—and they with him!" (68). Coverdale then sees Hollingsworth, Zenobia, and Priscilla "as the indices of a problem" he
means to solve (69). For Coverdale, whose hermitage is "an ob-
servatory" (99) as well as a retreat, all meaning of the Blithedale
experiment inheres in the machinations of the people he casts as
the characters in his "private theatre" (70). Eschewing participation and partisanship, he remains a spectator of all the realms in
which he dabbles: a cynic about the Blithedale enterprise, an un-
welcome bystander to the triangle of Zenobia, Hollingsworth,
and Priscilla, and, finally, an aging bachelor no longer writing.
The writer's encounter with utopia results not in the reformist
literary engagement urged by Hawthorne's transcendentalist contemporaries but in voyeuristic disengagement.[31] The poet who
would "turn the whole affair into a ballad" (223) relates a bachelor's romance, reveries of limited engagements.[32]

Voyeurism and Fetishism

Coverdale's disengagement shapes his narrative into a series of
disavowals in which he hedges on the accuracy or authenticity of

his observations. "What I seem to remember, I yet suspect may have been patched together by fancy," he remarks of the encounter between Zenobia and Westervelt which he reconstructs although he could not fully hear it (104). He similarly confesses to "a trifle of romantic and legendary license" in relating the events of Moodie's life (181). These rhetorical buffers to his representations allow Coverdale to circumvent commitment to his own words. The safety of the spectator is thus fortified in the uncertainty of his position as well as in the changeable—and exchangeable—aspect of his objects.

In Coverdale's practice of evasion and displacement we can recognize the consumerist dimensions of the psychology of voyeurism Freud later made familiar. The personal advantages of Coverdale's strategic consumerism become clear when we consider it in the psychic terms Freud made available. Since the safeties of uncertainty which anchor masculine individuality in *The Blithedale Romance* depend on the relation between uncertainty and identity operating in visual pleasure, it would be helpful to have in mind the logistics of that relation as conceived in both traditional (fundamentally androcentric) and revisionary psychoanalytic theories.

At stake in voyeurism, and in the pleasure of looking *The Blithedale Romance* explicates, is the maintenance of a particular masculine identity. Voyeuristic pleasure, according to Freud, is a fetishistic erotic practice, a substitute for genital sexual encounters. A fetish works as a penis-substitute, which "is not a substitute for any chance penis, but for a particular quite special penis that had been extremely important in early childhood but was afterwards lost. . . . To put it plainly: the fetish is a substitute for the woman's (mother's) phallus which the little boy once believed in and does not wish to forgo."[33] A defense against the knowledge of the mother's lack and against the threat of castration that the sight of that lack precipitates, fetishism represents a compromise in which the perception of castration is both registered and denied. In this typically male perversion, the fetish "remains a token of triumph over the threat of castration and a safeguard against it." And, as

Freud immediately adds, "it all saves the fetishist from being a homosexual by endowing women with the attribute which makes them acceptable as sexual objects."[34]

Freud defines homosexuality as an identification with the mother and her position in bourgeois culture as a sexual object. In Freud's narrative of "normal" sexual development, the child identifies with his father, who possesses the phallus. This identification occurs after the child realizes that the mother, the first and primary object of desire and identification, has no phallus; in contrast, in the case of what Freud calls homosexuality the child continues to fantasize a phallic mother and fails to align himself with his father's sexual identity. Yet even the "normal" path of development entails the same initial fantasy, which implies that all children are homosexual subjects until they realign themselves. Fetishism, or more precisely Freud's account of it, restages this difficulty in identity formation. Furthermore, as feminist readings of fetishism demonstrate, the Freudian theory functions to eliminate the homosexual moment in this process. What "saves" the fetishist even as he recapitulates the irresolution before "normal" sexual identification, Freud stresses, is that he, as it were, reendows woman with the penis. The fetishist's need to make women acceptable sexual objects by endowing them with penises has its corollary in the concept of penis envy, which characterizes women as wanting to be so endowed. The homophobic basis of both these remarkable formulations, Sarah Kofman points out, implies that homosexuality or fetishism "would be the *normal* destiny of the masculine libido." Indeed, under Freud's own logic "what becomes *abnormal* is heterosexuality."[35]

There is, then, a fetishistic defense organizing Freud's own account of fetishism: the erection of the penis against homosexuality and femininity. In Kofman's analysis, the defensiveness of Freud's fetishism arises from the fact that the fetish "is never a simple unequivocal substitute for the penis." Fetishism defends against its own equivocations, from its own "split between denial and affirmation of castration."[36] For Kofman and other feminist psychoanalytic critics interested in locating a specific female subject, this ambiguity in fetishism is a crucial symptom of a different sexual identity or of a difference within sexual identity. The "homosexual" structure of subjectivity Kofman analyzes exemplifies the difficulty and revision operating in normal identity formation. Following Lacan's revisionary exegesis of Freud, feminists focus on how Freud's account of the subject projects a self divided, a self always at odds with itself. In this light, Freud's attempts to stabilize his subject as heterosexual, surfacing in the "Fetishism" essay as censure of an ever present homosexuality or femininity, indicate that Freud futilely seeks to repress or resolve the uncertainties which in fact constitute and characterize the human subject. And, from the viewpoint of feminist psychoanalytic theory, this difficulty within subjectivity that Freudian homosexuality might be said to thematize is persistently associated in Freud's work with femininity. Femininity as Freud constructed it is thus not a site of sexual identity but a relation to sexual identity. Recognizing subjectivity as relational, Lacanian feminists locate the feminine in the operations and traces of the unconscious.[37]

I have rehearsed this discussion in order to clarify the sexual-identity issues at stake in both the phenomenon and the theory of fetishism. While fetishism, according to Freud, projects an account of homosexuality and homophobia, it also, and more meaningfully, images the conflicts and difficulties in subjectivity as homoerotics. Feminist revisionary readings of fetishism suggest something of the demonology in which the category of the homosexual has operated. The preceding synopsis of feminist psychoanalytic formulations of identity illuminates the displacements of erotic objects I have traced in *The Blithedale Romance* by explaining the self-protective psychic work Coverdale's visual pleasure performs. The point here is not to classify his strategies as homoerotic but to elucidate how they work. As much as Coverdale distances himself from erotic objects, his speculative interest in them keeps them ever present and, indeed, sustains him. The self-sustenance of his dispersed desire becomes clear when we consider further the defensiveness of fetishism.

Kofman frames the question of what fetishistic equivocations defend as being a question of sexual identity. Her analysis extends and particularizes Jacques Derrida's account of equivocation in fetishism in which he develops this matter as an epistemological question or, to be more precise, as an epistemological defense. Derrida takes what Freud called "the double attitude of fetishists" to be the fundamental point in fetishism: fetishism not only thematizes but indeed generates what Derrida calls undecidability. What fetishistic equivocations defend, Derrida proposes, is their very undecidability. And this undecidability fortifies the subject in a position of unassailability. As Derrida puts it, "the economy of the fetish is more powerful than that of the truth—decidable—of the thing itself or than a deciding discourse of castration (*pro aut contra*). The fetish is not opposable."[38] The doubleness of the fetish—its entertainment of both castration and the denial of castration—defines fetishism as a defense strategy. Simultaneously bound to contrary propositions, the fetish gains its undeniability by holding no truth to be unveiled. Fetishism in this view both *is* and operates a defense system in which identity is formed and sustained in its oscillations. Oscillation offers a means for holding a position by refusing to choose one.

From the anxious relations between persons and objects that Hawthorne discovers in public spectacles, *The Blithedale Romance* constructs both the psychological profile and the ontological status of fetishism. Again, I want to stress that what we recognize in this novel is not simply a paradigm of homoerotics; we see what might be called the objective of desire in keeping individual identity intact. The equivocations detailed by *The Blithedale Romance* and classified by psychoanalysis reflect the complications arising from the nineteenth-century representation of individuality in the feminine idiom. Fetishism, seen in the cultural context Hawthorne delineates, reprises the alignments through which the nineteenth century defined the self.

The fetishist's play with veils—a now-you-see-the-phallus, now-you-don't game—is typified in Coverdale's simultaneous curiosity and detachment. It is this double attitude that Zenobia's legend of "The Silvery Veil" attempts to critique as immoral. In this story the young man Theodore seeks to discover the Veiled Lady's identity. Gaining his object of viewing her without her veil, he loses her forever because he refuses to kiss the Lady before seeing her. To look behind the Lady's veil without "a pure and generous purpose, but in scornful skepticism and idle curiosity" (113) is to lose her: "to pine away, forever and ever, for another sight of that dim, mournful face—which might have been his life-long, household, fireside joy—to desire, and waste life in a feverish quest" (114). Taking her on faith (that is, kissing her without first seeing her) would mean aligning desire to a purpose, curiosity to investment, and hence would gain Theodore a happy domesticity. The moral of Zenobia's tale is not just that profane purposes get punished or that sexual knowledge entails loss; this parable cautions against Coverdale's lack of commitment. The intended lesson misses its mark, though, because unlike Theodore, Coverdale takes satisfaction in the perpetual desire that seeing the Veiled Lady generates. Like Theodore, he likes to peep behind veils and peer into private regions. Housefronts appear to him "a veil and a concealment," and he therefore posits that "there is far more of the picturesque . . . and vastly greater suggestiveness, in the back view of a residence. . . . Realities keep in the rear" (149). Putting his theory to practice, Coverdale, smoking in his Boston hotel room, watches through his rear window the rear of the boardinghouse opposite:

At a window of the next story below, two children, prettily dressed, were looking out. By-and-by, a middle-aged gentleman came softly behind them, kissed the little girl, and playfully pulled the little boy's ear. It was a papa, no doubt, just come in from his counting-room or office; and anon appeared mamma, stealing as softly behind papa, as he had stolen behind the children, and laying her hand on his shoulder to surprise him. Then followed a kiss between papa and mamma, but a noiseless one; for the children did not turn their heads. (150–51)

This portrait of domestic bliss seems to Coverdale "a prettier bit of nature" than anything at Blithedale Farm. He promises himself to pay the family "a little more attention, by-and-by" (151); but Coverdale is so addicted to his bachelor fascination with unveiling women that he soon forgets this resolution in favor of "sedulously watching" (162) "the faintest imaginable glimpse of a girl's figure" (155) through the windows of the floor below. Coverdale prefers to turn away from domestic intimacies and look elsewhere, "through the white curtain" of what proves to be "Zenobia's drawing-room" (161). He treats the sight of a domesticity he lacks like a commodity he enjoys looking at but has no interest in buying. Yet the objects that most powerfully compel his interest also are only for viewing: Zenobia appears at her window "like a full-length picture" (155). The fetishistic pleasure and safety of voyeurism find a fitting expression in Coverdale's utopian consumerism of only and always looking.[39]

Mesmerism, Voyeurism, and Romance

Coverdale's voyeurism depends on a regular panorama of objects for viewing. To satisfy this requirement of an ever present and always changing procession of objects, Coverdale's self-defensive spectatorship attributes a metamorphic property to the objects he looks at, their "transfiguration" (119) into more remote and even repellent forms. His erotic objects become, in mediumistic fashion, transparencies for yet other objects or concepts. It might be said that Coverdale loves the objects he views for the various paths of reference they map. Following Coverdale's optical series of displacing images, we can begin to see how the voyeur evades (as he courts) the danger of his own subjection through the referentiality of his objects.

As in the tableaux vivants the Blithedale residents perform, "in which scarlet shawls, old silken robes, ruffs, velvets, furs, and all kinds of miscellaneous trumpery converted . . . familiar companions into people of a pictorial world" (106), the accessories and ornaments that fascinate Coverdale constantly summon other images. For example, the hothouse tropical flower Zenobia wears as her customary ornament appears to him "a talisman" or "subtile expression of Zenobia's character" (45). Looking at this "daily flower," Coverdale begins to discern a "magical property" in it, moving him to declare Zenobia "an enchantress" and "a sister of the Veiled Lady!" (45). This pronouncement turns out to be "clairvoyant" (47), like the clairvoyance Coverdale attributes to Zenobia. A prophetic power seems to express itself in Zenobia's gesture of casting the exotic flower from her hair onto the floor. The "singular, but irresistible effect" of this act is to predict failure for the Blithedale socialist exploit: "[T]he presence of Zenobia caused our heroic enterprise to show like an illusion, a masquerade, a pastoral, a counterfeit Arcadia, in which we grown-up men and women were making a play-day of the years that were given to us to live in" (21). The train of thought generated by Zenobia's flower that brings to Coverdale this revelation also conveys the revelatory thought that "Zenobia has lived, and loved" (47).

If the supposition that "there is no unfolded petal, no latent dew-drop, in that perfectly developed rose" (47) excites (and eventually enervates) him, the mystery surrounding the appearance of the "flowerlike" (61) Priscilla, a "maiden" (49), equally enthralls him. Regarding the silk purses Priscilla sews as "a symbol of Priscilla's own mystery" (35), Coverdale wonders about the possible similarities between her and these intricate purses "whose peculiar excellence . . . lay in the almost impossibility that any uninitiated person should discover the aperture; although to the practised touch, they would open as wide as charity or prodigality might wish" (35).

The sexually charged ambiguity of Priscilla and her purses, their simultaneous inaccessibility and penetrability, also characterizes her role as Veiled Lady. Her disguised presence in public invites the disrobing and speculation described in Zenobia's cautionary tale about masculine interest in the Veiled Lady. Yet, as Coverdale remarks, "there was a singular self-possession in Priscilla" (142), and he "religiously" believes that "she had kept . . . her virgin reserves and sanctity of soul" (203) throughout her performances as the Veiled Lady. The paradox in her "visible obscurity" (201) also figures in her prophecies. On the first page of his narrative Coverdale mentions that the night before going to Blithedale Farm he consulted this celebrated "phenomenon in the mesmeric line," questioning her "as to the success of our Blithedale enterprise." "The response, by-the-by, was of the true Sibylline stamp, nonsensical in its first aspect, yet on closer study, unfolding a variety of interpretations, one of which has certainly accorded with the event" (5–6). These equivocations of the Veiled

Lady (which, as I indicated at the beginning of this chapter, resemble Coverdale's own ambiguous representations) mitigate the
more forthright statement Coverdale subsequently reads in Zenobia's disposal of her flower. Whereas the revelation Coverdale
takes from Zenobia's gesture clearly accords with later events, the
vague message he gets from the Veiled Lady only makes sense
after manifold interpretive machinations.

The paths from Zenobia's flower and Priscilla's purses to their
prophecies trace two different patterns of reference: direct correspondence and variable connection. The latter mode is clearly
more attractive to the voyeuristic project of holding erotic objects
at a remove. Zenobia's "womanly frankness" (47), the sheer physical fact of femaleness her body presents to Coverdale, makes him
"nervous" (48). In contrast to the unmistakable sexuality Zenobia
embodies, the Veiled Lady's identity appears allusive and indis-
tinct. She tantalizes Coverdale by constantly mystifying or defer-
ring her meaning. For voyeurs like Coverdale, the medium is the
message precisely because of her metonymic and metaphoric
possibilities.[40] Coverdale finds a perfect voyeuristic object in the
Veiled Lady: a sight that never solidifies into certainty. Both an
anonymous apparition and a public performer, she elicits and
eludes sexual and epistemological discovery. Her mesmeric performances restage the fetishist's pleasure in the ambiguity of his
objects. Ambiguity in his objects, however, does not obviate the
voyeur's subjection. It may preserve the mystique of the object,
but it illuminates a very definite correspondence: the identity of
the voyeur with the medium. We have already seen how Coverdale's interests habitually become his mediums, as Hollingsworth,
for instance, is "the medium of introducing" Priscilla (49). How
his interests make himself a medium becomes manifest in his encounters with the mesmerist Professor Westervelt. His dependence on mediums to maintain his balance between interest and
distance draws the spectator into the commercial network in
which they perform, and into a relation with the manager of this
business, the mesmerist. The mesmerist appeals to the voyeur's
desire, pandering to the voyeuristic interest in spectacles that are

themselves visual avenues to something else. In serving the voyeur the mesmerist subjects him.

Although Coverdale can resist subjection to the spheres of Zenobia and Hollingsworth, he succumbs to Westervelt's "influence" and finds himself looking "through his eyes" (101). This position entails a double violation, the usurpation of Coverdale's privacy and the pollution of his vision. "There are some spheres, the contact with which inevitably degrades the high, debases the pure, deforms the beautiful. It must be a mind of uncommon strength, and little impressibility, that can permit itself the habit of such intercourse, and not be permanently deteriorated," Coverdale notes (101). Against his own "impressibility" he forms an "infinite . . . dislike" (172) of Westervelt, "all the more," he frankly admits, "because a part of my own nature showed itself responsive to him" (102). The "contagion" with which Westervelt has "affected" (95) Coverdale causes a physical revulsion, "nothing less than a creeping of the flesh, as when, feeling about in a dark place, one touches something cold and slimy, and questions what the secret hatefulness may be" (172). The secret hatefulness proves to be Westervelt's penetration of Coverdale's own subjection, his own mediumship. With "a catlike circumspection," Westervelt turns Coverdale into a viewed object by "detecting and recognizing" him at his "post of observation" (158).

To be under the influence of the magician–businessman Westervelt is to be like the medium Priscilla, the victimized Veiled Lady whom D. H. Lawrence aptly called "a little psychic prostitute."[41] *The House of the Seven Gables* registered Hawthorne's horror of mesmerism in its representations of mesmeric power as rape and induced hysteria. In *The Blithedale Romance,* Hawthorne attaches such sordidness to mesmeric acts that the medium's public display of her virtue, which is the access she affords to transcendent spheres, appears as prostitution. Exhibiting Priscilla as the Veiled Lady, Westervelt conducts a traffic in mediums. This prostitution involves far more than the female body: the entire ideal of femininity, and thus of individuality, is undermined when the mesmerist makes commerce of individual penetrability. No beneficent mesmerism like Phoebe's homely magic appears in *The Blithedale Romance,* where Hawthorne pictures individuality as always vulnerable to a self-interested mesmeric control. Even Hollingsworth's rescue of Priscilla from Westervelt only places her in submission to another magnetic man who defines her "compass" (220).[42]

Mesmerists in general provoke "horror and disgust" in Coverdale because their power over others implies that "the individual soul [can be] virtually annihilated" (198). Asserting a "miraculous power of one human being over the will and passions of another," the mesmerist can change and control human dispositions:

> At the bidding of one of these wizards, the maiden, with her lover's kiss still burning on her lips, would turn from him with icy indifference; the newly made widow would dig her buried heart out of her young husband's grave, before the sods had taken root upon it; a mother, with her babe's milk in her bosom, would thrust away her child. Human character was but soft wax in his hands; and guilt, or virtue, only the forms into which he should see fit to mould it. (198)

Coverdale's examples of subjected persons are all female and the instances of their subjection are all departures from, if not repudiations of, their conventional roles. Under the influence of the mesmerist, women appear bound to none of their defining relations. While these arbitrary shifts in women's alignments clearly scandalize Coverdale, the mesmeric state of changeability also holds a certain attraction for him, despite his fear of being "beneath the influence of a man possessing this potency" (198). The swerves of affection that the mesmerized women exhibit—their variability and their rejection of fixed relations—bear an affinity with his own.

The identification between himself and mediums which Coverdale registers also encompasses the victimage of the medium to the mesmerist. Westervelt, "imbued throughout with a cold and dead materialism" (200), perceives in Priscilla's wraithlike physical condition (a condition of impressibility like Coverdale's own reduced corporeal state) a chance to capitalize on the popular association of femininity with immateriality and spirituality. Displaying the medium's signifying power, the mesmerist channels it for his own economic gain. He thus commodifies, reproduces, and distributes the medium's allusiveness. In "bondage" (112) to him, Priscilla "never [has] any free-will" (171). Priscilla in the role of the Veiled Lady medium repeats the history of her father, Moodie, who retains no character of his own, taking character from his circumstances. Moodie's fortunes, related in Coverdale's fairy-tale account ironically entitled "Fauntleroy," rise and fall. Subject to movement (and easily moved by the spirits Coverdale buys him), he represents the changeability and indeterminacy of life in the marketplace, the same commercial uncertainties Stowe attacked in *Uncle Tom's Cabin*. The danger of this life lies in the immanence of determinant operations which channel particular interests through permeable, unprotected individuals like Priscilla. It is this vulnerability to enslavement that Coverdale ultimately shares with Priscilla.[43]

What Westervelt has detected and revealed in Coverdale's spectatorship, then, is Coverdale's own mediumship—the fetishist's bondage to his objects. Westervelt shows that Coverdale's spectatorship is after all an enmeshment in others: he is a literally captive audience. Discovering Westervelt, Zenobia, and Priscilla in the boardinghouse across from his Boston hotel room fills Coverdale with "a positive despair, to find the same figures arraying themselves before" him (157). All his looking has left him with a "poor individual life, which was now attenuated of much of its proper substance, and diffused among many alien interests" (157). Even away from Blithedale, "the train of thoughts" his "three friends" have generated keeps "treading remorselessly to-and-fro" (153). These figures and thoughts "encroach upon" his dreams, where he is "impotent to regulate them" (153).

Having proved a vulnerable position, Coverdale's observational post requires defense. He thus insists on his "fitness for the office" of spectator, imagining that "of all possible observers," his objects "should have selected" himself (160–61). In this reversal of his previous characterization of himself as the "aloof" and "calm observer" (97), Coverdale now represents himself as desired by his objects. The imagination that his objects have chosen him, making him their object, removes Coverdale from his vulnerable voyeuristic state. For the object he imagines himself to be is subject only to himself: his voyeurism is an abstract subjection to his own "sympathies" to "pry with a speculative interest into people's passions and impulses" (154). It is such sympathy, Coverdale rationalizes, as he retrenches his position,

which impelled me (often against my own will, and to the detriment of my own comfort) to live in other lives, and to endeavor—by generous sympathies, by delicate intuitions, by taking note of things too slight for record, and by bringing my human spirit into manifold accordance with the companions whom God assigned me—to learn the secret which was hidden from even themselves. (160)

This charge to investigate Hollingsworth, Zenobia, and Priscilla proves, however, to be a "thraldom" (205) to Coverdale as he recognizes "how deeply my connection with those three has affected all my being" (195). "These three had absorbed my life into themselves," he realizes (194). If sympathy absorbs the voyeur into his objects, Coverdale finds some comfort in assuming that everyone shares this vulnerability:

Our souls, after all, are not our own. We convey a property in them to those with whom we associate, but to what extent can never be known, until we feel the tug, the agony, of our abortive effort to resume an exclusive sway over ourselves. (194)

Imagining everyone as under the sway of others, as mediums, the voyeur in effect elides his own subjection with a pervasive phenomenon. At the same time, projecting himself as a medium, the channel of others' desires, allows the voyeur to experiment safely with the subjection he fears. What is at stake here, as always, is the individuality of the voyeur—the safe play of his desires through his projective affinities. Thus Coverdale takes pains to reconstitute the individual spheres of his objects. After his admission of the mediumistic properties of self, he no longer desires to see scenes of Hollingsworth, Zenobia, and Priscilla, to whom he grants "a sphere of their own, where no other spirit can pretend to stand on equal ground with them" (213–14). He accordingly wants to relinquish any "right to be or breathe there" (214). His objects of interest can retain their own spheres, where, like Hawthorne's figures of romance, they "have a propriety of their own" (2). In their integrity the voyeur places the fate of his own individuality.

The defense Coverdale mounts for the integrity of his objects and for his interest in them extends what we can now recognize as the fetishistic logic of Hawthorne's famous apology for romance in the preface to *The Blithedale Romance*. Anxieties about his treatment of the ideals and idealists of Brook Farm prompt Hawthorne to claim "the romancer's license" to create an "atmosphere of strange enchantment." In such a "Faery-land," "the creatures of his brain may play their phantasmagorical antics." These creatures "are entirely fictitious," Hawthorne stresses. "It would . . . be a most grievous wrong to his former excellent associates, were the Author to allow it to be supposed that he has been sketching any of their likenesses" (1–2). Writing a "fancy-sketch" rather than "the outward narrative and the inner truth and spirit of the whole affair" (1, 3), Hawthorne maps the boundaries between his representations and any particular realities they might invoke. In the "theatre" the romancer establishes, he displays his objects of interest "without exposing them to too close a comparison with the actual events of real lives" (1). This theatrical romance projects an exhibition without access, following in this point the voyeur's convoluted preservation of the integrity of the viewed object. Placing his representations in their own sphere, where they have "a propriety of their own" (2), Hawthorne insulates them from whatever Brook Farm references they might suggest. The voyeur and the romancer in *The Blithedale Romance* thus work to fortify the individual spheres of viewed objects—to create and maintain the boundaries of displays.[44] Their ultimate aim is to place their exhibits in protected environments, "a little removed" (1) from both the exhibitor and the spectator.

Zenobia's Shoe

For all her indirection, the Veiled Lady leads the voyeur to a very definite point: the boundary marker between viewer and object.

The voyeur's peculiar consumerism without buying culminates in a custodial relation to his objects. This curatorship of his sights consists in foregrounding their physical and temporal limits. In this demarcation of the line between subjects and objects, voyeurism secures and sustains itself. The consolidation of voyeurism in this aesthetic relation emerges in *The Blithedale Romance* as Coverdale's newfound interest in the dead. Once he has admitted to the mediumistic properties of self and has adopted a respect for others' boundaries, his speculations focus on dead persons, figures with whom he has and can have no relation. Roaming the Blithedale woods, he stumbles "over a heap of logs and sticks that had been cut for firewood, a great while ago, by some former possessor of the soil" (211). "In the fitful mood that then swayed my mind," Coverdale relates, "I found something strangely affecting in this circumstance. I imagined the long-dead woodman, and his long-dead wife and children, coming out of their chill graves" (211–12). The image of death also attends his reencounter with Zenobia, who, he reports, "now looked like marble" (213). This image subsequently materializes at Zenobia's death, solidifying in "the marble image" (235) of her corpse. The "terrible inflexibility" (235) of her dead body terminates the prophetic train of images Coverdale pursues from "her death-like hue" (223) and "death-like" cold hand (227) to her discarded "delicate handkerchief" (230) to her abandoned "shoe" (231) to the dredging of her drowned body. No longer "compelled . . . to close" (44) his eyes before Zenobia's body, Coverdale sees his associations through to their final referent, the "rigidity" (235) of Zenobia's corpse.

The clarity of reference Zenobia's body attains in death recalls another remarkable moment of direct correspondence in the novel. Despite Hawthorne's disclaimer, one of his associates from Brook Farm days does appear in *The Blithedale Romance,* even in her proper name. Or, to be more precise, *as* her name. I am referring, of course, to Margaret Fuller, whose image Coverdale's visions of Priscilla summon when Priscilla delivers him a letter from his friend Fuller, "one of the most gifted women of the age" (51). Though not specifically invoked, Fuller might be said to appear again in Coverdale's description of Zenobia's death. An account of a feminist tragically drowning could not fail to summon associations of Fuller drowning in 1850.[45] Both these instances of interpenetration between fact and romance involve a woman's absence—her distance or her death. Encompassed in death, these figures can reside in the closed sphere of exhibition the voyeur and the romancer project. A memento mori simultaneously preserves the identity of the removed object and the viewer's train of associations. The death of his objects facilitates the voyeur's practice of entertaining certitude of reference alongside variability of reference.

An even better voyeuristic object than the Veiled Lady, a dead woman offers the perfect aesthetic display for the voyeur. Coverdale implements Poe's famous ghoulish dictum that the death of a beautiful woman is the most poetic topic. The richness of Zenobia's death for Coverdale's poetic and voyeuristic practice lies in "the spectacle" (235) it offers. Like all spectacles, it moves Coverdale to further speculations, specifically aesthetic ones about the ugliness of drowning. He cannot help but "suppose" that if Zenobia had foreseen "how ill" drowning "would become her, . . . she would no more have committed the dreadful act, than have exhibited herself to a public assembly in a badly-fitting garment!" (236). In Coverdale's judgment, she must have made an ill-informed aesthetic death choice based on pictures "of drowned persons, in lithe and graceful attitudes" (218). Attributing to Zenobia the desire to be viewed in her death, Coverdale to the last asserts his voyeuristic values. The effect of Zenobia's burial on him is thus to renew his "eager curiosity to discover some tangible truth" (239) about her relation to Westervelt.

It is in the proximity to death, however, that the voyeur's own secrets become manifest. Just before Zenobia's suicide, Coverdale has registered in his own body her grief at losing Hollingsworth. "[I]t seemed to me," he professes, "that the self-same pang, with hardly mitigated torment, leaped thrilling from her heart-strings to my own" (222). In this sympathetic state he "never once dreamed of questioning" his "right to be there" as he "had questioned it" earlier (222). As the limit of Zenobia's death approaches, Coverdale reiterates the rights of voyeurism. Sympathy with one's objects functions as an identity with them. And though Coverdale declares: "It suits me not to explain what was the analogy that I saw, or imagined, between Zenobia's situation and mine" (222), his narrative of voyeuristic practice has already revealed that he shares with Zenobia an erotic attachment and subjection to Hollingsworth.

The confession that he does make—that he "was in love— with—Priscilla!" (247)—only underscores his voyeuristic relation to all three which defends against Hollingsworth's magnetism. Choosing Priscilla when she is no longer available, like touching Zenobia when she is already "death-like," does not dispel voyeuristic disengagement. That Priscilla's marriage to Hollingsworth removes her as permanently as death removes Zenobia is underscored in Zenobia's image of her as passive wife to a "Bluebeard" (226).[46] Coverdale's confession simply reinforces what is already explicit: Coverdale's "bachelorship" (247) preserves an evasion of commitment. He finds the fitting end to his romance in the ends of these women.

Women's bodies eventually disappear along with women's work in *The Blithedale Romance*'s fetishistic vision of self-definition. Yet if Coverdale's voyeurism in effect buries Zenobia and Priscilla, it also revives them. For these figures continue to signify from their graves as Zenobia's "vindictive shadow" (243) haunts Hollingsworth, just as the dead woodman and his family in Coverdale's fantasy seem to come out from their graves. In this gothicization of the voyeur's objects, ghosts and ghostly relations defend his deferrals and attenuations of desire.

Through the voyeur's singular pleasure, Hawthorne channels the anxieties of individuality to which the sight of woman gives rise. Yet the narrative of this voyeuristic style of individuality does connect Coverdale with one feminine object. The train of images connected with Zenobia's body appropriately ends with her "kidshoe" of "French manufacture" with "a high in-step" (231), the sole object Coverdale takes and keeps from Blithedale. To the last, he attaches himself to objects that displace and replace other objects. We see once again the individualistic ethics of Coverdale's characteristically conspicuous consumption moderating the dynamic relation between the spectator and the objects he views. After Zenobia's death her discarded shoe has only one function: this object is just for looking. The custodianship of the single high-heeled shoe—a standard item of fetishistic paraphernalia—forever separates Coverdale from his erotic objects of interest even as it memorializes them.

The fate of women in this radically private order of individuality is to provide such memorials. Women's work and women's bodies move so far out of sight by the end of Hawthorne's Gothic Revival romances that their absence appears the very condition of individuality.[47] In the syllogistic formula of these romances of individuality, the elimination of work or women—the figures of anxiety—from the field of vision fully eliminates anxiety. The overkill of this logic and its misogynistic pattern are strikingly illustrated in Hawthorne's tales of such murderous egotists as Ethan Brand, Giacomo Rappaccini, and Dr. Aylmer. *The Blithedale Romance* presents a related type of personality, the individual produced and sustained in one particular masculine exposition of the domestic ideal of the private self.

The structure of erotic relations in *The Blithedale Romance,* essentially an encounter between two men played out through two women who are virtually interchangeable, prefigures what Freud deemed the perversion of fetishism. Visual pleasure in certain objects—here, women—defends against a homoerotic attraction. Initially a safeguard against mesmerization, the feminization of Coverdale as the "just looking" consumer and as the object of a magnetic gaze (first Hollingsworth's, then Westervelt's) ultimately must be avoided through another displacement: the fetishization of the female. A dead woman's shoe marks the horizon of an individuality vested in femininity that vitiates the female.

As the shoe substitutes for the woman who substitutes for the man, the clarity of the line between the viewer and his objects is reinforced. Fetishism thus forecloses on the very feminization it projects. Yet it would not be quite right simply to characterize *The Blithedale Romance* as an instance of homophobia translated into misogyny. Rather, these successive attitudes arise in the novel as strategies of safe spectatorship. In the consumerist pleasures and anxieties of looking that Hawthorne explores, homophobia and misogyny proscribe not specific sexes and sexualities, but the visibility of specificity: they prohibit the possibility of the spectator being static enough to be seen.

Part Three

Melville's Misanthropy

Chapter Five

Anti-sentimentalism and Authorship in *Pierre*

Seventeen books into the narrative of *Pierre; or, The Ambiguities,*
Melville abandons the chronology of Pierre's family history—the
stuff of the sentimental novel—to announce: "I write precisely as
I please."[1] This declaration of literary individualism heralds a sa-
tirical discussion of "Young America in Literature," as typified by
"the juvenile author" of "that delightful love-sonnet, entitled 'The
Tropical Summer'" (245). We now learn that Pierre has enjoyed
some success as the author of this sentimental sonnet and other
"gemmed little sketches of thought and fancy" (245).

The switch from the parodic Glendinning family plot to a lam-
poon of nineteenth-century American literary production sets the
individual who writes precisely as he pleases against prevailing
literary as well as domestic relations. For the remainder of the
book Melville chronicles not only Pierre's progression from idyllic
domesticity to incest and murder but his progress from celebrated
"juvenile author" of popular sentimental pieces to obscure author
of a "mature work." Under an individualistic imperative of authorship, Pierre flees both home and conventional literary celebrity. In what is perhaps the nineteenth century's most negative
portrayal of domestic values, Melville posits authorship as an an-
nulment of the curriculum vitae supervised by sentimental motherhood and popularized by sentimental literature. Literary subjec-

tivity as Melville imagines it demands and offers an alternative method of self-fashioning.[2]

The disengagement of individualism from domesticity related in *Pierre* removes it from the feminine sphere, establishing a standard of masculine individualism. Melville's proposal of an authorship independent of domesticitiy delineates what has become the androcentric bias of American literary tradition: the alignment of the individualistic self and its representations with anti-sentimentalism.[3] Unlike Stowe, who locates in sentimentalism the individual's independence of the market, Melville regards sentimentalism as identical with the market. To read *Pierre* is to follow the ways that literary individualism appropriates the anti-market rhetoric of domestic individualism in order to distinguish male individuality from femininity, "mature" from "juvenile" authors, and, ultimately, classic American literature from mass-market publications.

It is against the marketing methods promoting such literary works as "The Tropical Summer" that Melville asserts the prerogative of writing precisely as he pleases. *Pierre* explicitly identifies sentimentalism with the procedures of the nineteenth-century literary marketplace, procedures which threaten to eclipse the writer's individuality. The accessories and paraphernalia of publication proposed to Pierre—title pages, leather-bound editions, portraits and photographs of the author—all mass-produce the writer and his work. In Melville's sarcastic ruminations upon the literary economy, marketing concerns preempt the particularity of writer and work. Contemporary publishing and advertising techniques, particularly the puffing practice of prearranged favorable reviews, thus appear in the "Young America in Literature" chapter as the silly attempts of some tailors turned publishers to make Pierre "public property" (254) by "arraying" his "productions in the library form" (247).[4] The mutual admiration society of puffing reviewers is caricatured here as the publishing industry's notion of "the broadcloth of genius" (247) available for reproduction. Against this wholesale notion of literary value, Pierre removes himself from domesticity and commerce and, moreover, institutes a domestic and commercial relation among writer, work, and reader that preserves the writer's uniqueness. We might then recognize *Pierre* as a keynote address to the program of literary individualism and as a key text in the development of the domestic hostility that has so long characterized American formulations of the literary.[5]

Authorship and Anonymity

Melville's attack on sentimentalism in *Pierre* is thus not simply a revelation of his own difficulties with finding success in the mid-nineteenth-century literary marketplace where domesticity was the primary commodity but a disquisition on the commercial and familial relations inhibiting individuality.[6] Developing the mythology of literary individualism, *Pierre* features a cult of literary obscurity in contradistinction to the cult of popular sentimental literature. This alternative literary economy begins with Pierre's disengagement from all sentimental agents, from both his family and the literary marketplace. By imagining the elimination of literary relations—the public modes and publishing methods that threaten to erode the individualistic aims of the author—*Pierre* constructs the literary estate Melville cannot find in the nineteenth-century literary marketplace.

In leaving Saddle Meadows, the Glendinning family estate, Pierre renounces, not only his mother and the sentimental ethos she represents, but his successful career as a sentimental writer. The literary motives underlying Pierre's resolve to leave home and set up housekeeping with his illegitimate half-sister Isabel become manifest as "Pierre attempts a mature work" (282). This work entails divesting himself of all the appurtenances of literary career and sentimental taste that Melville lampoons.[7] Even before his departure with Isabel to New York, Pierre removes himself from the progression of that career by refusing a series of procedures to publicize and further his literary reputation. He demurs from an offer to publish a collected edition of his "fugitive pieces," from invitations to lecture at learned societies, from magazine requests for biographies and copies of his portrait and daguerreotypes, and even from ladies' pleas for autographs. All these attentions strike

Pierre as vulgar, causing him to consider "anonymousness in authorship" and to regret "that he had not started his literary career under that mask" (249). The advantage of "the inviolably anonymous method" is the "essential dignity and propriety" (249) it preserves.[8]

The system of anonymity contemplated in *Pierre* elaborates the ideas about exemplary authorship Melville conceived in his 1850 laudatory review of "Hawthorne and His Mosses." "Would that all excellent books were foundlings, without father or mother," Melville wishes, "that so it might be, we could glorify them, without including their ostensible authors." The anonymity of authors would enable and assure originality and genius, the marks of uniqueness. According to Melville, the author's anonymity preserves our fantasies about authors; "on a personal interview, no great author has ever come up to the idea of his reader. But that dust of which our bodies are composed, how can it ever fitly express the nobler intelligences among us?" In contrast to the reader's "ideal image of the man and his mind," the writer's own form betrays him as vulgar and commonplace.[9]

Because of this incommensurability, Pierre resists autographing as well as advertising his name. His autograph cannot match "the sublime poet Glendinning"; "owing to the very youthful and unformed character of his handwriting, his signature did not possess that inflexible uniformity, which . . . should always mark the hand of illustrious men" (253). From the opposite perspective, Pierre worries that his limited oeuvre does not merit the significance conferred by a leather-bound collected works edition. Either way, the presentation does not fit the writer.

"Anonymousness in authorship," of course, also may help the commercial success of the author, which proceeds independently of the writer's own form (249). This is the strategy adopted by nineteenth-century women writing under pen names: they assumed that under the name of an unknown man or woman, their work would not be defined by any aspect of their forms, whether sex or class or race. Anonymity also could operate as an effective publicity stunt, creating curiosity and gossip about the unknown author.[10] These commercial advantages in unknown authorship

become especially clear in *Ruth Hall,* the best-selling 1855 autobiographical novel by Fanny Fern, pseudonym of Sara Payson
Willis. In this satiric story of the rise of a sentimental writer, the
titular heroine also writes under a pen name, the sexually indeter-
minate single name "Floy." Just as the question of Fern's own
identity excited interest in the 1850s reading public, "there are
many rumors afloat" as to who Floy can be.[11] Anonymity here
publicizes the author; it epitomizes the literary commerce that
Melville's ideal anonymity would jettison.

Whereas Pierre seeks the inviolability of privacy, Ruth realizes
herself through public attention and approbation. For Ruth, the
literary marketplace holds the possibility of personal vindication,
the means for her to redress the failures of her family and associates. Another trenchant commentary on domestic myths and publishing practices, *Ruth Hall* portrays literary celebrity as the best
revenge against both family cruelty and an exploitative publishing
industry. Like *Pierre,* this novel aligns commercial with familial
relations. All these relations appear untrustworthy and, even
worse, malevolent in *Ruth Hall,* where grandparents abuse (in one
case fatally) their grandchildren, parents deride and neglect their
children, and publishers cheat their writers. But unlike Melville,
Fern takes pains to individuate these base actions, to tabulate how
the individuals in familial and commercial institutions may hinder
or help the struggling heroine.

Left penniless after her husband's death and refused support
from her in-laws and her own family, Ruth Hall must earn a living
for herself and her two daughters. When she turns to writing for
newspapers, her brother, a prominent editor, denies her aid, ad-
vising her "to seek some *unobtrusive* employment" (116). The editors and publishers Ruth meets as she tries to sell her writings
recognize her talent but are similarly stingy in the "mere pittance"
(140) they pay for her work. Quickly learning her "market-value"
as her writing sells and gains recognition, Ruth eventually finds a
properly "brotherly" publisher in John Walter, who gives her a
"just compensation" (142, 143, 142), granting her "talent the
moral right to a deserved remuneration" (141). In addition to
securing Ruth's "welfare" in a favorable "written contract" (143),

Walter makes it his business to admonish and embarrass those who had denied Ruth support. For Ruth Hall, successful publishing means getting wealth and fame, and getting back. Revenge is doubly sweet, for in this gratifying story of hard-won prosperity Fern/Willis exposed the uncharitableness of her brother Nathaniel P. Willis, the well-known editor and writer.[12]

The revenge motive in *Ruth Hall* disturbed contemporary reviewers of the book, because it seemed behavior unbefitting a woman writer. As a *New York Times* review stated:

If Fanny Fern were a man,—a man who believed that the gratification of revenge were a proper occupation for one who has been abused, and those who have injured us are fair game, *Ruth Hall* would be a natural and excusable book. But we confess that we cannot understand how a delicate, suffering woman can hunt down even her persecutors so remorselessly. We cannot think so highly of [such] an author's womanly gentleness.[13]

Though the author acknowledges in her preface that her book "is entirely at variance with all set rules for novel-writing" (3), she is not referring to rules of etiquette in this self-possessed statement about her writing style. Gentleness obviously is not a desirable quality to Fern/Willis, who was also departing from domestic womanhood in telling the story of how "our heroine had become a regular business woman" (173). The crucial gender boundary the book transgresses is the line between domesticity and the market. As Ruth finds a *"real, warm-hearted, brotherly brother,* such as she had never known" (144) in her publisher, familial relations are reformed and relocated in the market. More than this, *Ruth Hall* discloses the economic and social insecurity of domestic individualism for women and advocates that women pursue individualistic interests outside the domestic sphere.[14] In this endeavor, getting even is getting one's own. The real scandal of *Ruth Hall* lies in its unabashed commitment to market individualism.

Ruth Hall locates individuality in the celebrity mass publishing creates, in the market where Ruth's literary value is realized. All the fan mail Ruth receives—"letters of friendship, love, and business" (153)—confirms her sense of self-worth, so much so that she can invest in herself. On the basis of these "proofs that I have won the public ear" (153), she decides to keep the copyright to her work for greater gain when "my book will be a success" (163). Her readers provide commensurability between the writer and her worth. If Ruth's fans ask too much—some letter writers propose marriage; some request autographs or endorsements; others seek financial assistance; one dying woman begs Ruth to adopt her baby daughter—they do so because, as one correspondent writes her, they can "read your heart in your many writings" (165).

The sociability that Ruth's writing generates and through which she gains her "true valuation" (193) undermines individuality in *Pierre*'s vision of literary relations. Whereas *Ruth Hall* equates literary talent with commercial success—"'Floy' is a genius," Walter asserts, "hence her fame and success" (151–52)—*Pierre* repudiates such a connection between literary genius and market achievement. This withdrawal of literature from the market first takes the form of an assertion of masculinity.

It is "peculiarly distasteful for Pierre to comply" with "entreaties from the young ladies that he would be pleased to grace their Albums with some nice little song" (250). In this custom of "parlor society" where "you lose your own sharp individuality and become delightfully merged in that soft social Pantheism, as it were, that rosy melting of all into one" (250), Pierre discerns an emasculation of the author—"there no one draws the sword of his own individuality" (250)—analogous to literary publicists' violation of the author's privacy and uniqueness. In order to preserve his individuality amidst "that rosy melting" (250), Pierre selects a signature more personalized than his autograph: "I will give them the actual feeling of my hand, as much as they want. And lips are still better than hands. Let them send their sweet faces to me, and I will kiss *lipographs* upon them forever and a day" (251). Pierre enacts the spirit of this plan, blowing a kiss over all the albums and returning them "accompanied with a confectioner's kiss for each album, rolled up in the most ethereal tissue" (251).

In substituting lipographs for autographs Pierre both mocks and exploits the cult of celebrity. The other side of this masculine bluff of aggressive eroticism is, predictably, the fear of his own inadequacy being exposed. The form of publicity to which he most strenuously objects, the publication of his picture, in either portrait or photograph form, is particularly threatening and troubling to Pierre's desire for proper self-representation. If he allowed his editors to make copies of his portrait, the world would see the writer Pierre Glendinning as a beardless youth without the "most noble corporeal badge of . . . the illustrious author" (253), an image unequal to Pierre's fantasy of himself as bearded genius. If he permitted publication of his daguerreotype an even worse misrepresentation would occur, for Pierre believes daguerreotypes to be a vulgar mass production of the individual "dayalizing a dunce" rather than "immortalizing a genius" (254). In an age "when every body has his portrait published, true distinction lies in not having yours published at all" (254).[15] All these forms violate Pierre's sense of propriety, a self-proprietorship so extreme that nothing other than himself can represent him. Hence the kiss serves as his truest signature, his body's imprint, impossible to forge or copy.

The crucial point here is that Pierre's kiss cannot be published and marketed. Unlike Hawthorne's Coverdale, another young bachelor sentimental writer concerned with his individuality, Pierre sees no individualistic possibilities in consumer relations. So the relation between author and market that *Ruth Hall* forges exemplifies the literary commerce from which Melville would extricate the (male) author. Blowing kisses to female autograph seekers, Pierre dismisses a feminized reading public as well as the advertising practices directed toward it. His literary individualism opposes what Ann Douglas calls the feminization of American culture.[16] But the case of *Ruth Hall* makes clear that the distrust of the feminine and the commercial—more precisely, the distrust of the feminine in the commercial—rationalizes a masculinist monopoly of literary value. The business of literature which Pierre disdains is in fact run by men, Ruth Hall discovers, and the individuals most manipulated by this economic organization are women. This is why Fanny Fern celebrates Ruth's development of business sense: her story culminates in the pictorial image of a stock certificate, printed in the penultimate chapter, which Ruth purchases from her publishing profits. Ruth's accomplishment, like Pierre's early success as a sentimental writer, proves that any individual, even a woman writer, may succeed in the literary marketplace. The market and the publishers and writers who embody it therefore strike the masculinist literary individualist as unreliable, because too elastic, indices of value.[17]

Genius and Cannibalism

The anonymity of authors recommended in the *Mosses* review and followed in *Pierre* thus operates to distinguish literary value from market value. In celebrating Hawthorne's work Melville seeks to maintain the selectivity of the transcendent standard by which he measures him. The discrepancy between the bodily form of the author and the greatness of his literary work, the difference between his corporeality and his corpus (a punning association and dissociation Melville fondly elaborates throughout his own work), inaugurates a liberalized yet still selective critical standard of genius.[18] Melville speculates that the genius we attribute to great writers such as Shakespeare might in fact reside not in the man but in his membership in a brotherhood of genius: "May it not be, that this commanding mind has not been, and never will be, individually developed in any one man? And would it, indeed, appear so unreasonable to suppose that this greatness and overflowing may be, or may be destined to be, shared by a plurality of men of genius?"[19]

Melville simultaneously preserves the uniqueness of genius and extends it to new talents such as Hawthorne in his fancy of disembodied, collective genius. In this democratization of authorial achievement Melville elaborates the ideal of anonymous authorship as the submergence of the individual in the author. But the author does not disappear in this collectivity; rather, as a vehicle of brotherhood, he shines among men.[20]

This men's-club account of genius limits its membership, as *Ruth Hall* expressly demonstrates. Not all Ruth's readers recognize her "genius." Her brother brusquely tells her: "[Y]ou have no talent" (116). One of her correspondents, who signs himself "William Stearns, Professor of Greek, Hebrew, and Mathemetics,

in Hopetown College, and author of 'History of the Dark Ages,'"
makes it his business to inform her: "You are not a genius. . . .
Shakespeare was a genius. Milton was a genius," Stearns pro-
claims, and "the author of 'History of the Dark Ages,' which has
reached its fifteenth edition, was a genius." Stearns grants himself
the rank of genius because his work has warranted a "fifteenth
edition"; in short, because of its marketability. Realizing that Ruth
could make the same claim, Stearns adds that "the *female* mind is
incapable of producing anything which may be strictly termed
literature" (166). With this letter *Ruth Hall* exposes the misogyny
of the enterprise to define and assign literary genius.

In this book's feminist critique of literary criticism, even the
"brotherly" John Walter manifests masculinist assumptions about
a woman's writing. Though Walter declares and defends Ruth's
genius, he needs to isolate it as a phrenological phenomenon. He
would explain her talent as specific to her physiognomy. Con-
vincing Ruth to "have your head examined to please me," Walter
takes her to the phrenologist Professor Finman for an analysis of
the "bumps" on her head (167). Walter thinks the phrenological
reading confirms his own assessment of Ruth: "The Professor has
hit you off to the life" (171). Ruth, however, who has "not the
slightest faith in the science" (167), disagrees. The specific point
she challenges is the professor's contention that she cannot tolerate
criticism. Ruth quarrels "with no one who denies my writings
literary merit," but insists on "fair criticism" (172). Her disagree-
ment with the phrenologist becomes an indictment of prejudiced
literary criticism. Like the phrenological arbitrary categorization
of personality according to the accidents of physical composition,
criticism may misrepresent writings. Ruth allows reviewers "the
right to express" their views, but denounces their irresponsible
procedures:

But to have one's book reviewed on hearsay, by persons who never
looked between the covers, or to have paragraphs circulated, with words
italicized, so that gross constructions might be forced upon the reader,
which the author never could dream of; then to have paragraphs taken up
in that state, credited to you, and commented upon by horrified moral-
ists,—that is what I call unfair play. (172)

This rejoinder strikes at the presumptions of both phrenologists and critics, self-serving presumptions about "womanly nature" (172). Overall, Ruth gets fair play in the market, where she finds "another tribunal" (161) than her brother or Professor Stearns. For the critical program of defining genius according to Melville's masculinist prerogatives of literary individualism, it is then necessary, as the mission of Professor Stearns exhibits, to make the market a more selective index of value. Despite its anti-commercial rhetoric, Melville's literary individualism ultimately represents, not a rejection of the market, but the desire to limit it to the arbiters and adherents of a particular type of genius.[21]

In the validation of American literary genius advanced in the *Mosses* review, Melville accordingly imagines a different, masculinized, literary commerce in which the reader cannibalizes the author and his work. He speaks of having banqueted upon Hawthorne and his *Mosses,* of having "incorporated their whole stuff into my being."[22] In the process of advancing the author—of celebrating both Hawthorne and the advent of original American authorship, of a distinct American literature—Melville transforms the writer into object of consumption. The cannibalistic transfiguration of humans into food and useful resources rather curiously, and perversely, imitates and perfects the dynamics of the literary marketplace where books function as commodities. In the attempt to define a province of authorship not subject to the market delimitations Melville discerned in publishers' preferences for sentimental stories and other successful formulaic literary productions (in his own case, for the early sea tales that had sold well), Melville reenvisions literary commerce by transforming the author into his book.[23] That is, he forestalls the dissociation of the writer from his literary work when it goes to market by imagining the author as the commodity itself, the book to be banqueted upon.[24] Anonymity finally preserves the author for the right kind of commerce, in which he and his work may circulate.

Melville's feeding metaphor of literary relations reclaims and refines the metamorphoses from subjects to objects in the literary marketplace, situating subjectivity in the most extreme subjection of the self to its objective possibilities. Put more simply, the uniqueness of literary labor is secured in its consumption; the mark of authorship is most prominent when a literary production is consumed. That authorship emerges and endures in its proper commodification is the premise upon which Melville erects an American literary tradition. Far from dispensing with the consumerist relations of nineteenth-century literature so infamously associated with sentimentalism, Melville might be said to purify consumption to support literary individualism.

There could hardly be any more radical or terrifying anonymity than that of being eaten; yet this frightening reversal of anthropomorphism also images a perverse intimacy, a connection between bodies closer than kinship or sexual relations. As Melville's brotherhood of genius subsumes the individual author in order to elevate him, his incorporation of Hawthorne signifies a disappearing process that assures the perpetuation of the author: a presence so powerful as to penetrate and reside in other bodies. Anonymity appeals to the paradoxical desire of the writer to inhabit the crowd so as to be simultaneously both of and above it. In anonymity, as in orphanhood and the unknown familial status of the foundling, the self is most thinglike, least protected by the personifications of family and fame, and thus most original. The cannibalistic logic of Melville's aesthetics of anonymity works to highlight an autonomy of self. As this naturalized and masculinized literary economy is developed by *Pierre,* writing becomes a model of autogenesis.

Pierre implements the mythology of authorship Melville divulges in the *Mosses* review: in the course of the novel Pierre transforms himself into a self-generative and, ultimately, self-consuming author. This countdown to one, and then none, follows the procedure of Pierre's "lipographs," which replace standard literary relations with his own literary economy. More than a parody of the language of sentiment, the metamorphosis of autograph into kiss bespeaks the disappearance of the author's name, a system of anonymity wherein the author retains his individuality. The author's kiss translates into the candy kisses, delectable objects whose consumption recalls Melville's banqueting upon Hawthorne. Pierre also finds and protects his authorship in a model of cannibalism, a literary commerce so personal that, as we shall see, it resembles the mythology of the sentimental family it supersedes.

Bodies, Books, and Food

The consanguinity among author, book, and reader attained in Melville's vision of cannibalism and anonymity recapitulates the ideal of unity through food celebrated by nineteenth-century domesticians in popular cookery guides. Domestic advice writers imagined the achievement of democratic goals through food. According to William Alcott in *The Young Housekeeper, or Thoughts on Food and Cookery,* proper dietary habits would ensure "the happy day when all the family, however numerous and how little soever tied by ties of consanguinity, will be equal and free, dwelling together, eating and drinking together, and whether of one nation or another, always uniting around the same domestic altar."[25]

Preparation for this millennial moment of democracy and domesticity begins with "temperance in all things," Sarah Josepha Hale advised in her cookbook *The Good Housekeeper, or the Way to Live Well.*[26] The health and balance achieved by sensible family meals and the proper organization of the family unit prefigure the dissolution of the family into a larger family of nations. This millennial family, united through sacraments of food, implies both the expansion of domesticity (analogous to America's expanding market economy and geographical boundaries) and the disappearance of the sentimental nuclear family.

This double movement—the family magnified into great populations, the dissolution of family ties in the enlarged borders of the family—recurs in the strange mechanics of cannibalism in Melville's elaborations upon anonymity, but is there directed toward a different form of harmony. In the moment of literary brotherhood or "rosy melting," individuality is not subsumed by the community of individuals but consumed, incorporated by the masses. Melville's exemplary moment in literary relations retains the ambition of the writer, in a culture of consumption, to be consumed. This desire commits the author to the object-function at the communal feast, to becoming the meal. Furthermore, the aim of the strategy of anonymity is congruity with public taste: naturalization of the literary commodity so that the author's labor, understood as an extension of himself represented in his literary work, is preserved in the transmogrification of book to food. Melville envisions a radical intimacy like the universal endogamy of millennial domesticity but establishes his unity of relations on a perverse version of physical bonds and nurture arrangements. Whereas the apotheosis of domesticity signifies an implicitly so-cialistic political economy, a family transcending economic com-petition and fluctuation, *Pierre*'s culinary aesthetics exploit the individualistic possibilities of the literary marketplace. In this out-landishly egotistic version of commodification, the author endures in the consumption of himself.

Pierre thus advances a gastronomic organization of literary labor and consumption both to supplement and to supplant the domi-nant sentimental familial paradigm of literary relations. Melville's model of cannibalistic literary relations rewrites the millennial do-mestic meal as a literary feast, an individualistic perfection of consumerist practices in the literary marketplace. In the domestic apotheosis imagined in the great common meal, as in the ideal breakfast enacted in Rachel Halliday's kitchen in *Uncle Tom's Cabin,* all conflict and disunity are extinguished in the intimacy of eating together as one family. This ideal elaborates upon the nine-teenth-century iconography of intimate transmission from mother to child during breast-feeding. The mother's role in preparing for the perfection of domesticity, in guarding against "intemperance in eating" and forming "the habits of her children," followed from her proper regulation of breast-feeding.[27] Bad habits began in infancy, health reformer Orson Fowler warned, where "most mothers err in giving their children the breast . . . whenever they cry."[28] For Melville, such preoccupation with the effects of feed-ing, the implementation of education and disciplining through eating, marks precisely the sentimental family's intervention in the private life and intimacy it promises to protect.[29] If the individual becomes food, he circumvents the mediations feeding entails.

In *Pierre,* Melville satirizes these domestic investments in food and proper child-rearing in the breakfast scene between Pierre and his mother. Pierre, who "had an excellent appetite" (16), orders three bowls of milk, causing his mother to caution him playfully: "Don't be a milk-sop" (19). Yet Mary Glendinning wishes Pierre to "remain all docility" (20) to her and her "sweet programme" (19) for him. In contrast to the abundant meal of toast, tongue, pigeons, rolls, coffee, and milk in the Glendinning home, Pierre's first meal with Isabel, which he perceives as disloyalty to his mother, consists of only water and bread of Isabel's "own making" (162). Pierre calls their common meal of this bread a "real sacrament" (162), marking his flight from the maternal breast with a ritual of eating which introduces the new anti-sentimental organization of his life.

In this account of maternal nurture Melville reverses the popular sentimental metaphor of the prodigal son as a viper nursing at his mother's breast to identify the mother as the source of "such venom." Eschewing his mother's table, Pierre eschews "the too-seducing bosoms of clay" that alternately inspire flight and make men "glad to be uxorious" (180). Once Pierre has supped with his sister Isabel, prior meals seem to him like "rummaging in a pantry, like a bake-house burglar" (160); he is now resolved to leave his mother and "henceforth live together" and "eat in company" (160) with Isabel. Pierre thus rejects the table and the taste of the sentimental family, the nurture of the maternal breast, for Isabel's fare: poverty, anonymity, and finally her "death-milk," the vial of poison secreted between her breasts "where life for infants lodgeth not."

In *Pierre*'s parody of contemporary literary taste Melville literalizes taste, naturalizing the literary economy. This literalization revamps the spiritualization of nurture arrangements in domestic ideology so as to display the economy of consumption that sentimentalism simultaneously denies and propels. Melville's transubstantiation of author into book into the most natural and necessary of commodities projects a literary economy that will circumvent the marketplace variables affecting an author's success.

In imagining himself as food the author anticipates and exploits the objectification of people and literature through which culture and commerce operate.

Pierre's success as a sentimental author follows from the way his literary productions are taken to be in "Perfect Taste" (245), appealing to the consensus of literary value. To control and personalize his literary production, that is, to individuate it from other publications, Pierre eliminates the role of marketing agents—editors, publishers, biographers, and publicists—in his literary career. His literary practices compose not only a commentary on the vulgarities of the literary marketplace but an alternative literary economy. For "Pierre himself was a sort of publisher" at home (263), producing literary pieces on whatever scraps of paper he finds, strewing the house with his productions, and allowing anyone to take them gratis. So committed is Pierre to an organic relation between himself and his literary work that he needs no copyrights, no public record of himself or of his authorship other than the work itself. Indeed, he and his productions constitute an ecological system: he smokes cigars bought from his magazine publication earnings, lit by pages of his work—"His cigars were lighted in two ways: lighted by the sales of his sonnets, and lighted by the printed sonnets themselves." In this purification of the puffery system, Melville puns, "the puffs which indirectly brought his dollars were again returned, but as perfumed puffs" (262). Just as he would transform autographs into kisses and confections, literary signs into bodily gestures and pleasures, Pierre would translate literary production, both the work's materiality and its monetary value, into another oral pleasure, realizing the sentimental model of literary production as affective and nurturing.[30]

This closed cycle of literary and personal production is like the orbit of maternal influence, which is ideally a perfect congruity between the characters of mother and child. Pierre's distrust of marketplace methods of popularization, Melville's diatribe against publishers, editors, and literary hacks, expresses an absolute commitment to the model of literary production that sentimentalism seems to promote: an almost biological link between author and work analogous to the kinship between mother and son. So Pierre wants what the sentimental family and sentimental literature strive to achieve: a perfect domestic circle (like that of Rachel Halliday's kitchen) in which industry and individuality are independent from the marketplace; an intimacy between self and labor, writer and book, which assures the integrity of the individual. The representative form of this alternative formation of individuality is autobiography or, more precisely, a reconception of literature as fundamentally autobiographical—primarily self-expressive and self-determined.

In the spirit of this merger of writer with writing, Pierre imagines an autonomous, extrafamilial literary production, "too true and good to be published" (283). This perfection of sentimental ecology exacts a labor from Pierre which takes away his youth, his sight, his ambulation, his reason. His book, the book that (like its author) will not be published and placed in circulation, "whose unfathomable cravings drink his blood" and "consume all his vigor" (304–5), usurps his senses and his life; rather than extending or replicating the author's life according to the custom of the literary marketplace, Pierre's unfinished book cuts short the author by consuming him, thereby uniting the author and literary production in the anonymity of incorporation. By divesting himself of all sentimental investments, Pierre gets his wish—"in him you behold the baby toddler, . . . forced now to stand and toddle alone"—and the punishment for his Promethean desire to be original: "he lies still—not asleep as children and day-laborers sleep," but holding "the beak of the vulture" away from his heart (305). In the images of abandoned child and punished hero inhere the possibility of an achievement untouched by, uncontaminated by, and therefore uncommon to the public and its standards. The purest autobiography undoes its author, is unwritten or, rather, is inscribed upon the author's body, slated to appear only in the decomposition of that body.

The obvious problem with Pierre's literary economy is that the project of self-objectification finally destroys the self; yet it is objectification that empowers the circulation of self, author, and books in culture. Pierre deviates from his literary culture not so much in recognizing how subjectivity inheres in its "thingness"—in the fact that selves can be appropriated, even consumed and incorporated—but in imagining his objectification as self-generation.[31] The domestic iconography of mother and child preserves subjectivity in the image of pleasurable objectivity, in the figure of the nurtured child. That is, maternal nurture cultivates the emergence of the self and its circulation, reconciling subjectivity to the inevitability of its objectivity. Pierre would claim this maternal office for himself. And this is why *Pierre* initiates its reformation of the literary economy with the displacement of the mother.[32]

The Aesthetics of Incest

The plot against the mother which complements the literary plot generates still other movements that redouble the force of *Pierre*'s anti-sentimentalism. From these symmetrical developments emerges the creative principle of Melville's ambiguities: the generation of singularity from doubleness. Pierre replaces his filial relation with a sibling relation, only finally to replace that relation with solitude and solipsism. By the end of the book, father (already removed when the story begins), mother, sister, fiancée, cousin, and Pierre himself will have disappeared. But before Pierre and his family disappear, Pierre seems engaged in extending his family, by accepting Isabel as his sister and revivifying his father.

The subversion of motherhood and the sentimental family in *Pierre* begins with the recognition of something missing from Pierre's sentimental ethos. "So perfect to Pierre had long seemed the illumined scroll of his life thus far, that only one hiatus was discoverable by him in the sweetly-writ manuscript. A sister had been omitted from the text" (7). Prior to the appearance of Isabel, Pierre had used "the fictitious title" of sister for "his pedestaled mother" (7); but even his "romantic filial love" (5) cannot "supply the absent reality" (7). Melville soon supplies the text with the missing sister, granting Pierre's wish: "[H]ad my father but had a daughter!" (7).

Upon receiving Isabel's letter in which she confides her relation to him, Pierre "could not stay in his chamber: the house contracted to a nut-shell around him; the walls smote his forehead; bare-headed he rushed from the place, and only in the infinite air, found scope for that boundless expansion of his life" (66). Pierre's home cannot contain the expansion of self Pierre experiences in the news of his sister's existence; Isabel has fortified and augmented Pierre's selfhood by presenting him with a family history anterior and antithetical to domestic life with his mother. Once having seen Isabel's "henceforth immemorial face," Pierre feels "that what he had always before considered the solid land of veritable reality, was now being audaciously encroached upon by bannered armies of hooded phantoms, disembarking in his soul, as from a flotilla of specter-boats" (49). In this haunted state, Pierre finds "the face somehow mystically appealing to his own private and individual affections" (49); "most miraculous of all," he thinks "that somewhere he had seen traces of the likeness of that face before" (49). This invasion into his soul, into his most private and individual feelings, causes him to separate himself and his thoughts from his mother, making him "a falsifyer" to her (51).

As he withdraws from his mother, Pierre tries to account for the familiarity of Isabel's face and recalls "many an old legendary family scene, which he had heard related by elderly relations" (50). The text from which a sister had been omitted contained clues to her existence. Pierre remembers his dying father wailing "My daughter, my daughter!" (70). When Isabel appears, she confirms Pierre's childhood memory of his father as well as his wish for a sister. More important, she proves that Pierre's desire for a sister *is* his memory of his dying father.

Isabel's claim to sorority with Pierre, her claim to be the daughter of his father, thus raises issues of paternity less as questions of her parentage than as questions about the biography of the father. The "family legend" (73) that Isabel prompts Pierre to reconsider is his aunt Dorothea's story about the portrait of his father she had given him. This portrait depicted "a brisk, unentangled young bachelor" who was "airily and but grazingly seated, or rather flittingly tenanting an old-fashioned chair of Malacca" (73, 72). "The mother of Pierre could never abide this picture which she had always asserted did signally belie her husband" (72). "It is not he," Mary Glendinning maintained, and "the portrait which she held to do justice to her husband" was instead "a much larger one" that showed "a middle-aged married man," which she hung in the drawing room on "the most conspicuous and honorable place on the wall" (72). Yet Pierre's aunt Dorothea, his father's elder sister, had assured Pierre that the smaller "chair-portrait" was "an excellent likeness" (79). According to Dorothea, the portrait chronicles the senior Pierre Glendinning's love affair with a young French woman. A family cousin, Ralph Winwood, having decided to paint his relative as the wooer of the French woman, "slyly picked his portrait," secretly painting him just after his visits to the woman, hoping to "catch some sort of corresponding expression" on canvas (77). Suspecting that his cousin was painting him, Glendinning instructed Ralph to either hide or destroy the picture. Dorothea explains to Pierre "that the reason your father did not want his portrait taken was because he was secretly in love with the French young lady, and did not want his secret published in the portrait" (79).

Pierre's mother's "intuitive aversion" to this portrait and Isabel's letter informing Pierre of their relation seem to Pierre "reciprocal testimonies" to Dorothea's story (85). In Isabel, in the issue of a premarital affair, and in the premarital portrait Pierre discovers another truth about his father. The picture now seems to tell Pierre: "I am thy father as he more truly was . . . I am thy real father" (83). In this more true, more real father, Pierre finds the ideal of his literary economy: an author whose true likeness is reproduced. When the chair-portrait speaks to Pierre in the voice of his father, Pierre is replacing "the latter tales and legends of his devoted wedded love" (83) with the image of the father before his marriage. The portrait enables Pierre to imagine his father unconnected with his mother. Pierre now rejects the venerated paternal character to whom his mother has testified, finding a more accurate representation in the earlier chair-portrait. Though in taking Isabel's cause Pierre resigns his patrimony, he does so not as a renunciation of paternal inheritance but as an insistence on a more truthful account of his father. The preferred, antecedent portrait that "proves" to Pierre the fact of his father fathering Isabel provides him with a model of authorship independent of the sentimental family configuration he has known. His adherence to this model representation displaces his mother, who in her allegiance to the domesticated vision of Pierre's father signifies impediments to originality. The biography of the father, the truer representation of him, antedates the sentimental mother. Pierre identifies with what escaped or predated his mother's control, and it is with this sign of his father's character that Pierre identifies his own hopes for self-determination.

Isabel provides the occasion for Pierre to summon his father, not as proof of their relation, but as the model of authorship without maternal mediations, a type of his own self-generative potential. He invokes his father, or uses Isabel's claim as an invocation of the father, to inaugurate his own genealogy and commence his own nonsentimental narrative. In the ideal sentimentalist scenario of maternal influence, a good son carries into his career the good character of his mother.[33] But then it is finally the mother's portrait, a portrait of and by the mother, that the world sees. Pierre perfects the sentimental model of authorship by erasing the mother from the paradigm of literary relations and production. Choosing to link his destiny with his sister, Pierre divorces his literary endeavor from maternal supervision.

The domestic cult, however, ascribed to sisters a maternal role; they were to assist their mothers in "forming the moral, intellectual, and physical habits of their younger brothers and sisters." In his *Advice to Young Men* William Alcott stressed that sisters "may be made the instruments of a brother's moral regeneration."[34] Getting a sister, then, is like getting another mother. Satirizing and sexualizing the sentimental idealization of mothers and sisters, Melville remarks of Pierre's desire for a sister: "He who is sisterless, is as a bachelor before his time. For much that goes to make up the deliciousness of a wife, already lies in a sister" (7). Pierre conflates sister and wife as he conflated mother and sister. But he exploits the self-defining possibilities of having a sister, her signification not of maternity or wifehood but of her brother's individuality. A sister evinces both the progenitive power of the parent(s) and the difference between male and female identity. She thus assures her brother of his particular identity, of his individuality. Her difference underlines his originality. The female sexuality of the mother is not sufficient to offer this assurance, for the mother is not also an issue of the father, not a filial representation of the father. The conception of a daughter allows the son his self by both resemblance and dissimilarity, reinforcing the bond between father and son and preserving a genetic model of representation in which the son reproduces the father.

Given that Mary Glendinning is a widow and given the actual nineteenth-century patterns of remarriage and continuous childbearing, a more likely family plot would grant Pierre a sister through his mother.[35] But it is necessary to Pierre's reformation of the sentimental family to obviate the role of the mother in reproduction and nurture. The repudiation of the mother makes way for access to the father, a union removed from the mediations of mothers and markets in patriarchal perpetuation. At the outset of *Pierre*, Melville intimates that "this strange yearning of Pierre for a sister" derived from his solitary position as "the only surnamed male Glendinning extant" (7). Since Pierre's American Revolution heroic grandfathers, the family has "run off into the female branches" (8). Now Mary Glendinning, the sentimental mother, holds and wields "the old General's baton" (20); from this phallic mother Pierre seeks to wrest his authority and "have a monopoly of glory in capping the fame-column, . . . the tall shaft erected by his noble sires" (8). A sister by the same father reasserts the homosocial structure sentimentalism obscures, thus certifying male identity.[36]

In countering the hitherto accepted portraiture of Pierre's father, Isabel thus reinstates and affirms patrilinear authority, purifying it from the claims of nurture to the development of individual identity. As such she figures as the desirable dark woman of patriarchy—antidote to sentimental womanhood and society, affirmation of masculinity, the femme fatale whose appropriation reinforces masculine power. This reinforcement explains why Pierre's alliance with her alienates and kills his mother. More than an asocial projection of the masculine imagination and Melville's fantasy of an aboriginal woman, Isabel figures the removal of maternal nurturance, the proof of a nonsymbiotic identity.

The autobiography Isabel relates to Pierre begins with the declaration that she "never knew a mortal mother." Her lips "never touched a woman's breast"; she seems "not of woman born" (114). This Athenalike origin matches Pierre's fantasy of a life without a mother. Isabel projects the possibility of an alternative life and authorship in keeping with Pierre's desire for an autonomous mode of authorship and individuality, the fantasy of nature without nurture so celebrated in Melville's travel literature.[37]

Pierre accepts Isabel as his sister because she makes the claim most appealing to his ideal of selfhood: she invokes an anti-sentimental family history. This sister embodies for Pierre the fantasy of removing himself from the sentimental family. Despite Isabel's mysteriousness, the suddenness of her appearance in Pierre's neighborhood, her lack of proofs, her lapses into incoherent murmuring when she tells Pierre of her past, Pierre immediately believes her to be his father's daughter and his own sister. He requires neither legitimation of law nor corroboration of witnesses to prove Isabel's identity. Pierre becomes even more convinced of Isabel's story through her music, in which her claims merge with the sound of her guitar. "The guitar was human," Isabel tells Pierre. "It sings to me as I to it. . . . All wonders that are unimaginable and unspeakable; all these wonders are translated in the mysterious melodiousness of the guitar" (125). The wonder translated and offered to Pierre is the possibility of such a relation, the replacement of a literary economy based on the family with one assuring absolute identity between author and book. It is this unity of body and articulation, this composition of continuity between self and expressive gestures, that seduces and enthralls Pierre.

Isabel thus provides the occasion for a reconstruction of Pierre's history, a reconstruction beginning with the destruction not just of his sentimental filial relation with his mother but also of his paternity. He then dismisses as he protects his father in his bizarre moral imperative to take Isabel's cause; having replaced sentimental family authority with patriarchal authority, having discounted, that is, his mother's "over-fond" and "over-reverential . . . imaginary image" in favor of the chair-portrait of the "real father," Pierre then "strove to banish the least trace of his altered father" (87). In order "to hold his public memory inviolate" (198), Pierre determines to destroy his father's portrait, "the one great condemning and unsuborned proof" of his profligacy (197). But the protection of his father's memory is not Pierre's only motive. Now that Isabel has "become a thing of intense and fearful love for him" (197), the portrait reminds Pierre of her illegitimacy. Because "the portrait's painted *self* seemed the real father of Isabel," the portrait remains proof of Isabel's "sinisterly becrooked, bemixed, and mutilated" status (197). To save and purify Isabel's "sweet, mournful image," to free her of this undermining parentage, Pierre must "destroy this thing" (198), must eradicate the father-portrait. Just before leaving Saddle Meadows with Isabel he burns the portrait, performing funeral rites for his father "a second time" (198): "'Henceforth, cast-out Pierre hath no paternity, and no past; and since the future is a blank to all; therefore, twice-disinherited Pierre stands untrammeledly his ever-present self!— free to do his own self-will and present fancy to whatever end!'" (199). Pierre presents his fancy to the end of making Isabel (and himself) fatherless as well as motherless, so that in fashioning his life, in imagining an autobiography modeled after Isabel's, he might make himself an orphan. The orphan, like the foundling books Melville imagined in the *Mosses* review, might be untrammeled by origins, might map his own life.

Just as in Melville's mechanics of anonymity, in which originality is achieved by a simultaneous brotherhood and orphanhood, by an increase and an extinction of relations, Pierre undoes his family through his relation to Isabel. As soon as Pierre embraces Isabel as his sister, he in effect denies their sibling relation by making her his wife. They present themselves to the world as a married couple and their relation is presented by Melville as an erotic one.[38] From a conventional sentimental point of view, the scandalous motive of Pierre's perverse enlargement of his family lies in his incestuous desire for Isabel.[39] But from this same perspective, incest involves an even more scandalous aim: Pierre's goal of dissolving the family. He "marries" his sister to divest himself of his family, including his sister. A sister *qua* sister reminds her brother of parental origins, thereby checking the autobiographical fantasy of self-generation that subtends the myth of the author. Incest with the sister, violating sibling relation and family law, enables Pierre's renovation of family for the establishment of his literary economy, a mode of authorship embedded in a self-contained family, in the notion of the self as its own family.

Incest, in Pierre's reformed sentimental family, epitomizes and literalizes the sacred tenet in sentimentalism: the bond between mother and son. But more than exposing the domestic cult's deployment of the primary familial taboo in the service of education and socialization, Melville's story of Pierre's "doubly incestuous" situation, his eroticized relations with mother and sister, discloses the familial underpinnings of aesthetic projects: how family models inform and empower myths of the writer. In a dream just before the end of his life, Pierre identifies his literary project with the exploits of the Titan Enceladus. He imagines himself as a "heaven-aspiring" being "held down to its terrestial mother," caught between "man's earthly household peace, and the ever encroaching appetite for God" (347, 345). Pierre associates Enceladus with "the wild scenery" (344) of an unapproachable mountain. But it is not only the landscape of the sublime that attracts Pierre to Enceladus; it is the Titan's incestuous genealogy that makes him sublime to Pierre. Pierre sees Enceladus as a model of selfhood because the Titan is "son and grandson of an incest," "one issue" of an endogamous family (347).[40]

Taking his sister as wife, and later, when he admits Lucy to his lodgings in New York, taking his would-be wife as sister, Pierre simultaneously denies his family ties and revises those ties to create a more endogamous family, closer to his closed-circuit model of literary production. The endogamous, inbred family approaches the point of the family's disappearance; Pierre discovers in incest a foundation, a familial support in the form of no family at all, for his literary economy. Once established in his new familial arrangement, Pierre recedes into his work. His "author-hero Vivia" seems "directly plagiarized from his own experiences" (302). By writing this book Pierre is "thinning his blood and collapsing his heart. He is learning how to live, by rehearsing the part of death" (305). In this "accession to the personal divine" Pierre "can not eat but by force"; now become the sole source of his book, its subject and object of consumption, "his is the famishing which loathes all food" (305).[41] He famishes to be his book; in this corollary to Melville's literary cannibalism, the author is consumed by his production. The isolating movements of endogamy and incest culminate in the transformation of author into book.

A further consequence of *Pierre*'s exploitation of incest follows in an analogous change: the replacement of sentimental nurture networks by a system of self-generation. In this alternative dynamics of individualism, the unconsummated, nonprogenitive incest Melville describes between Pierre and Isabel approximates the condition of being one's own child. Pierre's "marriage" to Isabel accordingly makes him "foetal," infantilizing him as his writing debilitates him, leaving him blind and infirm, a "toddler" on his own. Subsumed by his book, his "Vivia," "Pierre was solitary as at the Pole" (338). The solitude of the autogenous self is such that nothing can intervene between the famishing author and the book that is his life. The singular literary economy projected from *Pierre*'s conversion of authors into (consumable) books, and domestic nurture into autogenesis, makes production and consumption identical: Melville's ideal (male) author *is* both the labor and the consumption of his production.

Crime and Punishment

The collation of *Pierre*'s perverse ecologies and genetics of family and authorship—the operations of anonymity, cannibalism, commodification, nurture, and incest I have been tracing through Melville's revision of literary economy—brings us, finally, to consider the function of death in literary individualism. If a certain misogyny inaugurated Pierre's quest for literary autonomy, a full-blown murderous misanthropy concludes it. All persons, even the person of Pierre, must disappear in this anti-sentimental narrative.

Once "isolated from the world, and intent upon his literary

enterprise" (285), Pierre learns that his mother has died, leaving Saddle Meadows to his cousin Glen Stanly, who has become Lucy's suitor. Replaced by Glen Stanly and reduced to a toddler, the disinherited Pierre is at last the orphan of his dreams. In the concluding events of the narrative, Pierre literalizes the violent solipsism of his literary project, killing his cousin and Lucy's brother, thereby "slaughtering the only unoutlawed human being by the name of Glendinning" (360).

In these crimes Isabel is the woman in the case, the cause of Pierre's murderous acts. Isabel affirms the sublimity of Pierre's solitary expedition by asserting that "God called thee, Pierre, not poor Bell" (159). In the prospect of allying his fate with his sister, Pierre conflates Isabel with God, his term for the polar opposite to the mother and household; "to him, Isabel wholly soared out of the realms of mortalness" (142), replacing Lucy and his mother, emblems of the sentimental impediments to his autobiographical quest. Yet when alone at his literary task, living in alternative domesticity with Isabel, Lucy, and the servant Delly, Pierre finds himself under the surveillance of a jealous wife. Isabel sees Lucy as an obstruction to their intimacy; once Lucy decides to live with them as "a nun-like cousin" (310), Pierre's relation to Isabel seems to her mediated "through another and an intercepting zone" (334). For Isabel, intercepting zones reinforce solitariness rather than interfere with it as Pierre fears. She seeks her brother in order to overcome individualness, for, as she tells him, "there is no perfect peace in individualness" (181).[42]

Both Isabel's possessiveness and Lucy's presence disturb the peace of Pierre's individualness; this populous polar region Pierre inhabits—it is also a New York tenement—exposes the inevitable problem of other people to the imagination of self-generation, the persistence of society in the fantasy of self-containment. Yet if Isabel as well as Lucy signifies the inescapability of relations, it is less as figures of sentimental culture than as instances of the problems of intersubjectivity which the sentimental family domesticates. The sentimental family reconciles the self with others, secures the notion of selfhood in relations with others that involve the objectification, nurture, discipline, and appropriation of the self by others. The problem of other persons remains when Pierre has left the sentimental family, because selfhood requires defining the self against otherness, because identity always entails relation. As the measure of Pierre's individualness, Isabel recapitulates the sentimental mother's function, the domestic standard in the process of individuation.[43]

At this convergence of the poles *Pierre* encompasses, two portraits again figure in Pierre's aesthetics of autobiography. Visiting a portrait gallery, Pierre searches for an intriguingly labeled picture, "No. 99. A stranger's head, by an unknown hand" (349). This doubly anonymous portrait, "a real Italian gem of art" amid a "most hybrid collection of impostures" (350), shows a "comely, youthful man's head, portentously looking out of a dark, shaded ground, and ambiguously smiling" (351). To Isabel, this face holds "certain shadowy traces to her own unmistakeable likeness"; "while to Pierre, this face was in part as the resurrection of the one he had burnt" (351). In their recognition of this portrait, "Pierre was thinking of the chair-portrait: Isabel, of the living face" she remembers of her father (351). This coincidence of two referents causes Pierre to wonder about whether the congruity between "Aunt Dorothea's nebulous legend" of his father's portrait and "Isabel's still more nebulous story of her father" (353) is not merely coincidence. "How did he know that Isabel was his sister? . . . the grand point now with Pierre was, not the general question whether his father had had a daughter, but whether, assuming he had had, *Isabel,* rather than any other living being, *was that daughter*" (353).

It is as if the recognition of Isabel's conventional relation to himself, her all too domestic claims, prompts Pierre to disown his brotherhood. But he retains the possibility of having a sister—his father still may have had a daughter. Melville sustains Pierre's literary fantasy by pairing the ambiguous picture with a copy of *The Cenci* of Guido, the portrait of the object and agent "of the two most horrible crimes . . . possible to civilized humanity— incest and parricide" (351). These portraits "exactly faced each other; so that in secret they seemed pantomimically talking over and across the living spectators below" (351). This association links Isabel with incest and parricide, so that even if she is not the orphaned sister of Pierre she is still identified with his project. Incest and parricide are crimes against relation, violations of the social (and legal) boundaries defining the family. Pierre would destroy these boundaries to rid himself of relations, of the very idea of relationship. The horror he discovers in the pictures is not the possibility that Isabel might not be his sister but the fact that she or some other remains necessary to his autobiographical project. His purified domestic economy cannot fully dispel the principle of relation. Isabel articulates this necessity of contrast to individuality when she tells Pierre: "I am called woman, and thou, man, Pierre, but there is neither man nor woman about it" (149). Sexual difference works to define not men and women but the possibility of self.[44]

Difference and resemblance, the conditions Pierre manipulates to form a self-generated, self-sustained life, bring Pierre back home to the inescapability of family. *Pierre* enacts a confusion between portraits and subjects, between representations and persons, writing and the body. The danger inherent to Pierre's fantasy of self-distinction through submersion in otherness is that of losing himself, becoming truly anonymous in anonymity. At play in the juxtaposition of the two pictures is the problem with a system of anonymous representation: the problem of determining and preserving originality when two or more representations coincide.

The quest for originality and the effort to defy the conventions of sentimental culture therefore eventually require methods of enforcement. Isabel's ultimate resemblance to Pierre's controlling sentimental mother, underscored by her resemblance to the Stranger's Head, alerts Pierre to the necessity of a law to uphold his model of the singular family. This is why the end of Pierre's mission is a chronicle of crime and punishment. His drama of individualness ends in prison, under the aegis of a legal administration of individuality. Pierre finally locates his literary economy not in heaven or at the North Pole or in any other sublime region

but in sentimental culture, on the wrong side of the law. In trans-
gressing the social order Pierre asserts his particularity and is sin-
gled out for his singularity.

Another domestic angel in Pierre's life, Isabel first enables and
finally circumscribes Pierre's autobiography. The doubts the portrait raises about her identity translate into threats to Pierre's literary enterprise and his character. Two letters precipitate Pierre's
resolve to shoot Glen Stanly and Lucy's brother, Frederic Tartan.
The first missive, from his ironically named publishers Steel, Flint
& Asbestos, accuses him of being "a swindler," of taking cash
advances "under the pretenses of writing a popular novel." The
publishers refuse to print any more of Pierre's "blasphemous rhap-
sody" and charge him for the "printing thus far" and the advances
(356). The second letter, from Stanly and Tartan, also charges
Pierre with a crime, denouncing him as "a villainous and perjured
liar" (356). This "scornfullest and loathesomest title for a man"
(357) echoes the doubt implanted in Pierre by the portrait resembling Isabel: the possibility that Isabel is not his sister but merely
the object of his lust, that his literary endeavor is "a detected
cheat" (357). Both his publishers and his kin strike at more than
Pierre's incestuous desires; they undermine his "intense procre-
ative enthusiasm," the myth of authorship elaborated by "his own
manifold and inter-enfolding mystic and transcendental persuasions" (353) about Isabel.

To acquit himself and "get a start of the wise world's abuse" of
his literary labor, Pierre spits upon his book and defies "all the
world's bread and breath" (357). Unable to realize in life his
Promethean quest for self-nurture, Pierre decides to meet his ac-
cusers and risk death, taking two pistols, "more wondrous" than
the "wondrous tools Prometheus used" (358). Still defending the
intent of his quest, the creation of a self-contained literary economy, Pierre plans the murder of his detractors as his response to
their letter, literally returning their words: "[F]or the top-wadding
[in the pistols], I'll send 'em back their lie, and plant it scorching
in their brains! he tore off that part of Glen and Fred's letter, which
more particularly gave the lie; and halving it, rammed it home
among the bullets" (359). In a last-ditch implementation of his

ecology of representation, he thus also literally returns his publishers' same accusation by translating steel, flint, and asbestos
into instruments designed to put an end to all commerce and
communication.

Murder and what is effectively matricide bring Pierre to prison
and a death sentence; now that "his own hand [has] extinguished
his house" (360), he can achieve his fantasy of self-nurture in the
only act of self-control remaining to him: suicide. In a last and fatal
act of self-nurture, he feeds himself to death with the poison Isabel
keeps between her breasts. The end of Pierre's story, though, is
not his but Isabel's. Joining him in death, gasping the last words
"'ye know him not!' . . . she fell upon Pierre's heart, and her long
hair ran over him, and arbored him in ebon vines" (362). Her
words seeming to testify to Pierre's impenetrability, to his independence from his sentimental past, Isabel's dying gesture and
"death-milk" actually return Pierre to the iconography of sentimental motherhood, ensconcing him in feminine bonds.

The Triumph of Sentimentalism

The return of the sentimental—the transformation of Pierre's anti-
domesticity into the final image of maternity—signifies that
Pierre's anti-sentimental literary quest is precisely the cautionary
tale by which domestic ideology defines and teaches individualism. Read this way, the fate of Pierre's literary individualism illustrates how bad boys get punished for blaspheming the family.
To erase the family from the writer's vista turns out to be only to
displace the family temporarily onto the geography of literary
quest. Returning Pierre to the sovereignty of domesticity, *Pierre*
exhibits a virtually paranoid sense of domestic governance. In this
narrative of maternal containment of the individual, sentimental
nurture blocks the writer from start to finish.

Nineteenth-century spellers, grammars, and readers represented the skills of reading and writing as extensions, if not de-
fenses, of family values. So, for example, in the didactic practice
characteristic of primer lessons which linked language usage with
familial goals, the child who correctly uses the articles *a* and *the*

successfully communicates the information that identifies a criminal as "the" man who had robbed and lamed her father.[45] The prominent recurrence of images of obedience and punishment in the pedagogies of reading and writing anchors literature in the family governance of individual behavior. The active and passive voices are imaged in one grammar book as an active adult figure with a whip standing over the passive child figure, reinforcing both the authority of the family and the individuality of the body the family alternately nurtures, shapes, disciplines, and punishes.[46] In the tradition of this sentimental education, Mary Glendinning tutors Pierre to make him "a fine, proud, loving, docile, vigorous boy," both "sweetly docile" to herself and "a haughty hero to the world" (20). For this she dies—and for that Pierre dies. If this seems an extreme view of domestic power and responsibility, it is by no means Melville's alone.

Pierre's history bears out the predictions of sentimental child-rearing literature, testifying not only to the dangers of domestic disobedience but also to the potential delinquencies in maternal nurturance. "It is because children have been prisoners in the domestic circle—in body, mind, and soul, that they afterwards become state prisoners," William Alcott warned in his advice to mothers.[47] This imprisonment involves not the oppressive "maternal tuitions" to which Pierre was "strangely docile" but, rather, their absence. According to the contemporary popular literature of child-rearing, the mother had to realize that "the quality and quantity of food and drink, drawn in by the child at the breast, tends . . . to propagate danger and error."[48] Because mothers "sow the seeds of nearly all the good and evil in our world," only their "watchfulness" can save their children from "the verge of destruction."[49] The memory of a mother's teachings might deter a son from "the temptations which come crowding upon him" in "the busy world. . . . Even though far away, in abodes of infamy, degraded and abandoned, he must occasionally think of a broken-hearted mother."[50] This means that filial criminality is the mother's responsibility and, moreover, evidence of maternal culpability. Thus, as one mothering manual admonishes, "[I]f you are unfaithful to your child when he is young, he will be unfaithful to

you when he is old."[51] In the nineteenth century's negative teleology of maternal nurture, the sins of the mother are visited upon
the son. Pierre's crimes and incarceration accordingly manifest
both the crime and the punishment of his mother.

When in capital punishment the birth cord is replaced with the
hanging noose, the mother is relieved of her governance and responsibility; she is negated as origin and agency in the son's career.
If criminality testifies to maternal neglect, and if punishment finally severs the criminal from the mother, then Pierre's crimes
enable him to attain the condition of the abandoned child which
sentimental criminology describes. He doubly detaches himself
from his mother by causing her death and, in his own death,
denying her maternity. It is the mother who is finally criminalized
and punished in *Pierre*'s exposition of the outlaw writer. In what
seems overkill—the excessive domestic violence of *Pierre*—
Melville espouses not merely his own misogyny but what might
be called the domestic tradition of misogyny.[52] For Pierre's repudiation of motherhood and home ultimately intensifies his domestic relations. His anti-sentimental literary quest is precisely the plot
and psychology by which the sentimental home forwards individualism. In this light, literary individualism appears less as an oppositional mode to domestic individualism than as a certain masculine expression of it.

When Pierre resolves to leave home, the narrator remarks on
the "dark, mad mystery in some human hearts, which, sometimes
during the tyranny of a usurper mood, leads them to be all eagerness to cast off the most beloved bond, as a hindrance to the
attainment of whatever transcendental object the usurper mood so
tyrannically suggests" (180). But once the individual, in order "to
embrace the boundless and unbodied air" (180), "breaks from
every enfolding arm, and puts to sea in the height of a tempest,"
he experiences not the freedom of his own pursuit but the memory
of the "household sun" he forsook (181). "For whoso once has
known this sweet knowledge and then fled it; in absence, to him
the avenging dream will come" (181). When Pierre renounces
home, he becomes "this self-upbraiding sailor; this dreamer of the
avenging dream" (181). Instead of adventure and the authority of

authorship, flight entails a reconstructed home and destructive sickness; to Pierre, "who would become as immortal bachelors and gods" (180), comes a bizarre domesticity and crippling disease. Homesickness, in Melville's exposition, is not simply the effect of flight but is embodied in the conditions motivating departure. The sickness of home is that it produces a sickness for home.

This reproduction of domesticity through its internalization, an internalization Pierre tries to radicalize into a separate society of one, attests to the productive function of misogyny and anti-sentimentalism in the domestic imagination. The desire to repudiate the mother, along with the market, is built into domestic individualism. In the genealogy of crime and punishment *Pierre* elaborates, domesticity perpetuates the demise of maternal power—the wide margins of maternal error repeatedly envisioned in nineteenth-century childcare literature—in order to preserve and replenish the sentimental legacy of individualism. *Pierre*'s testimony to domestic power suggests that the wish for self-valorization through matricide is part of what the ideology of sentimental motherhood dispenses and regulates. In this view, domesticity generates and reflects the myth of the author as the self's estrangement from the mother, a self-abandonment firmly anchored in the network called home.

Pierre's final and fatal bondage indicates that Isabel's function as the heroine through whom Pierre mirrors his ideal of individuality is ultimately in service to a sentimental literary economy. Isabel's pronouncement over Pierre's dead body to his friends that "ye know him not" (362) promotes the tale of misunderstood genius that has long circulated as the alibi of the American writer. As this tale issues from Pierre's death, he becomes the subject of a popular and frequently reissued narrative: the struggle of the male author in sentimental culture. Though Pierre fails in his authorial quest and *Pierre* failed with nineteenth-century readers, the mythology of authorship Melville expounded eventually found a select literary market—through the changing tastes and standards of the market.

The difficulty of *Pierre* and the failure of Pierre lie in the impossibility of imagining individualism outside either commerce or domesticity, of living outside the domain of self nineteenth-century America imagined—all of which is to say the impossibility of experiencing oneself as not oneself.[53] Perhaps the desire to be otherwise—to be outside the defining limits of self—is so constraining in *Pierre* because of the oppressive familiarity of alterity in individualism: the banality of utopianism in American visions of self.

Chapter Six

The Empire
of Agoraphobia

"Bartleby the Scrivener: A Story of Wall Street" puts into circulation the story of a man about whom "nothing is ascertainable." Because "no materials exist for a full and satisfactory biography of this man," the "few passages in the life of Bartleby" related by the narrator represent the life of Bartleby. Transforming this very impediment to biography into biographical copy, Melville's 1853 story of the "unaccountable Bartleby" both thematizes and reproduces a market economy ontology: Bartleby's history is a tale of the marketplace and, like other market productions, significant because circulating, effective because communicative and commercial.[1] Melville's entry into mass magazine circulation after the commercial failure of both *Moby-Dick* and *Pierre,* the tale exemplifies the mechanisms by which life in and of the marketplace is forwarded.

Unlike the moving copy the tale creates and disseminates, Bartleby himself is "a motionless young man" (45), "singularly sedate" (46), "stationary" (69). The curiosity "the inscrutable scrivener" provokes and the story he thus provides issue from this mysterious immobility, from "his great stillness" (53), his affinity to what is static in Wall Street: the walls of the buildings and offices where the circulation of property is ratified in deeds and titles, where changes in proprietorship are codified and copied. Amid this conveyancing, Bartleby remains in his partitioned office cubicle—walled in, facing more walls through his window, in his own "dead-wall reveries" (56). This enigmatic stance by which Bartleby removes himself from marketplace circulation also occasions his biography; "Bartleby the Scrivener," a tale of a stationary man, thus includes within its commerce a protest against commerce and, moreover, makes commerce of that protest, translating a wall into a scrivener, the scrivener's inscrutability into market reproduction.

Reiterating the market imperative to move, the circulatory fate of Bartleby demonstrates the crucial productivity of immobility. In the tautological procedures of the marketplace Bartleby's static, even ahistorical status, when transposed into literary currency, reprises life in the marketplace where movement is all. Melville's tale describes an itinerary of what might be called the immobility principle, the reproduction of circulation through tableaux of the stationary. Bartleby's arrested motion is one such tableau in the nineteenth-century American iconography of stillness featuring invalidism, woman, and home (and conflations of these) as predominant figures of restfulness.[2] The frail, sentimental heroine whose domestic angelicism marks her for death—imprinted in the American imagination by Stowe's 1852 invention of Little Eva, which was reproduced on the stage for the rest of the century—inaugurates and sustains this idealization of worldly retreat by a commercial society. Resembling the retreat of the invalid heroine into her home (Eva speaks of dying as going home to heaven), Bartleby's withdrawal invokes the domestic tableau in order to investigate its commercial peregrinations. How Bartleby's immobility moves is thus the story of how American culture deployed domestic stations and spaces of seclusion.

The Mechanics of Immobility

In order to understand how Bartleby's resistance ultimately enters and typifies commerce, or, to put it another way, how walls move, it is necessary first to see how and why, in nineteenth-century America, ordinarily mobile humans might become "dead-walls." The preeminent figure of immobility for the nineteenth century is the hysteric whose strange postures freeze normal bodily motion and activity.[3] Whereas Freud derived a theory of female sexuality from hysteria, American doctors focused on the characteristic hysterical symptoms of paralysis and nervous exhaustion. Nervous attitudes and hysterical presentations fit into a recurrent imagery of paralysis and exhaustion in American medical literature on nervous disorders. This discourse of immobility treats nervous poses and symptoms as social practices, variant implementations of a customary iconography. Postulating an evolutionary psychology in which mental diseases accidentally resuscitate formerly useful animal instincts, William James in 1890 associated "the statue-like, crouching immobility of some melancholiacs" with the "death-shamming instinct shown by many animals," the self-preservative immobility of "the feigning animal." This instinctual etiology, James believes, explains "the strange symptom which has been described of late years by the rather absurd name of *agoraphobia*. . . . When we notice the chronic agoraphobia of our domestic cats, and see the tenacious way in which many wild animals, especially rodents, cling to cover, and only venture on a dash across the open as a desperate measure," we are witnessing a prototype of the agoraphobic, who, in "terror at the sight of any open place or broad street which he has to cross alone, . . . slinks round the sides of the square, hugging the houses as closely as he can."[4]

This concern with the protection of walls and enclosures recurs throughout nineteenth-century case histories of agoraphobics which appeared after the classification of agoraphobia as a nervous disease in 1873.[5] A Connecticut man treated by Dr. William A. Hammond "would not go out into the street unless he went in a carriage" and, "in passing from the vehicle to the door of a house, he required the support of two men—one on each side of him."[6] The agoraphobic dependence upon walls of some kind is epitomized in nineteenth-century medical literature by a story about Pascal. After a 1654 carriage accident in which he was thrown into the Seine, Pascal "had [a] morbid fear of falling into a large space." To protect himself from chasms he imagined at his side, Pascal ever afterward kept a screen beside him. Nineteenth-century

French doctors posthumously diagnosed Pascal as agoraphobic. The agoraphobic dependence on enclosures or adjacent fortifications kept most sufferers within the walls of houses, safe from their terror of the street, where "everything was in motion."[7]

Many observers of the nineteenth-century American scene found such anxious house-hugging to be, not the anachronism James theorized, but, rather, a symptom specific to the conditions of American economic life, a response to the motions of commerce. The democratic opportunity and competition for economic advancement, the very mobility of American society, Tocqueville worried in 1835, were apt to render the individual "stationary."[8] Agreeing with this evolution of anxiety from economic freedom, Dr. George M. Beard declared in 1881 that the recent inventions of steam power, the periodical press, and the telegraph, as well as developments in the sciences and the increased mental activity of women, "must carry nervousness and nervous diseases." New technologies of transportation and communication enable "the increase in the amount of business" which has "developed sources of anxiety."[9] In the case of the agoraphobic man from Connecticut, Dr. Hammond noted that "there had been excessive emotional disturbance in business matters."[10] The anxieties and responsibilities of commerce, the famous Dr. S. Weir Mitchell believed, explain the "numerous instances of nervous exhaustion among merchants and manufacturers." According to Mitchell's notebooks of the 1880s, "manufacturers and certain classes of railway officials are the most liable to suffer from neural exhaustion"; merchants and brokers are the next most likely sufferers.[11] In the latter half of the century, the railroad figured prominently in American, German, and French lawsuits for mental health damages; it appeared to have created a fear of itself, the new phobia of traveling by railway.[12]

In these accounts of nervousness and anxiety, the mechanisms and modes of commerce ultimately immobilize the individual. Beard's and Mitchell's association of such conditions with economic developments in nineteenth-century life reflects anxieties about the effects of commerce notable in literature ranging from medical advice books to popular magazines such as *Putnam's,* where "Bartleby the Scrivener" first appeared. In this context, agoraphobia, the anxiety and immobility occasioned by the space and scope of streets, by the appurtenances and avenues of traffic, is an anti-commercial condition—literally, fear of the marketplace. The nosology of the condition as it emerged in America in the latter half of the century suggests, contrary to James, the aptness of the term *agoraphobia:* what inhibits the agoraphobe is the commerce that inhabits American life.

From the symptomology of immobility observed in nervous cases, an agoraphobic disposition emerges in social and medical discourse as the hallmark of American personal life. The recourse of the agoraphobic, when outside the house, to the protection of interiors or companions or shielding edifices represents an effort to retain the stability and security of the private sphere. Reproducing the enclosure and stillness of home in the deportment of the individual, agoraphobia approximates domesticity, often proclaimed as the nineteenth-century antidote to commercialism.[13] The antagonism between self and world manifest in agoraphobia reflects and replays the opposition between home and market that is upheld by domestic ideology. By maintaining the integrity of the private sphere, this opposition sustains the notion of a personal life impervious to market influences, the model of selfhood in a commercial society. In his propinquity to walls and his preference for his own wall-like impenetrable postures, Bartleby presents an extreme version of such a model: in "his long-continued motion-lessness" he achieves an "austere reserve," the ideal of domesticity on Wall Street.

Just as the isolate condition of hysteria translated into an anatomy of the self and its desires in Victorian society, the marginal phenomenon of agoraphobia furnished Victorian America with a paradigmatic selfhood associated with female experience or, more specifically, summarized and reproduced the tradition of selfhood established by domestic ideology. For nineteenth-century America, women signified the stability of the private sphere which Bartleby's wall-like stance exhibits, the standard of self-containment which the hysteric melodramatized. Thus the physicians who worried about the immobilizing effects of commerce directed much attention to preserving the tranquility of women and home, treating market-stricken men by attending to the maintenance of domestic womanhood. Both Beard and Mitchell decried non-domestic activity by women; Mitchell's *Wear and Tear; Or, Hints for the Overworked* treats the deleterious effects of commerce with advice on women's health. "It will not answer to look only at the causes of sickness and weakness which affect the male sex," Mitchell believes, because "if the mothers of a people are sickly and weak, the sad inheritance falls upon their offspring." To strengthen mothers for the American future, Mitchell designed his famous rest cure for nervous diseases. After undergoing a regimen of constant bed rest and severely restricted activity, women patients were to return to tranquil lives as wives and mothers. The rest cure countered the marketplace with a fortified domesticity.[14]

This fortified domesticity finally fortified the marketplace. The interest of physicians in the immobilizing effects of the marketplace signifies not an anti-market program but a foregrounding of domesticity from other images of the stationary. As the symptomology of immobility proliferates domestic attributes, the cure for immobility reiterates and recommends conventional domesticity. The aim of the rest cure, then, is not to limit market mobility but to reinforce a select domestic stillness, to underscore the healthy function of the stationary. In restricting women to bed, the rest cure in a sense demobilizes the domestic in order to recharge it for reproductive service to the market.

This interdependence of domesticity with the market emerges with greater specificity in nineteenth-century feminist critiques of the rest cure. Women such as Charlotte Perkins Gilman and the autobiographical narrator of her "The Yellow Wallpaper," whose nervous prostration did not benefit from the rest cure, used immobility to parody and protest against domestic confinement, to withdraw from household business. The protagonist of "The Yellow Wallpaper" withdraws into the world she sees in the wallpaper; oblivious to all else, she becomes indistinguishable from the paper and the woman she imagines behind it. It is impossible to distinguish where the woman "creeping" around the walls of her room is; her association with the wallpaper involves a traversal of conventional boundaries in which she simultaneously creeps along the walls of her room on both sides of the wallpaper and outside the house in "the long road under the trees."[15] The uncertainty of this woman's place, her identification with both the woman she imagines creeping behind the paper and the woman she imagines "creeping along . . . in the open country" (30–31), suggests that domestic borders vary and waver, that walls and women move.

In Gilman's portrait, the rest cure results in changing and disappearing walls, in a marketlike intensive domesticity. Nineteenth-century feminists from Charlotte Brontë to Charlotte Gilman explicated this delivery from home to market in their reinterpretations of domesticity. The feminist point of "The Yellow Wallpaper," and of other Madwoman in the Attic figures, is that domestic confinement ultimately destroys not only the woman but also the house; the real curative property of domesticity, then, would seem to be its elimination of barriers to the outside.[16] The final situation of the woman in "The Yellow Wallpaper" as she creeps "around the path by the wall" (36) is continual circulation.

That the domain of female circulation is madness appears to reaffirm the etiologies of the doctors who treated men suffering from the deleterious effects of commerce. The chronology unfolded by "The Yellow Wallpaper," however, illustrates a different movement: the domestic appropriation of the market, the mapping of its space within the interior of the home. The nervousness manifest in moving walls and in the dislocation of self replicates the conditions of commerce from which those walls ideally barricade the individual. Woman's nervousness thus bypasses the market outside, proceeding to a circulation of her own.

Gilman's subversion of domesticity launches a utopian transformation of the market, elaborated in the socialist-feminist collective households and redesigns of domesticity she advocated in her subsequent writings.[17] Raising market nervousness to a feminist power, "The Yellow Wallpaper" exploits the negative logic of commerce chronicled in accounts of American nervousness, revealing the market reflected and lodged in the walls of the home. This extension of the mechanics of immobility delineates and summarizes developments already visible in late nineteenth-century domestic architecture: the accentuation of open space within the domestic interior, the deemphasis on fixed enclosures that is exemplified in Frank Lloyd Wright's innovative windows, walls, and floor plans. Wright's homes appeared in the 1890s, but the century's best-known domestic ideologue, Catharine Beecher, had already advocated in the 1840s the advantages housekeepers might enjoy from open rooms and movable walls, changing the organization of domestic space to suit their various activities.[18] The mutability of domestic walls and the embrace of unbordered space described in "The Yellow Wallpaper" realize the value of mobility, the ethos of the market, already present in the domestic blueprint.

"The Yellow Wallpaper" and "Bartleby" are key moments in and representations of the mobilization of immobility that characterizes nineteenth-century American culture. If Gilman's story images both a consonant and a revisionary conclusion to an agoraphobic definition of selfhood, Melville's tale predicts and protests the circulation of the stationary that allows for such a conclusion. In the case of Bartleby, who does not even creep and whose walls do not move, Melville depicts an intransigent agoraphobia that admits no entry to the market, a tableau of the stationary in which walls stand still. The scrivener's motionlessness removes him from all forms of circulation; he does not even achieve the mobility of the woman who creeps around her room. To forestall the return of the agoraphobic to circulation, to circumvent the border movements of "The Yellow Wallpaper," Bartleby images an agoraphobia recalcitrant to the publicity in which the reformative discourses of disease place it. At the threshold of the American women's movement and the economic expansion of the latter half of the nineteenth-century, "Bartleby" presents an anxiety about the market anxieties that would propel physicians and feminists, as well as other commentators on American life, in the succeeding decades.

In the following exposition of nervousness about American nervousness it becomes clear that the agoraphobic model of self-integrity instantiates the market destiny of domesticity. The informing principle of domestic sanctuary, agoraphobia epitomizes the structure of individuality in a market economy. What finally makes agoraphobia paradigmatic, however, is not the domestic stillness it reproduces but the home-market circuit its theatrics of interiority restage. Agoraphobia's incarnation of commerce thus assures the market's future, the acceptance of its natural movements.

Market Fears and Phantoms

The logic animating Bartleby's motionlessness emerges with greater clarity in another nineteenth-century discourse inspirited by the agoraphobic imagination: the anti-feminist rhetoric of home protection. Nineteenth-century advice literature, sentimental novels, and women's magazines defined the home as a refuge from commercial life, an antithesis to the masculine marketplace.[19] Domestic literature such as *Godey's Lady's Book,* the century's most popular women's magazine, dedicated itself to the consolidation and cultivation of "the empire of home." Against men's struggle "for the mastery of the world," editor Sarah Josepha Hale urged women to stay home and engage in "a higher pursuit than the industrial arts afford," their "mission" as "guardians of whatsoever is good, pure, and lovely." Concurrent with the emerging consumerist role of women in the American economy, *Godey's* circulated an anti-commercial rhetoric on the virtues of staying home; stories celebrated heroines who eschewed the glamor of social life and the pleasures of shopping for their "quiet office" and frugal economies in "the empire of home."[20]

Like the physicians Beard and Mitchell, *Godey's* worried about women's part in contemporary economic revolutions, about the proliferation of commerce through women's work in the extra-domestic world. Anti-feminist polemics of the late nineteenth century amplified this concern in their scientistic characterizations of women as mentally inferior to men and subject to the reproductive function. This claim of biological determinancy advocates one form of reproduction over another; in opposition to the reproduction of commerce displayed by women's exercise of mental capacities and mobility, domestic traditionalists stressed "woman's nature" and "ministry at home."[21] Woman's participation in other occupations signals a degenerative movement, *Godey's* warned: "It is as though a star should strive to come down from its place in the calm sky and take the station of a gas-lamp in a crowded city street."[22]

To keep women from the crowded city streets, *Godey's* promoted domestic values and "never admitted any article . . . which is not intended to instruct either by example, sentiment, hints, or warnings."[23] As the American market economy developed and expanded and as women entered nondomestic situations, the magazine's instructive articles continued to hint about and warn against the dangers of the business domain. These anxieties about women in the marketplace surfaced most strikingly in an anonymous story of 1870 entitled "My Wife and the Market Street Phantom."[24] The stereotypical other woman opposed to the wife in the title is not a romantic rival, not a mistress or previous wife, but a "lady capitalist." The scandal is not sexual indiscretion but indiscreet business affairs.

George, the narrator, relates the story of the strain placed on his marriage by his reliance on creditors in his merchant business. He takes out a ninety-day loan to carry him over what loan offices now call a cash-flow problem, until he can collect on his own extensions of credit. His loan is passed on by one creditor to the dreaded Market Street Phantom, a "lady capitalist" notorious as much for her business methods as for her success. The lady's notoriety follows not only from the fact that she "is definitely a woman out of her sphere," but also from what the narrator calls her "peculiar style of doing business." When she buys up a loan note, she investigates the debtor:

She would look with the keenness of a merchandise broker at a stock of goods, count the boxes on the pavement before a store, inquire into the bank account of the drawer or city endorser, ascertain whether he was married or single, find it out if he kept a fast horse, and get a good look at him to see if he himself seemed to be a fast man.[25]

Then she enters into a familiar relation with the debtor, persistently calling on him to remind him of the due date on the note, assuming terms of "the most annoying cordiality" with him on every possible occasion. The worst of the Phantom's habits was "that she recognized all her debtors when she met them, that she spoke of them as her friends." For the duration of the loan period, the debtor is plagued by her presence—he is "under the spell of the Phantom." George compounds his predicament by not telling his wife the truth about his business affairs. The Phantom pays a call at the man's office the same day his wife is there. The wife immediately perceives her husband's embarrassment and is further disturbed when her husband refuses to tell her the truth about the Phantom's identity and her relation to him. Until the loan is repaid the marriage is in trouble and "agony." Finally, George pays his debt, confesses to his wife and brother-in-law, and "all the clouds that lowered upon our house were lifted."[26] The three laugh over the misunderstanding and in the future the husband goes to his brother-in-law for business loans.

The narrator has learned his lesson: the perils of credit in the marketplace and the perils of withholding in the marriage. His mistake was to conduct business affairs he could not reveal to his wife; he should have entrusted his business problems to domestic care. The conflict between credit and family is resolved not by the termination of the credit economy, as one might expect in a moral tale about the dangers of credit, but by the absorption of credit relations into the domestic circle. So the story finally rejects, not the principle of credit against which it protests, but the extra-familial phenomena that credit represents. That is, credit relations within the family are fine, but on Market Street they are scandalous, akin to adultery. The narrator triumphs over his situation when he is able "to cut the Phantom dead!"—when he is able to extricate himself from exogamous relations.[27] Domesticity withstands the impingement of marketplace immorality by simply nullifying the existence of extradomestic phenomena. The story thus consolidates the family state.

But while the story domesticates credit, it does not domesticate the lady capitalist. The lady capitalist is a homebreaker because she threatens to reverse the power relations that uphold domesticity. In a culture where woman can only be recognized as domestic, the lady capitalist is not merely aberrant but subversive. The story enables a reconciliation of the opposition between home and market in the home's acceptance of credit as a component of domestic life. The Phantom reverses the order of this accommodation: she brings the home under the aegis of the market. In assuming intimacy with her business associates, the Phantom behaves as if the market were the home; she insists on a chain of relations normally governed by domestic etiquette. She represents an untenable premise—not merely a woman out of her sphere, but domesticity outside the home.

Making the domestic an integral part of market relations, the Phantom makes explicit the continuity between home and market that domestic rhetoric disguised. And she does this by subsuming the home into the market, familiar relations into credit checks. When George's brother-in-law replaces the Phantom as family creditor, the proper hierarchy is restored. Instead of the home being invaded by the market, the home annexes the market.

But this domestic campaign itself risks the disappearance of domestic boundaries in the family's incorporation of credit practices. In order to safeguard against this blurring of distinctions between home and market, the story fortifies the domestic by scapegoating the lady capitalist. Imaged as a state being besieged, domesticity appears under attack from the female creditors who advance commerce, yet the ultimate enemy this domestic defense strategy addresses is the undomesticity of the home itself. When poltergeists haunt the marketplace, they are following the excursions of the home into the world. Thus, the goal of the effort to ostracize the lady capitalist is to deny both the Phantom's and the home's excursions, to affirm domestic integrity and isolationism. Home protectionism reaffirms domestic borders by disseminating fears of market manifestations.

For readers of *Godey's,* the "cutting dead" of the Phantom eliminated anxieties their consumer role raised about the integrity of the domestic sphere; exorcising the Phantom meant purifying the home. In this fear of the marketplace, this literal agoraphobia, the Phantom is a bogeyman whose expulsion enforces the division between home and market. Like bogeymen in the closet or under the bed, the Phantom's potential reappearance offers a continuous opportunity for reasserting domestic safety and tranquility. Although she figures as the credit economy's threat to the family, the lady capitalist in fact ensures the family's acceptance of credit. In this way she functions as the facilitating anxiety of the home's accommodation of change. The Market Street Phantom is thus the agoraphobic spirit governing consumerist domestic ideology.

Godey's cautionary tale assured its reader of the existence of a frightening exterior world from which to preserve herself, reaffirming the need for domesticity. The tale circulates the production of domesticity as a state of anticipatory defense. This construction of a vigilant domesticity that absorbs exterior threats is of course a model of capitalist consumption: the realization and reinforcement of personal life in the acquisition of things believed to be necessary for self-sufficiency. The story of a threatened domesticity sells a reinforced domesticity. This marketing of domesticity, the raison d'être of such magazines as *Godey's,* shapes the consumer role of women in the American economy. In order that the domestic remain a principle of stability, domestic consumerism requires the remapping of domestic boundaries, their extension into commercial spaces.

Reenacting this implementation of domesticity against its own changeability, the department store first attracted late nineteenth-century women shoppers by designing and advertising itself as a magnified model home, as embodying the unlimited possibilities of domestic space.[28] *Godey's* performed a similar negotiation: the magazine introduced women to products in the market and established continuity between consumerism and housekeeping. The market thus seemed in service to domesticity. The woman at home, Veblen's model of conspicuous consumption, came to represent the foundation of the market economy, her demands and needs its motivating purpose—or, in the more positive, progressive version, her virtues signified the economy's idealist aims of philanthropy, comfort, progress.[29]

The institutionalization of women as consumers that was accomplished by the incorporation of consumerist sites into women's sphere established the primarily public nature of women's new domestic performances, the visibility denoted in Veblen's "con-

6. "Shoe Shopping," *Godey's Lady's Book* 39 (August 1848). Courtesy of the Rare Book and Manuscript Library, Columbia University.

spicuous consumption."[30] (See figure 6.) So now, more than a century after the invention of the department store, the store itself figures as the dreaded open space in agoraphobic episodes. And women, who traditionally frequent shops and markets, predominate among agoraphobic cases. Most agoraphobic attacks take place within the walls of department stores or in vehicles on the way to stores. What might seem an environment more inducive of claustrophobia creates the same anxieties nineteenth-century agoraphobes associated with streets and open areas and similarly causes retreat into houses. Staying home, "playing a paragon of Victorian femininity," the female agoraphobic identifies and fears the store's quintessential market character.[31]

Recognizing the agoraphobic refusal to leave home as a refusal to shop, contemporary behaviorist treatments of agoraphobia conclude with a celebratory shopping spree at a department store. The behaviorist aim to make women shop reinforces as it remarks the market agenda inscribed in domesticity during the nineteenth century. In returning women to the market, the behaviorist treatment updates Mitchell's rest cure to suit a consumerist domesticity; returning women to the department store is identical to returning women to their domestic sphere. These rearrangements of domestic space in the treatment of agoraphobia and nervous diseases are reflected in the strategically changing geography traced by contemporary agoraphobics. The agoraphobic lives according to a world map delineating safe and dangerous zones; often she will alter the boundaries of safe spaces so that she may venture beyond home to a friend's house or some other selectively domesticated hostile territory—for example, one side of an unsafe street. Conversely, and as usually happens in the debilitating process of the agoraphobic condition, the danger zones in the outside world can multiply and eventually include even activities that connect the home to the external world, such as telephoning and correspondence.[32]

By expanding and contracting safety sites, agoraphobic manipulations of domestic borders continually manufacture the certainty of safe places, thereby reproducing domesticity. This productive circulation of domesticity elaborated in home protectionist rhetoric consolidates not only home but the marketplace where home is sold. The alternation of house-hugging and border-crossing in agoraphobic practice manifests an uncertainty about where the market is, suggesting that what is most terrifying about the market is its ubiquity, its inescapability. With each new retrenchment of barriers the marketplace advances ever nearer. For if home in fact embraces the world, there is finally no place for the agoraphobic to go except to market. A continual border operation, agoraphobia always assumes the traversal of the boundaries it sets, always presumes that the limits can or will change. Mirroring the market economy's circulatory generativity, agoraphobia ultimately multiplies and magnifies the marketplace. Through the logic of agoraphobia, through the productive persistence of domestic threats like the Market Street Phantom, the market circulates and expands.

Bartleby's Negations

A scenario of besieged domesticity, "My Wife and the Market Street Phantom" demonstrates this market economy expansion.

The economy associated with the Phantom triumphs when the family welcomes credit practices, thereby reconstituting market relations as domestic ones. The wife takes the place of the Phantom in her husband's thoughts and, in resuming that place, offers him credit from her brother. In this transposition domesticity subsumes the business of the ubiquitous lady capitalist, an assimilation perhaps most tellingly represented in Gilman's image of domesticity as woman's creeping confinement.

Replaying the mechanics of market expansion demonstrated in the *Godey's* story, the circulation of the woman in "The Yellow Wallpaper" "round and round and round and round" (29) her room also reiterates the agoraphobic association between selfhood and domestic enclosure. The woman finally doesn't "want to go outside"; having locked herself in her room, she prefers to stay where her "shoulder just fits in that long smooch around the wall" (35). Declaring that "you don't get *me* out in the road there!" she continues creeping on her "path by the wall" (35) just as Bartleby continues his agoraphobic behavior in prison, taking up a "position fronting the dead-wall" (72). These agoraphobic figures of self-preservation exemplify a more tenacious house-hugging than domesticity recommends; both retain their absolute interiority by identifying with and preserving themselves in the walls. But Bartleby's self-possession is more assured: when confined in prison (for the supremely ironic charge of vagrancy), "his face toward a high wall," he emphatically states: "I know where I am" (71). This is a knowledge the woman cannot, and need not, claim, because her attachment is to the movability of walls. Attaching herself to the wallpaper which changes and moves, she identifies with the wall she traces and traverses. Gilman's regrounding of female identity in unstable domesticity, in the uncertainty of a female form of commerce, imagines the benefits of not knowing where you are. Once the wall the woman becomes disintegrates in her domestic demolition project, she does not need to go out, because she has already attained a sphere of selfhood, however bizarre.

Gilman is offering this female circulation as a feminist *point d'appui,* as the situation from which to reimagine female roles. In Gilman's later, utopian *Herland* stories, the idea of female circulation culminates in the vision of a self-generating, all-female cul-

ture.[33] The exorcism of the Market Street Phantom by the *Godey's*
parable precludes such an alternative relation between women and
economics. What haunts the agoraphobic imagination in its management of the market, however, is not specifically the feminist
appropriation of circulation but the terminus of circulation an
alternative economy might institute. The real fear in the agoraphobic imagination is of circulations beyond even the alternative circulations of the female agoraphobic and "The Yellow
Wallpaper" heroine: the prospect of a utopian circulation, which
amounts to circulation nowhere, or no circulation, the immobili-
zation of mobility.

Against this possibility of an altogether different form of life,
the capitalist agoraphobic imagination summons the specter of the
lady capitalist, a woman out of her sphere. The home-protec-
tionist elimination of the lady capitalist limits and stabilizes ex-
pansionist market history; eliminating the lady capitalist prevents
the eventual evolution of the market into something different,
checking mobility from its own possible extremes. The feminist
progress suggested by the Phantom—her market perambulations—signifies the chaos and unfamiliarity of not only a woman
but a market unmoored from the modulations of immobility.
Without the tableaux of the stationary performed by women and
domesticity, the market approaches the uncertain state of the
woman in "The Yellow Wallpaper." Against its transformation
into a feminist or foreign circulation, the market economy incorporates feminism as a regulatory agoraphobic mechanism for its
own continuity. Premised as another threat to domesticity, feminism becomes the phantasm inspiring home defense. The ménage
à trois of husband, wife, and Phantom—other woman, or market,
home, and feminism, thus perpetuates the hegemony of consumerist domesticity.

At stake in this stabilization of circulation is the maintenance of
a domesticity in which one knows where one is. The dizzying
circulation "round and round and round and round" the room in
"The Yellow Wallpaper," an extreme version of the domestic
enclosure of the Market Street Phantom's perambulations, marks
the uncertainty of a self defined by walls that inevitably move. A

self dislocated by permutations in the standard tableau of the stationary signifies the continual risks to and relocations of selfhood induced by the capitalist agoraphobic imagination. The regulation of market progress introduced by the *Godey's* story stems the advance of the wall-moving woman of "The Yellow Wallpaper," whose movements reveal in turn that the greater risk in capitalist agoraphobic logic runs through its own regulatory movements: its propensity to change borders undermines the construct of a stable self. Shifting the walls that situate the self, agoraphobia is inevitably not agoraphobic enough. The emblematic market mechanism, it ventures too far from house-hugging to sustain the ideal of self-preservation its postures of immobility suggest. Thus the most thoroughgoing resistance to nineteenth-century consumerist domestic ideology and market operations comes from a figure antithetical to movement—the stationary, radically agoraphobic Bartleby.

Within these politics of agoraphobia, the dynamic between home and world manifested by consumption, emerges the meaning of Bartleby's negations and mysterious isolationism. Bartleby, who, in Elizabeth Hardwick's paraphrase, "shuns the streets and is unmoved by the moral, religious, acute, obsessive, beautiful ideal of Consumption," insists on a noncommercial domesticity.[34] In preferring "to be stationary" (69), Bartleby achieves an impenetrability the lawyer-narrator cannot alter or enter. What the lawyer recognizes as Bartleby's complete self-possession—"his great stillness, his unalterableness of demeanor under all circumstances" (53)—obviates the notion of exchange or intercourse, denies any form of commerce, including the conversation and charity the lawyer would readily extend.

In his agoraphobic responses or, rather, lack of responsiveness, Bartleby follows female agoraphobic modes of evading domestic consumerism and repudiating intercourse between private and public realms.[35] The encounter between the lawyer and the scrivener is one between two competing models of domesticity: commercial domesticity and the truly agoraphobic.[36] In this context the narrator appears as a kind of Wall Street housekeeper; however, his domesticated business practices are undermined by Bartleby's renunciation of the domestic pretensions of the "eminently safe man" in his "snug business" on Wall Street (40).

Although the lawyer belongs "to a profession proverbially energetic and nervous, even . . . turbulent," he permits "nothing of that sort . . . to invade [his] peace." He attributes to his office "the cool tranquility of a snug retreat" (40). The business of the lawyer's domestic commercial sphere chiefly involves overseeing and compensating for the unhealthy gustatory habits of his copyists. Turkey drinks and so cannot perform his duties during the afternoon; his fellow worker Nippers suffers from morning indigestion and does not work efficiently until afternoon. The office boy Ginger-nut seems to function mainly as "cake and apple purveyor for Turkey and Nippers" (45). For the lawyer, these concerns with food and drink are labor management issues: what his employees consume directly affects what they produce. In this office in the image of home, the eccentricities of appetite are accommodated in the business routine.

Into this domestic colony on Wall Street comes the "motionless young man" Bartleby (45), who initially seems to suit perfectly and even to optimize the narrator's domestic economy. The lawyer thinks "a man of so singularly sedate an aspect . . . might operate beneficially upon the flighty temper of Turkey and the fiery one of Nippers" (46). Bartleby's habits "at first" appear a model of balance between work and diet, consumption and production—his work *is* ingestion. "As if long famishing for something to copy," the lawyer notes, "he seemed to gorge himself on my documents . . . without pause for digestion" (46).

Indeed, Bartleby so much epitomizes for his employer the successful union of economic and individual attributes that his place in the office—in a screened corner of a partitioned-off section of the office, facing a window with a view only of a brick wall—makes a "satisfactory arrangement" in which "privacy and society were conjoined" (46). The lawyer thinks of Bartleby's office carrel as "his hermitage" (50), and Bartleby literalizes this domestic fantasy. His insistent denial of every request directed at him, his removal of himself into his "dead-wall reveries" (52), achieves the privacy, the hermitage, the lawyer imagines his establishment provides. Making the "office his constant abiding place and home" (56), Bartleby purifies his employer's domestic economy. While the lawyer attempts to domesticate business, to accommodate the fluctuations of production and consumption within the walls of his establishment, Bartleby seeks to empty the domestic of the economic, to establish an impregnable privacy. Counterspirit to the Market Street Phantom, the "apparition of Bartleby" (53) "haunting the building" (68) enforces the rhetorical boundaries of the private sphere.

Making the office home in fact, Bartleby is a missionary agoraphobic, incongruously claiming the walls of Wall Street as the protective borders of the private domain, preferring to the congenial agoraphobia of the narrator a doctrinaire, absolute one whose primary feature is not so much that he "never went anywhere," but that, as the lawyer observes, "he never went to dinner" (50). Rather than follow, in the fashion of the lawyer, the logic of agoraphobia, which ultimately admits and embraces the market, Bartleby "lives without dining" (73), perfecting the agoraphobic condition in anorexia, where the borders between world and self are traced (and ultimately erased) on the individual body. This radical refusal to partake of, and participate in, the world makes Bartleby "self-possessed" (54) and impenetrable: the traditional goal of domestic life. Simultaneously fulfilling and negating the logic of agoraphobia—establishing selfhood in the extinction of commerce—anorexia secures the agoraphobic division of self from world, home from market. A strict observance of this division, anorexia realizes the hermitage agoraphobia cannot obtain; expunging consumption, it halts agoraphobia's inevitable progress into the marketplace.

Anorexia and Anti-consumerism

The anorectic, almost always a woman, avoids the world by refusing the most basic form of consumption. By starving herself she suppresses her menstrual cycle, shutting down the process of her own reproductive functions. She maintains in her body the fantasy of domesticity Bartleby enacts: a perfect self-enclosure.

While anorexia hardly seems an ideal condition, it is the fulfillment of the ideal of domestic privacy, a state in which complete separation from the demands and supplies of the world is attained.

Anorexia, somewhat contrary to its name, is not the condition of being without desire but the enterprise of controlling desire. That is, the anorectic wants not to want and to this end tries not to consume, or to undo consumption. She devotes all her energy to regulating the passage of food to and from her body. Most anorectics do in fact succumb to eating binges and become bulimic, inducing expurgation after every meal. Or they adopt intensive exercise regimens and ingest large quantities of laxatives and diuretics. One anorectic reported to her therapist that she masturbated one hundred times each evening, believing the constant pressure would strengthen her sphincter muscles, thereby facilitating release of food through defecation.[37]

This effort to eliminate or control food frequently involves a preoccupation with the buying, preparation, and serving of food. An anorectic will insist on cooking for the family and will produce elaborate meals whose consumption she supervises but herself forgoes. One anorectic was brought to treatment by her mother because she was concerned about the weight gain her daughter was inflicting upon her. In this dedication to others' consumption, the anorectic bizarrely imitates the mother's housekeeping role. She thus controls the desire to consume, which she recognizes as a desire essential to the family. Another anorectic so insisted on having dominion over food that her wealthy father built her her own kitchen, separate from the kitchen where the family cook worked. Here the girl maintained her perfected domestic province, performing the central housekeeping role without consuming.[38] This case makes clear the anorectic's radical claim to domestic space, her Bartlebylike insistence on a privacy without commerce. The anorectic kitchen literalizes domestic ideals, perfecting domesticity in anti-domesticity.

Anorectic practices, like agoraphobic strategies, manifest domestic functions in extreme forms. Not surprisingly, some recent analysts and interpreters of anorexia read in this hyperbolic condition a radical realization and indictment of cultural dictates on women's bodies and functions. Anorectic body ideals seem to coincide with the contemporary valuation of female slenderness (another marketing of domesticity), prompting observers of anorexia to note the current "popularity" of this disease, its distinctive appeal to adolescent, middle-class girls.[39] Whereas cases of anorexia in the latter half of this century clearly reflect and address specific cultural values, the anorectic strategy in "Bartleby" stresses another agenda: the rejection of consumerist domesticity. Bartleby's anorexia would remove agoraphobia from domestic commerce, making impossible the connection between these diseases and domestic consumerism which nineteenth- and twentieth-century physicians and feminists variously register.

First recorded in medical history in 1689 as "A Nervous Consumption," in a treatise on tuberculosis, anorexia nervosa did not become a specific clinical entity until 1873, the same year agoraphobia was first classified and twenty years after the publication of "Bartleby."[40] The difficulty nineteenth-century doctors encountered in diagnosing anorexia, in identifying it as a specific disease, lay in the similitude between the symptoms of anorexia and those of consumption, now remembered as the great nineteenth-century disease. Although it is an incorrect paradigm for anorexia nervosa, the initial clinical classification of anorexia with consumption unwittingly points to the connection between these illnesses as metaphors, to the way the diseases, or the descriptions of the diseases, both exemplify economic models. Susan Sontag has pointed out the isomorphism between the economies of tuberculosis and nineteenth-century expanding capitalism. Tuberculosis exhibits "the negative behavior of nineteenth-century *homo economicus:* consumption; wasting; squandering of vitality."[41] The fluctuations characteristic of the illness—dramatic variances in appetite and energy—aptly reproduced marketplace disequilibrium and concomitant anxieties about saving and spending. Tuberculosis mysteriously consumed the body from within; the consumptive sufferer seemed to replicate on the body an apocalyptic view of economic progress, a state of simultaneous voraciousness and exhaustion. No Camillelike martyred heroine to this economy, the anorectic chooses illness as a repudiation of the marketplace and an expression of self-control. A refusal to replicate the economy in the body, anorexia is the paradoxical antidote to consumption, the negative behavior of *femina economica*.

The anorectic enactment of the self-destructiveness of self-denial surpasses the deaths of such angelic, tubercular heroines as Stowe's Little Eva and Alcott's Beth, translating domestic angels into skeletal women. Taking to the limit the sentimental ideal of true womanhood, the anorectic appears as the sentimental self-denying heroine par excellence. A macabre mockery of domesticity, the anorectic, like the agoraphobic and the hysteric, seems to offer another figure of resistance to domestic ideology, another feminist type of the Madwoman in the Attic.[42]

But since the anorectic opposes the economy of consumption of both feminist and traditional versions of domesticity, she resists canonization as a sentimental or feminist heroine. Indeed, feminist visions of women in the world epitomize the commercial possibility in the home-market relations from which the anorectic retreats. The circulation of the woman in "The Yellow Wallpaper" exhibits the tendency to mobility in agoraphobia which anorexia would prevent. Unlike agoraphobic or hysteric stances, anorectic body language refuses to represent any form of commerce. A purging of agoraphobia, anorexia replaces the economy of consumption with abstinence. Disappearing from sight and space, the anorectic creates her own purified version of nineteenth-century tableaux of the stationary, an approach to complete privacy and stillness.

It is finally death, the termination of self, rather than self-circulation through the elimination of cultural obstructions, that anorexia seeks. This anorectic cult of death differs from popular sentimentalist celebrations of death, such as Stowe's glorification of Little Eva's consumptive end, which circulated in nineteenth-century domestic literature.[43] Whereas sentimental death seeks the world and an audience, demands a public space in the world, anorectic death flees the world; the anorectic economy of self-denial redefines death as divestment from the marketplace. To realize the fantasy of controlling desire—to deny the existence of an outside, of anything exterior to the self—the anorectic inevitably must want to die. By rejecting the body she hates for its contiguity with the world, for its reminder of the desire to consume, the anorectic finally triumphs over desire. Paradoxically, her abstinence permits pure selfishness. Preferring, like Bartleby, not to eat, she detaches herself from the world and finally from the body that borders it, the last semblance of walls contiguous with the world. In the logic of anorexia's perfection of agoraphobia, death best preserves the self.

These are the anorectic politics of Bartleby's radical employment of immobility. Stringently restricting the agoraphobic imagination to its ethic of immobility, Bartleby elaborates death as the best method of self-preservation. He leaves the world in order to keep himself. If properly understood, the choice of divestiture, despite the obvious disadvantages of the disappearing self, is a powerful one. What better critique of domestic difficulties than the decision to live no longer? But as inevitable as the cult of death for the anorectic is the sentimentality of interpretation to which death is submitted and by which it is consequently misread. When Bartleby, entombed within the Tombs, sleeps "with kings and counsellors" (73), the narrator attempts to account for the bizarre life and death of his scrivener. In telling the scrivener's story he accepts the invitation to investigate and interpret this successful agoraphobic. The "vague report" (73) he offers as an epilogue satisfies *his* curiosity about Bartleby's motivations. If Bartleby worked in the Dead Letter Office in Washington, then his condition might be understood as a response to such close association with death, for do not dead letters "sound like dead men?" (73). Bartleby's condition seems to the narrator an intensified experience of human mortality. He therefore commemorates Bartleby's passage as a testament to the human tragedy, joining the man and the crowd in his closing lament, "Ah, Bartleby! Ah, humanity!" (74).

The narrator's sentimental closure to Bartleby's story links Bartleby with the very chain of existence he preferred to avoid. This conjunction of Bartleby with humanity—the agoraphobic's nightmare—also elides the differences between the domestic preferences of Bartleby and those of his employer, thus diffusing the force of Bartleby's renunciation of commercial domesticity. By ignoring the alignment between circulation, life, and death which Bartleby signifies, the narrator's solution preserves the commerce domesticity tacitly transacts. The narrator would have us believe that Bartleby, continually witnessing letters on doomed errands of life, speeding to death, suffered from an overexposure to death, when death is precisely what Bartleby sought. The very idea of an errand—of letters reaching their destination—is anathema to Bartleby, who evades every form of intercourse, whose preferences cannot even attach to an object. The anorectic tries to deny to food and body any relation, by transforming objects of consumption into threatening, alien forces; she asserts the body's independence from the objects of its desires. Similarly, Bartleby detaches himself from things and all activities involving things, refusing even to commit himself to predicates that would signify subject-object relations, that would connect his negation to something external to himself. Bartleby hardly exemplifies the tragedy of death; his anorexia attests, rather, to the tragedy of circulation. What impels him or inters him is not the disconnections caused by death but the connections produced by life.

The success of a suicide mission depends on the proper interpretation of the suicidal intention. Bartleby's final act of refusal secures him no recognition for his cause, no canonization by fellow adherents. Despite the intended enunciation of the scrivener's death, the lawyer interprets the tragedy as confirmation of his own sentimentality. Whereas Bartleby sought to dissociate himself from all forms of economy, the narrator returns the copyist to the sentimental economy. Imagining Bartleby among kings and counsellors, the lawyer invokes Job's artificial death wish: in his lament on the misfortunes of his life, Job cries that he would have been at rest with kings and counsellors if he had died in the womb, or if his birth and nurturance had been prevented by the knees and breasts.[44] This lament almost comically shifts both the responsibility for Job's unhappy existence and the termination points of that existence; the logic of his wish delivers him to a resting point only imaginable in history, only possible for having lived. Job, then, does not wish that he had never been born—but that is precisely what Bartleby wishes when he prefers not to. The lawyer would return Bartleby to history when Bartleby would prefer not to have sucked, to have aborted his existence altogether.

The lawyer's interpretation of Bartleby's death, the tale's circulation of Bartleby's life, subsumes the radical act into the chain of existence and the chronicle of history, into literary currency. This final domestication implies that elimination of the body achieves only partial secession from the commercial. Interpretation invades death's privacy, taking death as a communiqué. Bartleby's imagination of an aborted self, a broken circuit, offers to the sentimental imagination an annexation of the unknown, widening the boundaries of what we think of as the world and women's sphere. In the agoraphobic imagination structuring selfhood in a market economy, death becomes another province, another border to be crossed—the final domestic station to be mobilized. The narrator's attempt to find a transcendent meaning to the Bartleby enigma is thus precisely the triumph of sentimentalism and consumerism, the perpetuation of a preoccupation with private property and personal provinces.

Even death, whether imagined as an escape by Bartleby or invoked as a principle of coherence by the lawyer, repeats the expansion-and-contraction patterns of the various sects of domestic perfectionists. The agoraphobic structure of domestic ideology, which Bartleby takes to the limit, includes and utilizes mortality within the logic of home protection. The life and death of Bartleby recirculate the imagination of being besieged which persists in shaping and defining the economies of capitalism and the economies of private life. Even in death, commerce continues; this is the errand of life on which letters speed to and from death.

Afterword

What happens when the markers of self-definition in nineteenth-century America begin to fade? This is the question Henry James addressed in *The Bostonians,* where he famously considers "the situation of women, the decline of the sentiment of sex, the agitation on their behalf"—or, in the terms of this study, the waning of domestic womanhood.[1] In James's 1886 epilogue to the literature of domestic individualism, a new public femininity displaces domestic femininity, changing the coordinates of individuality. The three nineteenth-century phenomena that for Stowe, Hawthorne, and Melville signify the outer limits of the self—slavery, mesmerism, agoraphobia—thus figure crucially in *The Bostonians* as techniques for redrawing the boundaries of self.

When Basil Ransom first sees Verena Tarrant perform, he immediately responds to the medium, and not the message, of "her strange, crude, absurd, enchanting improvisation" on women's rights.[2] To this "stiffest of conservatives, . . . it was simply an intensely personal exhibition, and the person making it happened to be fascinating" (84). He regards her "as a vocalist of exquisite faculty, condemned to sing bad music"—to utter the "inanities" of feminist rhetoric with which Basil assumes "she had been stuffed" by her father, the mesmeric healer Selah Tarrant (85). Verena's liberal Bostonian audience holds a more mystical and sympathetic view. A "mesmerist's only child," Verena is said to possess a "talent for conversation" facilitated by her father (70).

Under the strokings of "his long, lean hands, . . . some outside power seemed to flow through her" (80–81).

To Olive Chancellor, Basil's Bostonian cousin, "Verena's genius was a mystery" akin to immaculate conception; "her precious faculty . . . had dropped straight from heaven, without filtering through her parents." In Olive's eyes, Verena appears the expression of a sort of feminist providence, for the young girl seems to exhibit "the same tenderness, the same pity for women that she herself had." Unlike Basil, the feminist reformer Olive sees Verena's "power" as coextensive with the feminist sentiments she voices. Olive then can quite readily explain Verena's "gift" as a transhistorical sisterly empathy: "she seems to have lived in imagination through all ages" (104).

The determination of Verena's control forms the plot of *The Bostonians,* as her "golden voice" (263) inspires the erotic, political, and commercial desires of her audience. She is pure medium, a channel for any interest her auditors wish to recognize. Through this perfect vehicle *The Bostonians* follows the progress of female individualism and the reactionary male individualism it provokes as women in postbellum America cross the gender lines of domesticity. As a woman speaking in public for the political rights of women, Verena exemplifies the permeability of domestic boundaries. More than this, she virtually embodies a principle of passively itinerant womanhood, which may serve various interests. Verena in effect passes from one mesmerist, one set of "grotesque manipulations" (83), to another, from her father to Olive to Basil—from public entertainment to political cause to private relationship. With the oratorical power to "resolve" her audience "into a single sentient personality" (265), Verena is an invaluable channel for any set of convictions, be it her father's mesmerism or women's rights or male individualism.

The contest for Verena accordingly takes on the dimensions of the Civil War as the Southern conservative and the Northern reformer fight for different concepts of the feminine sphere in support of different forms of individualism. In this sexual rehearsal of the nation's great conflict, Olive and Basil struggle not simply for Verena but for the right to delimit her influence, for the exclusive right to her talent. Verena's public femininity provokes a property battle over her representation—over who will run her and whom she should represent. At stake in the control of Verena is the representative character and function of femininity. Her fate, the question of whom she serves, encapsulates the future of femininity's service to individualism.

The Bostonians emphasizes the commercial character of this battle and of the female public figure. Representing the commercialization of femininity as a traffic in women, the novel's narrative of feminist progress reverts to a narrative of slavery. Verena comes into Olive's possession and into full service to the cause of women's rights when Olive gives the Tarrants "a cheque for a very considerable amount" to leave her and Verena "entirely alone" (176). If this seems a supremely ironic situation, it also, and more significantly, appears congruent with Olive's wish to "rescue the girl from the danger of vulgar exploitation" (104), a danger she associates with the Tarrants who, after all, "embraced, tenderly, the idea of a pecuniary compensation" (177) for their daughter. In line with Stowe's logic of sentimental possession, Olive wants to own Verena in order to protect her from commercial usages and to make her expressive of all Olive's own feelings.

Though Olive rebuffs, along with the mesmeric Tarrants, the commercial interest of the press in Verena, her political commitment to women's rights and democracy means she still must make public use of Verena, giving others access to her. "Conforming herself to a great popular system" (415) for the sake of her cause, Olive must finally promote and defend Verena's public life. The last battle between her and Basil is not over Verena—Basil's sexual magnetism has already brought the girl under his power—but over Verena's anticipated performance at the Boston Music Hall. Basil, whose agoraphobia on Verena's account runs so deep that he believes there is "no place in public" for a woman (328), recognizes his real adversary in "that roaring crowd." "You are mine, you are not theirs," he tells her (425), reinstating the lines of the domestic sphere.

Taking Verena from "vulgarizing influences" (330) to keep her "at home" (328), Basil reinforces domestic distinctions "to save" his sex "from the most damnable feminization" (327). The "ugliness" of his beliefs is manifest in the way that his redrawn domestic boundaries exclude and excoriate not simply external commerce but the persons in it, whom he calls "senseless brutes" (430). If agoraphobia in *The Bostonians* fortifies masculinity, it does so by codifying the persons and places from and by which individuality is distinguished. In its chronicle of feminist and reactionary redefinitions of femininity this novel also records the new measures of personal identity provided by regional and sexual types: the Southerner, the New Englander, the Bostonian, the lesbian, the masculine man. These types furnish easily distinguishable identities at the very time when antebellum delineations of geographical and gender boundaries have faded. Typing provides a local color of individuality, situating individuals as surely as domesticity once placed them.

The symmetry of Verena's experience as she passes from one control to another suggests that the current of the novel runs inexorably toward reinstatement of domestic womanhood. Even progressivism contributes to this backward movement. In the horror of "the exhibition of enterprise and puffery" (415) registered in *The Bostonians,* the new trends of mesmerism and feminism through which women move into public space before "the gaze of hundreds" (331) resemble that prior commercial custom which placed women on platforms: slavery. Yet much as the agoraphobic attitude toward public womanhood invokes the stock nineteenth-century menaces of individuality, it also reflects the exhaustion of that inventory, the need for new representational strategies of self demonstrated by a conservative reliance on a rhetoric already superseded by events that have carried women out of the domestic sphere. A documentary of conservative backlash, *The Bostonians* at the same time introduces the counter-movement sure to come and the new lines along which individual claims would form. For James clearly does not endorse the final removal of Verena to the domestic sphere. Indeed, in the narrator's final prediction of the "tears" that "she was destined to shed," he strikes the note of inevitable domestic sorrow: the irreconcilable differences arising from the conflicting requirements of two individualities. As Basil takes Verena from the Boston Music Hall, the novel provides a glimpse of this new domestic site: the terrain of marital discord through which the fiction of James, Howells, Chopin, Norris, Gilman, Dunbar-Nelson, Wharton, and Larsen would delineate changing properties of femininity and of the self it anchors.

Notes

Introduction

1. C. B. Macpherson, *The Political Theory of Possessive Individualism: Hobbes to Locke* (New York: Oxford University Press, 1962).

2. This dating is based on the Oxford English Dictionary's attribution of the first use of the term *individualism* to Tocqueville in 1835, and on other reports discovering the term in the 1820s. Niklas Luhmann, "The Individuality of the Individual: Historical Meanings and Contemporary Problems," in Thomas C. Heller, Morton Sosna, and David E. Wellerby, eds., *Reconstructing Individualism: Autonomy, Individuality, and the Self in Western Thought* (Stanford: Stanford University Press, 1986), 313–25; K. W. Swart, "'Individualism' in the Mid-Nineteenth Century (1826–1860)," *Journal of the History of Ideas* 23 (1962): 77–90; Stephen Lukes, *Individualism* (New York: Oxford University Press, 1973).

3. Alexis de Tocqueville, *Democracy in America,* vol. 2, trans. George Lawrence, ed. J. P. Mayer (New York: Anchor-Doubleday, 1969), 506–7.

4. I borrow this phrase from the title of Christopher Lasch's *Haven in a Heartless World* (New York: Basic Books, 1977). In this study Lasch takes domestic rhetoric quite literally as he defends domesticity as the last refuge from capitalistic progress. I shall be demonstrating throughout this book that domestic values are in fact integral to capitalist development.

5. Catharine Beecher, *A Treatise on Domestic Economy* (1841; rpt. New York: Schocken, 1977), 18, 14.

6. Recent comprehensive studies of eighteenth- and nineteenth-century capitalism demonstrate an integral relation between the emergence of domestic ideology and the expansion of capitalism. See Julie

Matthaei, *An Economic History of Women in America: Women's Work, the Sexual Division of Labor, and the Development of Capitalism* (New York: Schocken, 1982); Elizabeth Fox-Genovese, "The Ideological Basis of Domestic Economy: The Representation of Women and the Family in the Age of Expansion," in Elizabeth Fox-Genovese and Eugene Genovese, *Fruits of Merchant Capital: Slavery and Bourgeois Property in the Rise and Expansion of Capitalism* (New York: Oxford University Press, 1983), 299–336.

7. Elizabeth Cady Stanton, "Solitude of Self," address before the United States Senate Committee on Woman Suffrage, February 20, 1892. Reprinted in Mari Jo Buhle and Paul Buhle, eds., *The Concise History of Woman Suffrage: Selections from the Classic Work of Stanton, Anthony, Gage, and Harper* (Urbana: University of Illinois Press, 1978), 325–27.

8. Stanton, "Solitude," 326.

9. For an interesting account of nineteenth-century feminism as a critique of possessive individualism, see William Leach, *True Love and Perfect Union: The Feminist Reform of Sex and Society* (New York: Basic Books, 1980).

10. Although Matthiessen does not include Poe among the literary representatives of the American Renaissance, I do, because his works are regularly studied in classes on antebellum American literature. Matthiessen's reason for the exclusion—that Poe did not represent democratic sentiments—can easily be dismissed. From the perspective of domestic individualism, Poe's extenuations of psychic states fit perfectly within the democratic value of self-cultivation. Matthiessen himself cannot fully deny Poe, but regularly invokes him as a contrast to Hawthorne: F. O. Matthiessen, *American Renaissance: Art and Expression in the Age of Emerson and Whitman* (New York: Oxford University Press, 1941).

11. Jane P. Tompkins coined the term "the Other American Renaissance" in her examination of Susan Warner's *The Wide, Wide World* (*Sensational Designs: The Cultural Work of American Fiction* [New York: Oxford University Press, 1987]; also published in Walter Benn Michaels and Donald Pease, eds., *The American Renaissance Reconsidered* [Baltimore: Johns Hopkins University Press, 1985]). Historian Mary Kelley calls this rise of women writers in America "literary domesticity": *Private Woman, Public Stage: Literary Domesticity in Nineteenth-Century America* (New York: Oxford University Press, 1984). I shall not be concerned here with the problems in women's literary careers that Kelley treats informatively, nor shall I be delineating the features of the Other American Renaissance. My exposition of domestic individualism, indeed, will suggest some of

the problems in separating male and female traditions, a separation which itself reflects an effect of domestic ideology.

12. Leslie Fiedler, *Love and Death in the American Novel* (New York: Criterion, 1960), xx–xxi.

13. Ann Douglas, *The Feminization of American Culture* (New York: Knopf, 1977); Henry Nash Smith, "The Scribbling Women and the Cosmic Success Story," *Critical Inquiry* 1 (September 1974): 47–70.

A few words are in order to clarify the difference between my premise of the nineteenth-century domestication of individuality and Douglas's thesis of the feminization of American culture. In proposing that individuality is aligned with and based on the feminine sphere, I am not suggesting that women direct the values of individualism or that the commercialism identified with domestic literature establishes "the anti-intellectual tradition in American culture." If American culture is feminized in the nineteenth century (and I share Douglas's belief that it is, while holding a different view of what that means—I do not see this as a degenerative movement), this feminization represents an androcentric society's deployment of as well as dependence on the domestic. And far from debasing intellectual activity, domestic individualism introduces new imaginative strategies of self-definition, exemplified in nineteenth-century fiction. My account of the feminized self to some extent follows from the traditional association of interiority with the female or feminine, described in Ian Watt, *The Rise of the Novel* (Berkeley and Los Angeles: University of California Press, 1967); and more recently developed in Myra Jehlen, "Archimedes and the Paradox of Feminist Criticism," *Signs* 6 (Summer 1981): 575–601; Frances Ferguson, "Rape and the Rise of the Novel," *Representations* 20 (Fall 1987): 88–112; and Nancy Armstrong, *Desire and Domestic Fiction* (New York: Oxford University Press, 1987).

As Ferguson points out in her analysis of *Clarissa* and eighteenth-century rape laws, the psychological complexity of subjectivity that the novel represents does not make mental states transparent but, rather, institutes a contradictory relation between an individual's stipulated mental state and her actual one. Instead of expressing interiority, the novel form identifies the conflict between at least two accounts of self. So to propose, as Jehlen provocatively does, "that this interior life, *whether lived by a man or woman, is female*" is to shift focus to a resolution of identity. The identification of interiority with femininity, carefully studied in Armstrong's rereading of Watt and British fiction, emerges as a historical function: the rise of the domestic woman and the novels representing her facilitate and reflect new organizations of economy and class. I thus want to emphasize the feminization or, to be more precise, the domestication of self as a dynamic process, related to similar economic developments in America. Registered in American literature as an embattled individuality, this self consists in a state of conflict that resonates as much with the sets of contradictions we call male as with those we call female.

14. Nina Baym, *Woman's Fiction: A Guide to Novels by and about Women in America, 1820–1870* (Ithaca: Cornell University Press, 1978), 27; Nina Baym, "Melodramas of Beset Manhood: How Theories of American Fiction Exclude Women Authors," *American Quarterly* 33 (Summer 1981): 123–39. Besides Baym, Tompkins, and Kelley, a host of feminist critics have amplified the theme of an American female cultural tradition. See, for instance, Elizabeth Ammons, "Stowe's Dream of the Mother-Savior: *Uncle Tom's Cabin* and American Women Writers before the 1920s," in Eric J. Sundquist, ed., *New Essays on Uncle Tom's Cabin* (New York: Cambridge University Press, 1986), 155–95; Annette Kolodny, *The Land before Her: Fantasy and Experience of the American Frontiers, 1630–1860* (Chapel Hill: University of North Carolina Press, 1984); Cheryl Walker, *The Nightingale's Burden: Women Poets and American Culture before 1900* (Bloomington: University of Indiana Press, 1982); and, in a slightly different vein, Carroll Smith-Rosenberg, "The Female World of Love and Ritual: Relations between Women in Nineteenth-Century America," in her *Disorderly Conduct: Visions of Gender in Victorian America* (New York: Knopf, 1985), 53–76.

15. The prevalence of corporeality here exemplifies Sharon Cameron's point that American fictions seem preoccupied with conceptions of identity conceived in corporeal terms. Cameron particularizes the customary depiction, in American literature, of the self outside the confines of a social context into a concern with the "problems of human identity predicated in terms of the body": Sharon Cameron, *The Corporeal Self: Allegories of the Body in Melville and Hawthorne* (Baltimore: Johns Hopkins University Press, 1981), 6.

Chapter One

1. Harriet Beecher Stowe, *The Key to Uncle Tom's Cabin* (1853; rpt. New York: Arno Press, 1969), 257.

2. Harriet Beecher Stowe, *Uncle Tom's Cabin; or, Life among the Lowly* (1852; rpt. Columbus, Ohio: Charles E. Merrill, 1969), 1: 297. This edition is a reprint of the first edition published in 1852 by John P. Jewett and Co. The long serial appearing in *The National Era* from 1851 to 1852 became a two-volume book. Except as noted, all future references will be to this edition; volume and page numbers are given in parentheses in the text.

3. I am here following Elizabeth Fox-Genovese's definition of domestic economy as "an integral component" of the ideology of "any system of political economy" that it "intersects, reinforces, and counters." Fox-Genovese provides an excellent description and analysis of the role of domestic economy as the "handmaiden of emerging capitalism" in nineteenth-century France. See her "The Ideological Basis of Domestic Economy."

4. *Ladies Magazine* 3 (January 1830), quoted in Nancy C. Cott, *The Bonds of Womanhood: Woman's Sphere in New England, 1780–1835* (New Haven: Yale University Press, 1977), 68. For another informative account of the distinction made by the domestic cult between the home and the marketplace, see Mary Ryan, *Womanhood in America* (New York: New Viewpoints, 1979), 75–117.

5. Abolitionists often associated slavery with what the Reverend George B. Cheever called the contagious marketplace "spirit of gain." Wendall Phillips lamented that their plan "to plant the self-sacrifice of a rigid Anti-Slavery" in America was frustrated by a "money-loving country, intensely devoted to the love of material gain." Quoted in Ronald G. Walters, *The Antislavery Appeal: American Abolition after 1830* (Baltimore: Johns Hopkins University Press, 1976), 112, 113.

6. For an exposition of Stowe's fear of slavery "as an emblem of market economy," see Walter Benn Michaels, "Romance and Real Estate," in his *The Gold Standard and the Logic of Naturalism: American Literature at the Turn of the Century* (Berkeley and Los Angeles: University of California Press, 1987), 85–112. Michaels elaborates the constitutive role of desire in the market economy in *"Sister Carrie's* Popular Economy," also in *The Gold Standard,* 31–58. My own interest is in Stowe's presentation in domestic terms of the fear of both the market economy and the desire that characterizes it. For a valuable discussion of the transposition of public issues to the private, familial realm in English industrial novels contemporaneous with *Uncle Tom's Cabin,* see Catherine Gallagher, *The Industrial Reformation of English Fiction: Social Discourse and Narrative Form, 1832–1867* (Chicago: University of Chicago Press, 1985). Family life in the industrial novel, Gallagher argues, is "presented as society's primary reforming institution" and therefore must "be separated from and purged of the ills infecting the public realm" (115).

7. Quoted in Stowe, "Introduction to the 1881 Edition," *Uncle Tom's Cabin* (1881; rpt. New York: Collier Books, 1978), 33–37; Ellen Moers, *Literary Women* (Garden City, New York: Doubleday, 1976), 37. Moers also points out that for Stowe "the true horror was not the inhumanity of slavery but its very human, easygoing alignment with the normal procedures of the marketplace" (86).

8. Douglas, *The Feminization of American Culture*, 11–12; Jane P. Tompkins, "Sentimental Power: *Uncle Tom's Cabin* and the Politics of Literary History," *Glyph* 8 (1981): 81–82.

My own exploration of Stowe's political domesticity is indebted to Douglas's landmark study of sentimental values and American Victorian culture, to Tompkins's valuable reassessment of sentimentalism's revisionary force, and to Elizabeth Ammons's insightful observations of Stowe's critique of capitalism and masculine practices of power. Ammons notes Stowe's advocacy of "cooperativism" and "love" "as possible foundations for social organization": Elizabeth Ammons, "Heroines in *Uncle Tom's Cabin*," *American Literature* 49 (May 1977): 173.

9. Tompkins, "Sentimental Power," 83.

10. Douglas, *The Feminization of American Culture*, 13.

11. Beecher, *A Treatise on Domestic Economy*. All subsequent references are noted in parentheses in the text.

12. Sermon by Henry Ward Beecher, October 1849. Quoted in Martin Rugoff, *The Beechers: An American Family in the Nineteenth Century* (New York: Harper and Row, 1981), 371.

13. On the Beechers and their role in nineteenth-century America, see Rugoff, *The Beechers;* William G. McLaughlin, *The Meaning of Henry Ward Beecher: An Essay on the Shifting Values of Mid-Victorian America* (New York: Knopf, 1970); Kathryn Kish Sklar, *Catharine Beecher: A Study in American Domesticity* (New York: Norton, 1976).

14. For a detailed treatment of the social changes domesticity accompanied, see Cott, *The Bonds of Womanhood;* Thomas Dublin, *Women at Work: The Transformation of Work and Community in Lowell, Massachusetts, 1826–1860* (New York: Columbia University Press, 1979); Matthaei, *An Economic History of Women in America*.

15. George Fitzhugh, *Cannibals All! Or, Slaves without Masters* (1857; rpt. Cambridge: Belknap Press of Harvard University Press, 1973), 198. Eugene Genovese explicates the slaveholders' critique of capitalism in "The Logical Outcome of the Slaveholders' Philosophy: An Exposition, Interpretation, and Critique of the Social Thought of George Fitzhugh of Port Royal, Virginia," in his *The World the Slaveholders Made* (New York: Vintage, 1971), 118–244.

16. Rugoff, *The Beechers*, 321.

17. Barbara Welter describes in detail the rhetoric of domestic sanctity in "The Cult of True Womanhood," in her *Dimity Convictions: The American Woman in the Nineteenth Century* (Athens: Ohio University Press, 1976), 21–41.

18. It is interesting that once slavery was abolished, Stowe could fully endorse Beecher's domestic economy. After the Civil War, Stowe col-

laborated with her sister in revising the *Treatise;* it was republished as *The American Woman's Home* in 1869. (Catharine Beecher and Harriet Beecher Stowe, *The American Woman's Home: Or, Principles of domestic science; being a guide to the formation and maintenance of economical, healthful, beautiful, and Christian homes* [New York: J. B. Ford, 1869].) They now shared a utopian matriarchal project: the establishment of "the model Christian Neighborhood." The Beecher sisters' contributions to feminist architectural designs are discussed in Dolores Hayden, *The Grand Domestic Revolution: A History of Feminist Designs for American Homes, Neighborhoods, and Cities* (Cambridge: MIT Press, 1981).

The term *patriarchal* as it appears in my argument about alternative matriarchal organizations does not refer to the specific historical organization of the household under the authority of the father, modeled after the political authority of the king. Lawrence Stone discusses this phenomenon in *The Family, Sex, and Marriage in England, 1500–1800* (New York: Harper and Row, 1977), 239–40. Rather, I am invoking the general sense of the word as government or rule by men, a sense which has evolved from the tradition of men holding political authority over the household. Many feminists adopt this nonhistorically specific usage in order to highlight the gendered structure of political power that follows from such androcentric organizations of society.

19. Stowe, *The Key to Uncle Tom's Cabin,* 257. For similar observations on Rachel's ministerial function in a redemptive matriarchal order, see Ammons, "Heroines in *Uncle Tom's Cabin,*" and Tompkins, "Sentimental Power."

20. Harriet Beecher Stowe, "Appeal to the Women of the Free States of America on the Present Crisis in Our Country," *The Liberator,* March 3, 1854.

21. Catharine Beecher, "An Essay on Slavery and Abolition with Respect to the Duties of American Females" (Philadelphia: Anti-Slavery Society, 1837).

22. Angelina Grimke, "Letter XI," in *Letters to Catharine Beecher* (Boston: Isaac Knapp, 1836), 103–4.

23. Angelina Grimke, "Appeal to the Christian Women of the South" (New York: American Anti-Slavery Society, 1836); reprinted in Gail Parker, ed., *The Oven Birds: American Women on Womanhood, 1820–1920* (New York: Anchor, 1972), 124.

24. Sarah Grimke, "Letter VIII," *Letters on the Equality of the Sexes and the Condition of Woman* (Boston: I. Knapp, 1838); reprinted in Alice Rossi, ed., *The Feminist Papers: From Adams to de Beauvoir* (New York: Bantam, 1974), 315.

25. Southern diarist Mary Boykin Chesnut saw slavery's humiliation

of white women in terms of the adultery and miscegenation practiced by their husbands: "Mrs. Stowe did not hit the sorest spot. She makes Legree a bachelor": August 1861 entry in *A Diary from Dixie*, ed. Ben Ames Williams (Boston: Houghton Mifflin, 1949), 121–22. Chesnut's diary has recently been reprinted in a new edition titled *Mary Chesnut's Civil War*, ed. C. Vann Woodward (New Haven: Yale University Press, 1981), 168.

26. Gerda Lerner, *The Grimke Sisters from South Carolina: Pioneers of Women's Rights and Abolition* (New York: Schocken, 1975). On the abolitionist roots of the women's rights movement see Barbara Berg, *The Remembered Gate: Origins of American Feminism, the Woman, and the City, 1800–1860* (New York: Oxford University Press, 1980); Ellen Carol Dubois, *Feminism and Suffrage: The Emergence of an Independent Women's Movement in America, 1848–1869* (Ithaca: Cornell University Press, 1978).

27. Quoted in Barbara Welter, Introduction to Elizabeth Cady Stanton, *The Woman's Bible* (1895; rpt. New York: Arno Press, 1974), xxii–xxiii.

28. Harriet Beecher Stowe, *Women in Sacred History* (New York: J. B. Ford, 1874), 1.

29. Harriet Beecher Stowe, *The Minister's Wooing* (1859; rpt. New York: AMS Press, 1967), 2.

30. Quoted in Walters, *The Antislavery Appeal*, 103.

31. Kenneth Lynn also remarks on the primacy of domestic values in the novel in his Introduction to *Uncle Tom's Cabin* (Cambridge: Belknap Press of Harvard University Press, 1962). On the theological force of domesticity in *Uncle Tom's Cabin*, see Alice Crozier, *The Novels of Harriet Beecher Stowe* (New York: Oxford University Press, 1969), 3–33.

32. See also the discussions of the sexual manifestations of the ideology of nondesire in Nancy C. Cott, "Passionlessness: An Interpretation of Victorian Sexual Ideology, 1790–1850," in Nancy C. Cott and Elizabeth H. Pleck, eds., *A Heritage of Her Own* (New York: Simon and Schuster, 1979), 162–81, and Carroll Smith-Rosenberg, "Sex as Symbol in Victorian Purity: An Ethnohistorical Analysis of Jacksonian America," in John Demos and Sarane Spence Boocock, eds., *Turning Points: Historical and Sociological Essays on the Family* (Chicago: University of Chicago Press, 1978), 212–47.

33. Quoted in Walters, *The Antislavery Appeal*, 98.

34. On the cult of Little Eva and the sentimental novelists' domestication of death, see Douglas, *The Feminization of American Culture*, 1–13, 240–72.

35. For a discussion of the transformation of Eva's token of hair into

the lock of hair Simon Legree received from his mother, see Crozier, *The Novels of Harriet Beecher Stowe,* 29–31.

36. Harriet Beecher Stowe, letter to Gamaliel Bailey, March 9, 1851, Garrison Collection, Boston Public Library.

37. Charlotte Perkins Gilman, *Moving the Mountain,* serialized in her monthly magazine *The Forerunner* 2 (January and February 1911); reprinted as a separate volume (New York: Charlton, 1911). Gilman also serialized her other utopian novels: *Herland* appeared in *The Forerunner* 6 (January–December 1915); *With Her in Ourland* appeared in *The Forerunner* 7 (January–December 1916). *Herland* was also published as a book, edited by Ann J. Lane (New York: Pantheon, 1979).

38. For a similar account of Stowe's elimination of men from positions of power, see Tompkins, "Sentimental Power," 98.

Chapter Two

1. It is this alternative feminine economy that feminists stress as the revisionary power of the sentimental ethos. A term coined by Jane Tompkins and collaterally developed by a number of scholars working in nineteenth-century American studies, *sentimental power* has come to signify a feminine—if not feminist—counter-tradition in literary history, an oppositional mode to the masculinist, capitalist, individualistic, and imperialist values operating in American culture. Against these values, the domestic work of women, in their sentimental literary productions or in their household practices, promotes virtues of maternity, cooperation, sympathy, and charity, comprising an alternative vision of American political economy. Stowe's exploitation of these matrifocal values instates such an alternative vision, and, as Tompkins and other critics argue, an alternative American literary tradition. Thus, as Elizabeth Ammons asserts, "No book matters more to the literary history of women in America than *Uncle Tom's Cabin*": see "Stowe's Dream of the Mother-Savior," 155.

In the wake of this reevaluation of sentimental values, *Uncle Tom's Cabin* has emerged as a touchstone for Afro-American literary traditions, a framework defining black literary representations in America from the nineteenth century to the present. We now witness a decorous alliance of feminist and black literary criticism under the banner of sentimental power that effectively erases racism from the spectrum of sentimental effects. In this chapter extending and complicating my discussion of *Uncle Tom's Cabin,* I want to reconsider the racist features of sentimentalism that the notion of sentimental power elides as it elaborates the literary properties of women and blacks. More specifically, I will be concerned with the liberal property relations that structure both the feminist polemic of sentimental power and Stowe's anti-slavery polemic.

I do not mean to say here that black literary scholarship ignores the racism in the novel; I *do* mean to point out that the feminist claims for the revisionary force of the novel have set the terms of discourse about *Uncle Tom's Cabin* in such a way that the attempt to consider the relations between racism, sentimentalism, and the feminine sphere would appear an ungallant if not anti-feminist act. Hortense Spillers has called this the "muting of 'race.'" Spillers's comment appears in a footnote to her essay "Changing the Letter: The Yokes, the Jokes of Discourse, or, Mrs. Stowe, Mr. Reed," in Deborah E. McDowell and Arnold Rampersad, eds., *Slavery and the Literary Imagination: Selected Papers from the English Institute,* 1987 (Baltimore: Johns Hopkins University Press, 1989), 25–61 (note 21).

Black literary critics have treated the novel's influence on Afro-American literary representations more fully. See, for example, Robert Stepto, "Sharing the Thunder: The Literary Exchanges of Harriet Beecher Stowe, Henry Bibb, and Frederick Douglass," and Richard Yarborough, "Strategies of Black Characterization in *Uncle Tom's Cabin* and the Early Afro-American Novel," both in Sundquist, ed., *New Essays on Uncle Tom's Cabin,* 135–53; 45–84. Such work enlarges and complicates the notions of the novel's "power," but the powerful alliance Stowe forges between abolitionism and racism in the white literary imagination has not yet been fully explored. For some useful perspectives on this configuration as it appears in the writings of Lydia Maria Child and Mark Twain, see Karen Sanchez-Eppler, "Bodily Bonds: The Intersecting Rhetorics of Feminism and Abolition," and Eric J. Sundquist, "Mark Twain and Homer Plessy," both in *Representations* 24, Special Issue on America Reconstructed, 1840–1940 (Fall 1988), 28–59; 102–28.

2. Theories of the democratic state and the rights of individuals secured in such a state date back to the seventeenth century, when they were founded in opposition to divinely sanctioned authority and patriarchy. Since then, this originally white-based and androcentric defense of the individual has been applied to the civil rights of women and blacks; in these applications, as I will show, some of the contradictions within possessive individualism become manifest. See Macpherson, *The Political Theory of Possessive Individualism.*

3. In this light, the fact that Stowe changed the original subtitle of the novel from "The Man That Was a Thing" to "Life among the Lowly" seems to suggest that her concerns were better represented by terms of race or class distinctions than by distinctions between persons and things.

4. Feminist criticism has in effect jettisoned the issue of racism, focusing on what Jean Fagan Yellin calls "woman's role in the slavery crisis," a role that is understood to be reformist, if not revolutionary ("Doing It Herself: *Uncle Tom's Cabin* and the Woman's Role in the Slavery Crisis," in Sundquist, ed., *New Essays on Uncle Tom's Cabin,* 86). My aim in this essay is to illuminate the connections between abolitionism and racism in Stowe's work: to examine the varieties of affection operating in sentimentalism. This exploration pursues questions not addressed in my analysis of Stowe's critique and reformulation of domestic values presented in Chapter One and previously published as "Getting in the Kitchen with Dinah: Domestic Politics in *Uncle Tom's Cabin,*" *American Quarterly* 36 (Fall 1984): 503–23, an analysis which locates the revisionary force of *Uncle Tom's Cabin* in Stowe's reformation of sentimental values but does not investigate the limits of that reformation.

5. Philip Fisher, "Making a Thing into a Man," in his *Hard Facts* (New York: Oxford University Press, 1985), 87–127.

6. On the sentience of human artifacts (both within and without the scope of domesticity), and the significance of this personification in human practices and institutions, see Elaine Scarry, *The Body in Pain: The Making and Unmaking of the World* (New York: Oxford University Press, 1985).

7. Once free, that is, paid for after she has escaped north from slavery, Jacobs can enjoy not only her liberty but the fact of having gotten herself at a bargain—at "so small" an amount of her value. She fantasizes confronting her former owner so "that he might have mourned over the untoward circumstances which compelled him to sell me for three hundred dollars": Harriet A. Jacobs, *Incidents in the Life of a Slave Girl, Written by Herself* (1861; rpt., ed. Jean Fagan Yellin, Cambridge: Harvard University Press, 1987), 199–200.

8. Ann Douglas also describes the relation between *Uncle Tom's Cabin,* artifacts of sentimentality, and consumerism in the introduction to her *The Feminization of American Culture,* 1–13. Documentation of the culture industry of *Uncle Tom's Cabin* can be found in E. Bruce Kirkham, *The Building of Uncle Tom's Cabin* (Knoxville: University of Tennessee Press, 1977); James D. Hart, *The Popular Book: A History of America's Literary Taste* (Berkeley and Los Angeles: University of California Press, 1950), 111–12; Stephen A. Hirsch, "Uncle Tomitudes: The Popular Reaction to *Uncle Tom's Cabin,*" in Joel Myerson, ed., *Studies in the American Renaissance* (Boston: Twayne, 1978), 311.

9. For an excellent history of conceptions of the market as the maximization of democratic principles and individual powers, see C. B.

Macpherson, *Democratic Theory: Essays in Retrieval* (New York: Oxford University Press, 1973).

10. For a related discussion of the attainment of property rights through the transcendence of personal claims and limits, see Howard Horwitz, "*O Pioneers* and the Paradox of Property: Cather's Aesthetics of Divestment," in Jack Salzman, ed., *Prospects: An Annual of American Cultural Studies* 13 (New York: Cambridge University Press, 1988), 61–93.

11. Stowe's 1864 series of *Atlantic* articles were collected in her *House and Home Papers* by Christopher Crowfield [pseud.] (Boston: Ticknor and Fields, 1865); essays appearing in the *Atlantic* from January to September 1865 were reprinted in *The Chimney Corner* by Christopher Crowfield [pseud.] (Boston: Ticknor and Fields, 1868). These two collections were later published in one volume called *Household Papers and Stories,* volume VIII in the Riverside Edition of the Writings of Harriet Beecher Stowe (Boston: Houghton, Mifflin, 1896).

12. Harriet Beecher Stowe, "The Ravages of a Carpet," *House and Home Papers,* 1–22. In an unpublished essay fittingly called "Sentimental Empathy," Lynn Wardley has given an eloquent exposition of the influence of domestic surroundings.

13. Lucy Larcom, *A New England Girlhood, Outlined from Memory* (1889; rpt. Boston: Northeastern University Press, 1986), 148–50.

14. Harriet Beecher Stowe, "Home-keeping versus House-keeping," *House and Home Papers,* 23–47.

15. Stowe, "The Ravages of a Carpet," 8.

16. Letter to Gamaliel Bailey, March 9, 1851, Garrison Collection, Boston Public Library.

17. On the mid-nineteenth-century popular cult of George Washington, see George Forgie, *Patricide in the House Divided: A Psychological Interpretation of Lincoln and His Age* (New York: Norton, 1979).

18. In this case, the sentimental object impressed into use comes from Stowe's own collection of memorabilia, from her own loss of a son. Her grief for a lost child is rewritten here as an occasion of empathy between white and black mothers. (Charles Edward Stowe, *Life of Harriet Beecher Stowe Compiled from Her Letters and Journals* [Boston: Houghton, Mifflin, 1890], 123–24).

Stowe's empowerment of domestic objects with transformative if not redemptive effects suggests an affinity with the Roman Catholic belief in sacred objects and relics. Her sentimental Christian matriarchal values likewise attract Stowe to the veneration of motherhood in the cult of the Virgin Mary, as is evident throughout her *Woman in Sacred History.* One possible way to read Stowe's hostility to Irish immigrants (discussed later in this chapter) is to understand it as a mechanism of distinguishing and distancing her Protestant domestic values from the Catholic logic of mediation that they approximate.

19. Karl Marx, *Capital,* vol. 1, ed. Friedrich Engels, trans. Samuel Moore and Edward Aveling (New York: Modern Library, 1906), 81–96; Walter Benjamin, *Charles Baudelaire: A Lyric Poet in the Age of High Capitalism,* trans. Harry Zohn (London: New Left Books, 1973), 55. Mary Ann Doane has noted that the alignment of consumerism with empathy Benjamin describes is also an alignment of consumerism with the feminine: *The Desire to Desire: The Woman's Film of the 1940's* (Bloomington: Indiana University Press, 1987), 31–32. The intimate relations between persons and commodities projected in commodity fetishism (which Benjamin excoriates) and the feminine sphere these relations invoke are precisely what Stowe's sentimental possession tries to achieve.

The now classic statement of consumer society's reification of intimate human relations is Max Horkheimer and Theodor Adorno, *Dialectic of Enlightenment,* trans. John Cumming (New York: Continuum, 1987). See also Jean Baudrillard, "The Ideological Genesis of Needs," in his *For a Political Critique of the Political Economy of the Sign,* trans. Charles Levin (St. Louis: Telos, 1981), 63–87.

20. I here revise Marx's famous passage: "Could commodities themselves speak, they would say: Our use-value may be a thing that interests men. It is no part of us as objects. What, however, does belong to us as objects, is our value." (*Capital,* 95.)

21. Marx, *Capital,* 96–97.

22. The identification of freedom—specifically, women's freedom—with consumerism is nicely described in Rachel Bowlby's *Just Looking: Consumer Culture in Drieser, Gissing, and Zola* (London: Methuen, 1985), 18–34. Bowlby quotes Elizabeth Cady Stanton's injunction to "GO OUT AND BUY!" as an example of how women's emancipation was linked to their shopping. Not only could women obtain labor-saving machines to aid them at home, but shopping would bring them into the public sphere. As Bowlby points out, shopping itself becomes another form of nineteenth-century feminine influence. For Stowe, such economic power is eschewed because it is the very force she wishes to transmute.

23. See Fitzhugh, *Cannibals All!*

24. Harriet Beecher Stowe, "A Family Talk on Reconstruction," *Household Papers and Stories,* 284–85.

25. Stowe, "A Family Talk on Reconstruction," 288, 298.

26. Stowe, "A Family Talk on Reconstruction," 294.

27. Harriet Beecher Stowe, "The Lady Who Does Her Own Work," *House and Home Papers,* 125–47. This 1864 essay and Catharine Beecher's chapter on "The Care of Domestics" from her *A Treatise on Domestic Economy* were combined to form the chapter on "The Care of Servants" in their *The American Woman's Home,* published in 1869. The co-authored chapter joins Beecher's maternalism toward servants with Stowe's ideal of republican labor.

28. Stowe, "The Lady Who Does Her Own Work," 126, 128.

29. Stowe, "The Lady Who Does Her Own Work," 136.

30. Stowe, "The Lady Who Does Her Own Work," 145, 140.

31. The "servant problem" or "domestic service problem" was a prominent topic in women's magazines and domestic advice literature from at least the 1830s well into the twentieth century. Stowe characterizes it as a problem of the housekeeper's skill, self-possession, and self-reliance, but for most commentators the servant problem meant the scarcity of domestic servants. Late in the nineteenth century, reformers identified the problem as that of the exploitation of servants. The major nineteenth-century study of both employers and employees was Lucy Maynard Salmon's *Domestic Service* (New York: Macmillan, 1897). An informative study of all these aspects of the issue is David M. Katzman, *Seven Days a Week: Women and Domestic Service in Industrializing America* (New York: Oxford University Press, 1978).

32. Stowe, "The Lady Who Does Her Own Work," 138–39, 145.

33. Harriet Beecher Stowe, "Servants," *House and Home Papers,* 221.

34. Stowe, "Servants," 219.

35. Stowe, "A Family Talk on Reconstruction," 298. Although the imperative to domestic enclosure and sanctity in Stowe's reconstruction essays in effect eliminates blacks from the domestic economy, Stowe did represent a black servant as one of "our folks" in her revisionary historical novel *Oldtown Folks* (Boston: Fields, Osgood and Company, 1869). There she recast the establishment of American democracy and domesticity as a project in white and black freedom and intimacy.

36. Stowe, "Servants," 222–23. These statements are reiterated in Beecher and Stowe, *The American Woman's Home,* 13, and in another Stowe article, "A Model Village," *The Revolution* 1 (April 2, 1868): 1. On Stowe and Beecher's contributions to the cooperative housekeeping movement in nineteenth-century America, see Hayden, *The Grand Domestic Revolution,* 54–63.

37. It is Frado's color that her evil mistress Mrs. Bellmont tries to intensify, by making her work hatless in the sun, so that her "inferiority" will be unquestionable: Harriet Wilson, *Our Nig; Or, Sketches from the*

Life of a Free Black, in a Two-Story White House, North, Showing That Slavery's Shadow Falls Even There (1859; rpt. New York: Vintage, 1983).

In an essay on Lydia Maria Child's 1867 novel on interracial marriage, *A Romance of the Republic,* Carolyn Karcher traces the "hierarchy of color" that persists even in abolitionist visions in which amalgamation is imaged as a lightening of blacks: "Lydia Maria Child's *A Romance of the Republic:* An Abolitionist Vision of America's Racial Destiny," in McDowell and Rampersad, eds., *Slavery and the Literary Imagination,* 81–103.

Karen Sanchez-Eppler puts the case of literal white supremacy even more strongly when she observes that the sentimental emancipation of blacks "depends upon the black being washed white. The problem of antislavery fiction is that the very effort to depict goodness in black involves the obliteration of blackness" (Sanchez-Eppler, "Bodily Bonds," 39).

38. Eric J. Sundquist, in his "Mark Twain and Homer Plessy," demonstrates how post–Civil War American legal decisions worked to undo precisely this effect of miscegenation which logically should have secured entitlements to free blacks.

39. On the domestic purity and sanitation movement, see Barbara Ehrenreich and Deirdre English, *For Her Own Good* (New York: Anchor Press/Doubleday, 1979), 141–82; on anti-immigrant and racist sentiments, see Katzman, *Seven Days a Week,* 146–265; Alice Kessler Harris, *Out to Work: A History of Wage-Earning Women in the United States* (New York: Oxford, 1982), 119–41.

Jacques Derrida has recently analyzed the relations between apartheid and capitalism, explaining a configuration of progress and racism similar to the one I am delineating in Stowe's formulations of domesticity. See "Racism's Last Word," *Critical Inquiry* 12, 1 (Autumn 1985): 290–99; and "But, beyond . . . (Open Letter to Anne McClintock and Rob Nixon)," *Critical Inquiry* 13 (Autumn 1986): 155–70.

Chapter Three

1. The disestablishment of women from the spheres of economic productivity has been well documented by many historians. See, for example, Cott, *The Bonds of Womanhood;* Matthaei, *An Economic History of Women in America.* The term *disestablishment* comes from Ann Douglas's apt identification of the relegation of women to the domestic sphere of private life with the social disempowerment of the ministry in the nineteenth century, elaborated in her pioneering work *The Feminization of American Culture.* On individualism and the rise of domesticity, see Eli

Zaretsky, *Capitalism, the Family, and Personal Life* (New York: Harper Colophon, 1976). The privatization of self (and its governance through this recategorization and the complementary invention of social agencies to supervise private life) has been delineated in Jacques Donzelot, *The Policing of Families* (New York: Pantheon, 1979), and Michel Foucault, *The History of Sexuality*, vol. 1: *An Introduction*, trans. Robert Hurley (New York: Vintage, 1978). In what follows I will not be tracing a history of American individualism and concepts of femininity as consolidations of state power in the private sphere; rather, I am interested in the cultivation of private practices that Donzelot and Foucault have illuminated as sites of power relations as a particular formation of American culture, a representation of individuality drawn from and against changing conditions in the division of labor. Moreover, I shall focus on the function of the imagery of the physical and the feminine in nineteenth-century American formulations about private life.

2. In *Uncle Tom's Cabin*, the exemplary blacks besides the Christlike Uncle Tom are the devout Eliza, her converted husband, George, and the educated Topsy, who becomes a missionary.

3. Catharine Beecher, "Statistics of Female Health," in her *Letters to the People on Health and Happiness* (New York: Harper, 1855). Reprinted in Parker, ed., *The Oven Birds*, 165–78.

4. Beecher's copious housekeeping instructions typify the thoroughness of nineteenth-century domestic advice literature. Her 1841 *A Treatise on Domestic Economy* was reprinted annually from 1842 to 1857 and issued in revised form under various titles through the 1870s. For accounts of the work housekeepers performed, see Susan Strasser, *Never Done: A History of American Housework* (New York: Pantheon, 1982); Ruth Schwartz Cowan, *More Work for Mother: The Ironies of Household Technology from the Open Hearth to the Microwave* (New York: Basic Books, 1983).

5. Catharine Beecher, "An Address to the Christian Women of America," in her *Woman Suffrage and Woman's Profession* (Hartford: Brown and Gross, 1871), 171–202. On the effort to raise the status of housework see also Beecher, *A Treatise on Domestic Economy*, 39–40; Stowe, "The Lady Who Does Her Own Work."

In her reading of eighteenth- and nineteenth-century British conduct books, Nancy Armstrong notes the spiritualization of domestic work. Armstrong analyzes this as a representational strategy to define women by their depth rather than their surface. See her chapter on "The Rise of the Domestic Woman" in her *Desire and Domestic Fiction*, 59–95.

6. I am drawing this account of the representation of women's work (i.e., housework) from a study of Beecher's many advice books and

some forty other nineteenth-century domestic guides housed in the Schlesinger Library on the History of Women in America at Radcliffe College, Harvard University. Harriet Robinson's reminiscences appear in *Loom and Spindle, Or, Life among the Early Mill Girls* (1898; rpt. Kailua, Hawaii: Press Pacifica, 1976). See below for a discussion of the evocation in accounts of housekeeping of the lady and her leisured status.

7. E. H. Dixon, *Woman and Her Diseases* (New York: Charles H. Ring, 1846), 133. For examples of hysterical symptoms recorded in mid-nineteenth-century America see Gunning S. Bedford, *Clinical Lectures on the Diseases of Women and Children* (New York: Samuel S. & W. Wood, 1855), 373; Buel Eastman, *Practical Thesis on Diseases Peculiar to Women and Girls* (Cincinnati: C. Cropper & Son, 1848), 40. The best introduction to nineteenth-century American instances and views of hysteria remains Carroll Smith-Rosenberg's ground-breaking essay "The Hysterical Woman: Sex Roles and Role Conflict in Nineteenth-Century America," *Social Research* 39 (Winter 1972): 652–78, reprinted in her *Disorderly Conduct: Visions of Gender in Victorian America* (New York: Knopf, 1985), 197–216.

8. Beecher, "Statistics of Female Health."

9. Smith-Rosenberg, *Disorderly Conduct,* 198. Hysteria is also presented as a phenomenon of the bourgeois woman and family in Ann Douglas's important article "The Fashionable Diseases: Women's Complaints and Their Treatment in Nineteenth-Century America," *Journal of Interdisciplinary History* 4 (Summer 1973): 25–52, reprinted in Mary Hartman and Lois W. Banner, eds., *Clio's Consciousness Raised: New Perspectives on the History of Women* (New York: Harper Colophon, 1974), 1–22.

10. Beecher, "Statistics of Female Health," 174. Smith-Rosenberg also notes the prevalence of hysteria (especially among men) in the lower socioeconomic classes; see her nn. 5 and 14 in *Disorderly Conduct,* 331, 332. She cites (among others) the work by E. H. Van Deusen, "Observations on a Farm of Nervous Prostration," *American Journal of Insanity* 25 (1869): 447, which discovered a high incidence of "nervousness, hysteria, and neuresthenia" among farm workers.

11. Inquiry into how the hysteric may expose or experiment with the limits of the domestic cult of the disembodied and disenfranchised female figure has resulted in some intriguing feminist readings of nineteenth-century culture. See, in addition to the works by Ann Douglas and Carroll Smith-Rosenberg already cited, Elaine Showalter, *The Female Malady* (New York: Pantheon, 1985), 121–64.

In this chapter I will not be asserting a teleology of domesticity in which housework leads to hysteria (although the autobigraphical accounts of Harriet Beecher Stowe, Elizabeth Cady Stanton, and Charlotte

Perkins Gilman, to mention only three of many, offer ample evidence for this chronology), but be stressing the simultaneity of these feminine forms, their common heritage in domestic ideology's disconnection of woman from her work and body. I am interested here in the role of the romanticization of labor in the invention of the hysterical woman. This relation of representations of housework to the nineteenth-century proliferation of hysteria suggests that the problematic nature of hysteria—its presentation of bodily symptoms without physiological sources—might be understood as an extension (or even the perverse perfection) of contradictions within the logic of an individuality that locates personal integrity in the denial of women's self-expression of labor. The economy of work and women that produces the iconographic figures of the housekeeper and the hysteric, and the integral relation between them, shapes and informs the phenomenology of identity in market society. I am therefore proposing that an analysis of hysteria might begin with its productive relations—what hysteria contributes to nineteenth-century society, as well as what it costs women.

12. Beecher and Stowe, *The American Woman's Home*, 260. Beecher and Stowe do not address here the possibility that housework itself involves an imbalance. Feminists such as their grandniece Charlotte Perkins Gilman would later identify the housekeeping role as a cause of hysteria and nervous disease: *The Living of Charlotte Perkins Gilman* (1935; rpt. New York: Harper Colophon, 1972), 90–106. Stowe also registered the neurotic or unhealthy effects of housekeeping in her accounts of rigid housekeepers such as Miss Ophelia in *Uncle Tom's Cabin* and Miss Asphixia in *Oldtown Folks*.

13. Scarry, *The Body in Pain*. Scarry's brilliant analysis of the processes of embodiment, disembodiment, and reembodiment in work—the relation between body and artifact, sentience and representation—offers an important new reading of materialism in which subjectivity is not effaced but, on the contrary, constructed and reconstructed in the production of objects. That the subject can be traced through its objects and labor is particularly significant for a feminist cultural materialism: in this framework, housework signifies at least two histories, a history of female experience and a history of the social relations women's work creates, performs, and maintains.

14. Examples of the literary figure of the deformed worker include the characters in Rebecca Harding Davis's "Life in the Iron Mills": the "sickly" Janey; Hugh Wolfe, "known as one of the girl-men"; and Deborah, who was "almost a hunchback." This story first appeared in the *Atlantic Monthly* 7 (April 1861): 430–51. It is reprinted in book form as *Life in the Iron Mills, or The Korl Woman* (Old Westbury, N.Y.: Feminist

Press, 1972). Elizabeth Stuart Phelps's factory tales "The Tenth of January" (*Atlantic Monthly* 21 [March 1868]: 345–62) and *The Silent Partner* (Boston: J. R. Osgood, 1871) also focus on injured or deformed workers: the hunchback Asenath and the deaf—and eventually blind—Catty Garth. The novel and short story are reprinted together in *The Silent Partner, A Novel, and "The Tenth of January"* (Old Westbury, N.Y.: Feminist Press, 1983).

15. Beecher, *A Treatise on Domestic Economy*, 18.

16. Scarry, *The Body in Pain*, 265–66.

17. Foucault has described the "hystericization of women's bodies" as one major strategy by which sexuality was deployed in the nineteenth century to ensure a labor force and its reproduction: to avoid "any wasted energy, so that all forces were reduced to labor capacity alone." Foucault stresses "the production of sexuality rather than the repression of sex" in this politics of sex and recommends that we "shift our analysis away from the problem of labor capacity and doubtless abandon the diffuse energetics that underlies the theme of a sexuality repressed for economic reasons": *The History of Sexuality*, 1: 103–14. I want to suggest that the analysis of hysteria, long identified with accounts of female sexuality, could benefit from another reorientation: before abandoning "the diffuse energetics" underlying the theme of repressed sexuality, it would be useful to consider how these energetics have underwritten a repression of female labor. The hystericization of women's bodies is a representation (and production) of work as well as of sexuality. In the case of women, a double repression operates that subtends the production of ideologies of sexuality and of work.

18. The concept of an ideally alienated labor I am describing obviously departs from customary accounts of alienation. According to Marx, "The performance of work appears in the sphere of political economy as a *vitiation* of the worker, objectification as *loss* and as *servitude to the object,* and appropriation as *alienation.*" It is one of the features of alienation that the worker "creates his own production as a vitiation, a punishment, and his own product as a loss." That "he does not fulfil himself in his work but denies himself" is reflected in a spatialization of the experiences of working and being: "The worker, therefore, feels himself at home only during his leisure time, whereas at work he feels homeless." Or, as another translation of the same passage puts it, the worker "feels at ease only outside work, and during work he is outside himself. He is at home when he is not working and when he is working he is not at home." (Karl Marx, "Alienated Labor" [1844] in Marx, *Early Writings,* trans. T. B. Bottomore [New York: McGraw Hill, 1964], 120–34; and in Marx, *Writings of the Young Marx on Philosophy and Society,*

trans. Lloyd D. Easton and Kurt H. Guddat [Garden City, N.Y.: Anchor Books, 1967], 292–93.)

Jean Baudrillard has recently analyzed the function of alienation as a myth of loss and transcendence in Marxist thought. For Baudrillard, the concept of alienated labor supports the narrative of a fall from a unity of work and being, a unity identified with an ideal of use value. This valuation of use over exchange or symbolic value and its accompanying myth of origin and transcendence (an originary pure state and the effort to recoup it), Baudrillard has pointed out, are themselves produced by the governing political economy, by capitalism. "Exchange value is what makes the use value of products appear as its anthropological horizon." Marxism fails to challenge capitalism, Baudrillard charges, because it cannot recognize its own abstract work, its own function as a critical fiction and useful apology. "It convinces men that they are alienated by the sale of their labor power, thus censoring the much more radical hypothesis that they might be alienated as labor power, as the 'inalienable' power of creating value by their labor." If alienability is not a feature of exchange value but is in fact inherent to the notion of labor, then the Marxist idealization of labor (or human production) must be seen as instrumental to the perpetuation of the vision of capitalist political economy: the production and productivity of human development. ("The Concept of Labor," in his *The Mirror of Production,* trans. Mark Poster [St. Louis: Telos Press, 1975], 21–51.)

As a myth of loss and reunion, alienation in Baudrillard's view signifies the hegemony of capitalism. His analyses have been enormously influential for their demonstrations of the breadth and depth of the achievement (this, of course, is not a word he would use) of capitalism. There is, then, for Baudrillard an absolute correspondence between capitalism and its effects. Capitalism appears as the referent of all experience.

In the particular development of capitalism (i.e., the rise of domestic ideology) I am tracing in this chapter, I am not substantiating the hypothesis of containment Baudrillard proposes but exploring further the productive or creative function of alienation: the formations of individuality—and femininity—it reflects and generates. What is for Baudrillard the determinant and scandalous closure of the capitalist system is in my view only one coordinating narrative to arise among possible permutations. In other words, referentiality makes both capitalism and its alternatives possible; capitalism is itself shaped by particular reorganizations of work that reflect shifting relations in the meaning of work. One instance of how referentiality works as a principle of change, thus generating various ends, can be seen in the representation of women's work.

19. My thinking on issues of identity and corporeality in Hawthorne

has benefited from Sharon Cameron's penetrating investigations of boundaries of the self and body in her *The Corporeal Self.*

20. Nathaniel Hawthorne, *The House of the Seven Gables,* vol. 2 of the Centenary Edition of the Works of Nathaniel Hawthorne (Columbus: Ohio State University Press, 1963–   ), 314–19, 64–65. All subsequent references to this edition of the novel will be noted in parentheses in the text.

21. The rise of domesticity and the socioeconomic transformations it accompanied are well described in Cott, *The Bonds of Womanhood,* 63–100; the history of American textile manufacture is traced in Dublin, *Women at Work.* A similar description of domesticity's nostalgic function appears in my essay "Nuclear Domesticity: Sequence and Survival," *Yale Journal of Criticism* 2 (Fall 1988): 179–91.

22. Emma Hewitt, *Queen of the Home: Her Reign from Infancy to Age, from Attic to Cellar* (Philadelphia: Miller-Megee, 1892).

23. On the emergence of the department store in the 1850s, see Susan Porter Benson's chapter "The New Kind of Store" in her *Counter Cultures: Saleswomen, Managers, and Customers in American Department Stores* (Urbana: University of Illinois Press, 1986), 12–30; Michael Miller, *The Bon Marché: Bourgeois Culture and the Department Store, 1869–1920* (Princeton: Princeton University Press, 1984).

24. Andrew Jackson Downing, *Rural Essays* (New York: Leavitt and Allen, 1853), 243. This was a posthumous collection of essays and editorials from Downing's periodical *The Horticulturalist,* which appeared in 1846. A helpful description of Downing's relation to the cult of domesticity can be found in Patricia Bunkle's 1974 unpublished paper "Domestic Piety and the Gothic Revival," stored at the Schlesinger Library on the History of Women in America, Radcliffe College, Harvard University.

25. Andrew Jackson Downing, *Cottage Residences* (1842; rpt. New York: Dover, 1981), 23, and his *The Architecture of Country Houses* (1850; rpt. New York: Dover, 1969), 323.

26. Downing, *Cottage Residences,* 12–13.

27. John Ruskin, *The Seven Lamps of Architecture* (1848; rpt. New York: Noonday Press, 1961), 174, 173. This book appeared in an unauthorized edition in New York in 1849; it was then issued twenty-five times up to 1894, attesting to the influence of Ruskin on American architecture and aesthetics throughout the century.

28. Ruskin, *The Seven Lamps of Architecture,* 170–73.

29. Downing, *The Architecture of Country Houses,* 3.

30. Downing, *The Architecture of Country Houses,* 265, 269, 267, 270. An excellent discussion of Downing's "Americanization" of the English Gothic Revival and of his place in nineteenth-century American archi-

tectural history appears in Vincent Scully, *The Shingle and the Stick Style: Architectural Theory and Design from Downing to the Origins of Wright* (New Haven: Yale University Press, 1977), xxiii–lix.

31. Downing, *The Architecture of Country Houses*, 269, 261, 269, 262.

32. For an apposite discussion of how ideology works for the rationalization of capitalism in the expression "A man's home is his castle," see Eve Kosofsky Sedgwick, *Between Men: English Literature and Male Homosocial Desire* (New York: Columbia University Press, 1985), 14–15.

33. Andrew Jackson Downing, *A Treatise on the Theory and Practice of Landscape Gardening* (New York: Wiley and Putnam, 1841), viii.

34. Downing, *Cottage Residences*, 1–3.

35. Thorstein Veblen, *The Theory of the Leisure Class* (1899; rpt. New York: New American Library, 1953), 41–80.

36. Caroline Matilda Kirkland, *The Evening Book, or Fireside Talk on Morals and Manners* (New York: C. Scribner, 1853), 17.

37. Barbara Welter, "The Cult of True Womanhood," in her *Dimity Convictions*, 21.

38. Stowe, *The Minister's Wooing*, 2. The Metropolitan Museum's 1989 costume exhibit of women's aprons documents another mode through which the domestic came to signify the distinction of leisured classes. The recurrent vogue in decorative aprons displayed in this show (including one belonging to Queen Victoria) reflects a long-standing Western tradition of invoking the domestic to represent a distance from actual domestic labor.

39. *Letters of Hawthorne to William D. Ticknor* (2 vols.; Newark: Carteret, 1910), 1: 78.

40. See, for example, Phelps's prefatory note to *The Silent Partner* (Old Westbury, N.Y.: Feminist Press, 1983), in which she cites the reports of the Massachusetts Bureau of Statistics of Labor on the abuses of the factory system. Specific accounts of the daily endangerments to life and health can be found in the letters of millgirls collected by Thomas Dublin in *From Farm to Factory* (New York: Columbia University Press, 1981).

41. Maria Tatar emphasizes the sexual nature of mesmeric power in this novel, pointing to the attraction the Maule men hold for the Pyncheon women. See her suggestive and informative *Spellbound: Studies on Mesmerism and Literature* (Princeton: Princeton University Press, 1978), esp. 200–217.

42. Jean-Martin Charcot, *Oeuvres Complètes* (Paris: Progrès Médical, 1866), vol. 1, 320–33, 427–34, 436–39; Paul Richer, *Etudes Cliniques sur la Grand Hystérie* (Paris: Delahaye & Lecrosnier, 1885). These works are discussed in George Frederick Drinka's excellent history of *The Birth of*

Neurosis: Myth, Malady, and the Victorians (New York: Simon & Schuster, 1984), esp. 74–107.

43. André Pierre Brouillet, *A Clinical Lesson of Dr. Charcot at the Salpêtrière* (Rare Book Room, Countaway Library of Medicine, Harvard University). A copy of this picture hung in Freud's office and it appropriately reappears as the cover illustration to Charles Bernheimer and Claire Kahane, eds., *In Dora's Case: Freud-Hysteria-Feminism* (New York: Columbia University Press, 1985), and in Elaine Showalter's feminist history of hysteria, *The Female Malady* (New York: Pantheon, 1985), 149. On Blanche Wittman, see Drinka, *The Birth of Neurosis,* 123–51; Catherine Clément, *The Weary Sons of Freud,* trans. Nicole Bell (London: Verso, 1987), 51–55. There is now a vast feminist literature, especially in film studies, treating hysteria as a spectacle. I mention only a few of the most powerful and provocative treatments: Joan Copjec, "Flavit et Dissipati Sunt," *October* 18 (Fall 1981): 21–40; Mary Ann Doane, "Clinical Eyes: The Medical Discourse," in her *The Desire to Desire,* 38–69; Jacqueline Rose, *Sexuality in the Field of Vision* (London: Verso, 1986).

44. Charcot's work on hypnotism and hysteria was available in America beginning in 1879. See, for example, the article he co-authored with Georges Gilles de la Tourette, "Hypnotism in the Hysterical," *Dictionary of Psychological Medicine,* 2 vols., ed. Daniel Hack Tuke (Philadelphia: Blakiston, 1892), 1: 606–10. Hypnotism was also central to other studies of hysteria such as Hippolyte Bernheim, *Hypnotisme, Suggestion, Psychothérapie: Nouvelles Etudes* (Paris: Doin, 1891), and his *Suggestive Therapeutics,* trans. Christian A. Herter (New York: Putnam, 1889). By the end of the century, Freud and William James, among others, explained mesmeric states as hysterical ones: Sigmund Freud and Joseph Breuer, *Studies in Hysteria 1893–1895,* trans. James Strachey (New York: Basic Books 1957), 215–22; Eugene Taylor, *William James on Exceptional Mental States: The 1896 Lowell Lectures* (Amherst: University of Massachusetts Press, 1984), 35–72. I am suggesting that the association between hysteria and mesmerism was already in place in the 1850s: that the structural similarities of mesmeric and hysteric performances had already long been manifest, and that Hawthorne in *The House of the Seven Gables* represents commerce as homologous with these structures of behavior.

45. Nathaniel Hawthorne, *Love Letters of Nathaniel Hawthorne* (Chicago: Defobs Society, 1907), reprinted in his *The Blithedale Romance,* ed. Seymour Gross and Rosalie Murphy (New York: Norton, 1978), 242–44.

46. Ibid.

47. I draw this list (a partial one) from the 1850s title listings of the

publishers Fowler and Wells, who had offices in New York, Boston, and Philadelphia.

48. Joseph Haddock, M.D., *Psychology, or the Science of the Soul* (New York: Fowler and Wells, 1850), 8, 18, 56, 41–42, 57–58. The nervous system is now understood to be composed of a four-part brain: the cerebrum, middle brain, cerebellum, and medulla. Voluntary and involuntary nerves are contained in the spinal cord, which is continuous with the lower brain. Some nerves enter and traverse the spinal cord without ever passing into or from the brain: Randolph Lee Clark and Russell W. Cumley, eds., *The Book of Health* (New York: Van Nostrand Reinhold, 1973), 377–83.

On the popularity and influence of mesmerism, see Drinka, *The Birth of Neurosis*, 127–30; R. Laurence Moore, *In Search of White Crows: Spiritualism, Parapsychology, and American Culture* (New York: Oxford University Press, 1977). On the intellectual and political history of mesmerism, see Robert Darnton, *Mesmerism and the End of the Enlightenment in France* (Cambridge: Harvard University Press, 1968). Logie Barrow traces this history through nineteenth-century British society and its importance for labor movements: *Independent Spirits: Spiritualism and English Plebeians, 1850–1910* (London: Routledge & Kegan Paul, 1986).

49. Haddock, *Psychology*, 55.

50. Mesmer's theories are published in F. A. Mesmer, *Mesmerism*, trans. George J. Bloch (Los Altos, Calif.: William Kauffmann, 1980); John Bovee Dods, M.D., *The Philosophy of Electrical Psychology, in a Course of Twelve Lectures* (New York: Fowler and Wells, 1850), 54, 58, 71. In the late nineteenth century George M. Beard developed ideas about electricity and the nervous system into a theory of neurasthenia and electrotherapeutics: "The Elements of Electrotherapeutics," *Archives of Electrology and Neurology* 1 (1874): 17–23, 184–94. Beard's best-known work, *American Nervousness: Its Causes and Consequences* (New York: Putnam, 1881), emphasizes the strain socioeconomic conditions imposed on the nerves.

51. Although the nostalgia promoted by domesticity implies that consumer relations are less familial and familiar than the relations associated with an economy of home production, commerce in *The House of the Seven Gables* is imagined as productive and personal. Recent work by Susan Strasser on personal networks and modes of distribution, redirecting assumptions about the culture of consumption, offers a historical verification of Hawthorne's characterization. See her *Satisfaction Guaranteed*, forthcoming from Vintage Books.

52. Downing, *The Architecture of Country Houses*, 269.

53. See Michaels, *The Gold Standard and the Logic of Naturalism*, 88. The political agenda of romance, that is, the question of whether Hawthorne's romance forecloses on democratic innovation or embraces it, preoccupies recent criticism of *The House of the Seven Gables*. My reading of the inner workings of the romance's transformative operations, foregrounding the women's work which enables Hawthorne's romance of commerce, investigates how this novel encompasses change so as to make it seem tradition. The very configuration of progressivism versus conservatism is thus abrogated here, as Michaels also has argued. The actual operations of change in this romance suggest that the central issue here is the role of women in nineteenth-century social and political transformations: the aesthetics through which a certain profile of political economy emerges. For different views, see Brook Thomas, "*The House of the Seven Gables*: Reading the Romance of America," *PMLA* 97 (March 1982): 195–211; Michael T. Gilmore, *American Literature and the Marketplace* (Chicago: University of Chicago Press, 1985), 96–112.

Chapter Four

1. Nathaniel Hawthorne, *The Blithedale Romance*, vol. 3 of the Centenary Edition of the Works of Nathaniel Hawthorne (Columbus: Ohio State University Press, 1964). All page references are to this edition and are given in parentheses in the text.

2. The character of Coverdale has accordingly provoked and pervaded much criticism on *The Blithedale Romance*. See, for example, Kent Bales, "Coverdale's Mean and Subversive Egotism," *Bucknell Review* 21 (1973): 60–82; Nina Baym, "*The Blithedale Romance*: A Radical Reading," *Journal of English and German Philology* 67 (October 1968): 545–69; William Hedges, "Hawthorne's *Blithedale*: The Function of the Narrator," *Nineteenth-Century Fiction* 14 (March 1960): 303–16; James Justus, "Hawthorne's Coverdale: Character and Art in *The Blithedale Romance*," *American Literature* 47 (1975): 21–36; Joan D. Winslow, "New Light on Hawthorne's Miles Coverdale," *Journal of Narrative Technique* 7 (1977): 189–99; and Annette Kolodny's Introduction to *The Blithedale Romance* (New York: Viking Penguin, 1983), vii–xxx.

3. In *Rear Window*, one pole of the manipulation dialectic in the spectator is wittily enacted in Thelma Ritter's massage of the injured Jimmy Stewart; Stewart in turn reverses the passivity of his spectatorship when he uses his camera as a weapon to stop Raymond Burr's attack. Many Hawthorne tales (as well as notebook entries) examine watching as an active and aggressive practice: "Ethan Brand" and "Wakefield," to

mention the most striking instances, starkly exhibit the egomania of relentless looking. The other side of spectatorship, its passivity and malleability, is the subject of *The Blithedale Romance*. For this content and for its intensely visual style, the novel invites consideration in the cinematic terms of voyeurism and spectatorship that Hitchcock's films, perhaps more than any others, have generated. See, for example, Leland Poague and Marshall Deutelbaum, eds., *A Hitchcock Reader* (Ames: Iowa State University Press, 1986); Tania Modleski, *The Women Who Knew Too Much: Hitchcock and Feminist Theory* (New York: Methuen, 1988).

In Hitchcock as in Hawthorne, the viewed object is always female. The gendered structure of visual pleasure and spectatorship has been most fully developed by feminist film critics. See Laura Mulvey, "Visual Pleasure and Narrative Cinema," *Screen* 16 (Autumn 1977): 6–18, reprinted in Gerald Mast and Marshall Cohen, eds., *Film Theory and Criticism: Introductory Readings* (New York: Oxford University Press, 1985), 803–16; Christine Gledhill, "Recent Developments in Feminist Film Criticism," *Quarterly Review of Film Studies* (1978): 457–93, reprinted in Mary Ann Doane, Patricia Mellencamp, and Linda Williams, eds., *Re-Vision: Essays in Feminist Film Criticism* (Los Angeles: AFI Monograph Series, 1983), 18–48. More criticism has considered the historical and psychological specificity of female spectatorship. For example, see Doane, *The Desire to Desire*; Miriam Hansen, "Pleasure, Ambivalence, Identification: Valentino and Female Spectatorship," *Cinema Journal* 25 (Summer 1986): 6–32. Carol Clover has complicated the question of gender in spectatorship further in her analysis of the gender-crossings operating in both the characters and the audiences of the slasher films: "Her Body, Himself: Gender in the Slasher Film," *Representations* 20 (Fall 1987): 187–228.

In this chapter I will be tracing what most of these critics would call a male spectatorship and masculine pleasure and identity formation. The aim of my exposition of Coverdale's voyeurism, though, is not to situate *The Blithedale Romance* in this critical framework but to illuminate the relation of voyeurism to nineteenth-century formulations of individuality, whose market dimensions of spectacle and spectatorship pre-date, as they prepare for, the invention of film.

4. See the discussion of Hawthorne's horror of the public nature of mesmerism in Chapter 3, above.

5. Throughout this discussion the reader will recognize the ideas of Thorstein Veblen, whose conceptualization of conspicuous leisure as a psychology of looking and being looked at (*The Theory of the Leisure Class*) aptly describes the manifestations of nineteenth-century consumer culture Hawthorne was already apprehending in the 1850s.

6. Utopian socialists were addressing problems they perceived in early nineteenth-century political economy. An illuminating discussion of utopianists' critiques which has influenced my thinking on utopianism and consumerism can be found in Anne C. Rose, *Transcendentalism as a Social Movement, 1830–1850* (New Haven: Yale University Press, 1981), 109–207.

7. Coverdale's languor has seemed to many readers an index of Hawthorne's views of the efficacy of either art or reform. A tradition of *Blithedale* criticism thus turns on the question of failure: the failure of reform, or art, or romance.

A contemporary reviewer declared: "Hawthorne discards all ideas of successful human progress" (unsigned review in the *American Whig Review* 16 [November 1852], reprinted in *The Blithedale Romance,* ed. Gross and Murphy, 282). Over a century later, Irving Howe characterized Coverdale's relation to utopia as Hawthorne's treatment of "what happens when a hesitant intellectual attaches himself to a political enterprise": *Politics and the Novel* (New York: Horizon, 1957), 167. More recently, Michael Davitt Bell has argued that "the failure of American Romanticism is the great subject of *The Blithedale Romance.*" This is "the failure of the artist and his society to confront the true nature of the originating spirit of literary and social order." It takes the form of Coverdale's repression of "truly imaginative self-discovery" in favor of "sentimentality": *The Development of American Romance: The Sacrifice of the Relation* (Chicago: University of Chicago Press, 1980), 185–93.

Such readings follow a moral agenda, which differs in content according to the critical perspective of the "best" category of value: the political, the aesthetic, or the personal. However these readings may vary, they are all committed to assessing the failure of the novel to represent the fulfillment of one of these programs. My reading is concerned with what is accomplished in the novel's thematics of limitation—with limitation as a strategy of individualism.

8. My own reading builds upon Richard Poirier's observation that Coverdale exemplifies "the transformations of a sort of Emersonian man into a Dandy": *A World Elsewhere: The Place of Style in American Literature* (New York: Oxford University Press, 1966), 93–143.

9. Downing, *The Architecture of Country Houses,* 23.

10. Veblen, *The Theory of the Leisure Class,* 41–60. Zenobia at one point remarks that Blithedale provided an "Arcadian freedom of falling in love" across class ranks, and wonders why Coverdale did not take advantage of this freedom "to fall in love with Priscilla." It will become clear in the following discussion that maintaining lines of distinction is crucial to Coverdale's keeping from falling in love with anyone.

11. Downing, *The Architecture of Country Houses,* 23.

12. Georg Lukács has described this critical distance as the contemplative mode. For Lukács, this is the state of reified subjectivity: a false consciousness because it emanates from an economic system (capitalism) distinguished by its falsification of real or true value. That is, capitalism's implementation of exchange value alters the basic relations of labor value, thus producing subjects who internalize this perversion in value: "Reification and the Consciousness of the Proletariat," in his *History and Class Consciousness,* trans. Rodney Livingstone (Cambridge: MIT Press, 1983), 83–222.

While Coverdale might seem to exemplify the reified subject, his perversion, that is, his contemplative detachment, does not stem from his subjection to economic conditions. Rather, it represents the machinery and work of his self-production—the laborious desires by which he sustains himself. Ironically, the notion of reification fails to acknowledge an entire realm of production, the psychic and social modes of self-production and distribution. To assume a process of reification is to assume a set of productive relations that were not exchange relations and also to assume a consciousness that could be independent of exchange relations. Readings of Coverdale as an ideological case—whether failed reformer or ineffectual aesthete—thus measure him, or Hawthorne, against a phantasmic standard. My point here is that individualism and its ethics of privacy arise in (nineteenth-century) market society: individual consciousness in this society accordingly reflects it.

13. The difference between *The Blithedale Romance*'s account of consumer consciousness and the post-Marxist conceptualization of reified subjectivity can be best demonstrated by altering the concluding sentence to Horkheimer and Adorno's essay "The Culture Industry: Enlightenment as Mass Deception." Whereas Horkheimer and Adorno assert that "the triumph of advertising in the culture industry is that consumers feel compelled to buy and use its products even though they see through them," *The Blithedale Romance* suggests that the triumph of consumerist culture is that consumers feel compelled to see (and see through) its products even though they do not necessarily buy and use them: Horkheimer and Adorno, *Dialectic of Enlightenment,* 167.

14. Beecher, *A Treatise on Domestic Economy,* 12–14.

15. "Domestic inventions were perhaps the communitarians' best advertisement": Dolores Hayden, *Seven American Utopias: The Architecture of Communitarian Socialism* (Cambridge: MIT Press, 1979), 225–29.

16. The best study of the meaning of work in nineteenth-century America is Daniel T. Rodgers, *The Work Ethic in Industrial America, 1850–1920* (Chicago: University of Chicago Press, 1974). On the significance

of work with respect to women, see Dublin, *Women at Work;* Alice Kessler-Harris, *Out to Work: A History of Wage-Earning Women in the United States* (New York: Oxford University Press, 1982). The importance of the unpaid women's work that constituted the full-time careers of middle-class women is discussed in the previous chapter.

17. A good general history of the emergence of alternative economic communities in America is Arthur Bestor, *Backwoods Utopias: The Sectarian Origins and the Owenite Phase of Communitarian Socialism in America,* 2d ed. (Philadelphia: University of Pennsylvania Press, 1970).

18. For information on 1840s experiments in social organization, see, among others, Mark Holloway, *Heavens on Earth: Utopian Communities in America, 1680–1880* (New York: Dover, 1966), 117–97; Hayden, *Seven American Utopias,* 9–61, 149–85, and her *The Grand Domestic Revolution,* 34–63; Ronald G. Waters, *American Reformers, 1815–1860* (New York: Hill and Wang, 1978), 39–75.

19. Quoted in Holloway, *Heavens on Earth,* 104.

20. George Ripley, letter to Emerson, November 9, 1840, quoted in Anne Rose, *Transcendentalism as a Social Movement,* 133–34.

21. Anne Rose, *Transcendentalism as a Social Movement,* 133–34.

22. Nathaniel Hawthorne, letter to Sophia Peabody, August 22, 1841, reprinted in *The Blithedale Romance,* ed. Gross and Murphy, 236.

23. Anne Rose, *Transcendentalism as a Social Movement,* 130–61.

24. Bronson Alcott, "Days from a Diary," *Dial* 2 (1842): 409–37. On the Alcott family's experience at Fruitlands, see Anne Rose, *Transcendentalism as a Social Movement,* 197–206; Madeleine Stern, *Louisa May Alcott* (Norman: University of Oklahoma Press, 1950), 16–45.

25. On the Shakers and their radical alternative economy that abjured sexual reproduction, see Edward Deming Andrews, *The People Called Shakers: A Search for the Perfect Society* (New York: Oxford University Press, 1963); Hayden, *Seven American Utopias,* 65–103; Lawrence Foster, *Religion and Sexuality: The Shakers, the Mormons, and the Oneida Community* (Urbana: University of Illinois Press, 1984), 21–123.

26. Anne Rose, *Transcendentalism as a Social Movement,* 198–206.

27. Rachel Bowlby (*Just Looking,* 32–33) has proposed that the notion of "just looking" expresses "the suspended moment of contemplation before the object for sale—the pause for *reflection* in which it is looked at in terms of how it would look on the looker." In Bowlby's view, this moment marks "an insatiable interplay between deprivation and desire" in the consumer who lacks what she looks at. In what follows I will be suggesting a different account of what it can mean just to look: far from exacerbating the consumer's sense of lack, looking can confirm the spectator's self-definition, his or her subjection *of* the viewed object, as well

as his or her subjection *to* the viewed object. It is the possibility of over-identification, of the viewer's transformation, that concerns Hawthorne. This dynamic of looking in *The Blithedale Romance* applies to a male spectator, defining a masculine identity within the consumer sphere historically aligned with the feminine.

28. Lauren Berlant also notes the homoerotics of the Coverdale-Hollingsworth relationship, reading it as part of a discourse on love and utopianism: "Fantasies of Utopia in *The Blithedale Romance*," *American Literary History* 1 (Spring 1989): 36–38. While my reading of *The Blithedale Romance* is intended to open discussion on the role of homoerotics in representations of femininity and individuality, I am not here pursuing the directions such a discussion of Hawthorne's work might take. Recent provocative treatments of the circuits of desire and power that homoerotics (and an accompanying homophobia) have buttressed offer possible routes. I have in mind here particularly the work of Sedgwick, *Between Men,* and Christopher Craft, "Tennyson's Strange Manner of Address," *Genders* 1 (Spring 1988): 83–101, and "Kiss Me with Those Red Lips: Gender and Inversion in Bram Stoker's *Dracula*," *Representations* 8 (Fall 1984): 107–33.

29. The transfiguration of Priscilla into Margaret Fuller also dispels her erotic attractiveness, just as the attraction to her dispels the erotic attractiveness of Zenobia and Hollingsworth. The obsessive system of equivocation and displaced desire I am describing here is nicely captured in Frederick Crews's observation of the "erotic furtiveness which pervades the narrative": *The Sins of the Fathers: Hawthorne's Psychological Themes* (New York: Oxford University Press, 1966), 194–212.

30. Emerson points out the confusion between expiation and true philanthropy and stresses the priority of self-reformation to social change in "New England Reformers: Lecture at Amory Hall" (1844), reprinted in *The Collected Works of Ralph Waldo Emerson,* Vol. 3: *Essays: Second Series,* ed. Joseph Slater, Alfred R. Ferguson, and Jean Ferguson Carr (Cambridge: Harvard University Press, 1983), 149–67.

31. Emerson advocated an American poetry that would "revive and lead in a new age": "The American Scholar" (1837), reprinted in *The Collected Works of Ralph Waldo Emerson,* Vol. 1: *Nature, Addresses, and Lectures,* ed. Robert E. Spiller and Alfred R. Ferguson (Cambridge: Harvard University Press, 1971), 52. Margaret Fuller identified the exemplary utopian potential of American culture in contemporary "attempts of external action, such as are classed under the head of social reform": "American Literature, Its Position in the Present Time, and Prospects for the Future" (1846), reprinted in *Margaret Fuller: American Romantic,* ed. Perry Miller (Ithaca: Cornell University Press, 1970), 227–50.

32. My reading accords with Philip Rahv's well-known argument that "the emotional economy of this story is throughout one of displacement . . . the whole point of Coverdale's behavior is to avoid involvement": "The Dark Lady of Salem," *Partisan Review* 8 (1941): 377. But whereas Rahv takes the relationship of Coverdale to Zenobia to be the displaced crucial erotic connection, I suggest that the relationship of Coverdale to Hollingsworth is the primary erotic connection Coverdale evades, along with all others. Another reading that identifies Zenobia as the real object of desire displaced by Coverdale's confession to being in love with Priscilla is Ellen Morgan's "The Veiled Lady: The Secret Love of Miles Coverdale," in C. E. Frazer Clark, Jr., ed., *Nathaniel Hawthorne Journal* (Dayton: Microcard Editions, 1971), 169–81.

33. Sigmund Freud, "Fetishism," trans. Joan Rivière, in Philip Reiff, ed., *Sexuality and the Psychology of Love* (New York: Collier, 1972), 215.

34. Freud, "Fetishism," 216.

35. Sarah Kofman, *The Enigma of Woman: Woman in Freud's Writings,* trans. Catherine Porter (Ithaca: Cornell University Press, 1985), 84. Challenging the dictum that fetishism is a specifically male perversion, Naomi Schor has explored the sexual problematic in fetishism from the point of view of a woman: "Female Fetishism: The Case of George Sand," in Susan Rubin Suleiman, ed., *The Female Body in Western Culture: Contemporary Perspectives* (Cambridge: Harvard University Press, 1986), 361–72.

36. Kofman, *The Enigma of Woman,* 88, 86.

37. Freud's major statements on homosexuality appear in the essays "The Sexual Aberrations," in his *Three Essays on the Theory of Sexuality,* ed. and trans. James Strachey (New York: Avon, 1962), and "The Psychogenesis of a Case of Homosexuality in a Woman," trans. Barbara Low and R. Gabler, and "Certain Neurotic Mechanisms in Jealousy, Paranoia, and Homosexuality," trans. Joan Rivière, both in *Sexuality and the Psychology of Love,* 133–59 and 160–70. Excellent discussions of Lacan's insistence on the difficulty and radical division in subject formation can be found in the lucid introductory essays by Juliet Mitchell and Jacqueline Rose to their translation of Lacan essays, *Feminine Sexuality: Jacques Lacan and the Ecole Freudienne* (New York: Norton, 1985), 1–57. The work of Julia Kristeva has most persistently identified the feminine with the unconscious and with the function of the unconscious in language which she calls the "semiotic." See Kristeva's account of fetishism in her *Revolution in Poetic Language,* trans. Margaret Waller (New York: Columbia University Press, 1984). Also see Jacqueline Rose's eloquent defense and explication of Kristeva's work in "Julia Kristeva—Take Two," in Rose's *Sexuality in the Field of Vision,* 141–64. For yet another

direction a feminist appropriation of the unconscious might take, see Mary Jacobus, *Reading Woman: Essays in Feminist Criticism* (New York: Columbia University Press, 1986).

38. Jacques Derrida, *Glas,* trans. John P. Leavey, Jr. and Richard Rand (Lincoln: University of Nebraska Press, 1986), 227.

39. Coverdale's fetishization of objects can also be considered in the light of Marx's concept of commodity fetishism. Marx attributes "the enigmatical character of the product of labour, so soon as it assumes the form of commodities" to the social relations in which the commodity is produced. In a capitalist economy, "every commodity might be regarded as a symbol," not of its labor value, as Marxists would wish, but of its exchange value—of money, itself also a symbol. In their symbolic character, commodities thus appear to take on a life of their own, removed from the processes of production: Marx, *Capital,* 1: 82 and 103.

In *The Blithedale Romance* the fetishistic character of commodities provides a model of individuality. Coverdale's objects attract him precisely because he cannot ascertain their referentiality, their fixed meaning. This impenetrability of the pictures before Coverdale images his fantasy of an impenetrable self.

40. Roy R. Male also uses the Marshall McLuhan line to describe Coverdale's investment in Priscilla. In Male's quite different allegorical reading, Priscilla figures the imagination or fantasy, the medium with which Coverdale falls in love: "Hawthorne's Fancy, or the Medium of *The Blithedale Romance,*" *The Nathaniel Hawthorne Journal* (1972): 67–73.

41. D. H. Lawrence, *Studies in Classical American Literature* (New York: Viking, 1968), 107. The hypothesis that Priscilla is in fact a "working-girl" has been advanced by Barbara F. Lefcowitz and Allan B. Lefcowitz, "Some Rents in the Veil: New Light on Priscilla and Zenobia," *Nineteenth-Century Fiction* 21 (1966): 263–75.

42. Richard Brodhead has treated Hawthorne's figuration of love as a mesmeric relation and a "model of domination" in "Hawthorne among the Realists: The Case of Howells," in Eric J. Sundquist, ed., *American Realism: New Essays* (Baltimore: Johns Hopkins University Press, 1982), 25–41.

43. Recent feminist analyses of nineteenth-century mesmerism suggest an alternative characterization of the medium or female spiritualism. Her very lack of personal control—her representation of a higher authority—could authorize her unconventional acts and utterances, ones such as the rejections of female duties mentioned in Hawthorne's description of mesmeric power: Alex Owen, "The Other Voice: Women, Children and Nineteenth-Century Spiritualism," in Carolyn Steedman, Cathy Urwin, and Valerie Walkerdine, eds., *Language, Gender, and Childhood*

(London: Routledge & Kegan Paul, 1985), 34–73; Judith R. Walkowitz, "Science and Seance: Transgressions of Gender and Genre in Late Victorian London," *Representations* 22 (Spring 1988): 3–29.

Any study of mesmerism and nineteenth-century literature must take note of Maria Tatar's informative and illuminating *Spellbound*. My reading of mesmerism as a model of individualism closely parallels Tatar's identification of mesmerism as a model of psychological domination in Hawthorne's fiction. But whereas Tatar emphasizes Hawthorne's concern with the role of the mesmerist, I am interested in his fascination with the vulnerability of the medium. On Hawthorne and nineteenth-century mesmerism, also see Taylor Stoehr, *Hawthorne's Mad Scientists: Pseudoscience and Social Science in Nineteenth-Century Life and Letters* (Hamden, Conn.: Archon, 1978), 32–63.

44. An intriguing and somewhat parallel discussion of the perverse desiring machinery consumer displays set in motion can be found in Stuart Culver's striking analysis of window dressing in "What Manikins Want: *The Wonderful World of Oz* and *The Art of Decorating Dry Goods Windows,"* *Representations* 21 (Winter 1988): 97–116.

45. Though Fuller never resided at Brook Farm, she visited there, and of course Hawthorne also knew her from her visits to Emerson's home and his own home in Concord. In drawing the parallel between Fuller's and Zenobia's deaths by drowning I am not reviving the debate on whether Hawthorne was representing Margaret Fuller in his portrayal of Zenobia. It is clearly part of the referential play of this novel to link Fuller alternately with Priscilla and then Zenobia. I am interested in how Hawthorne's use of his dead friend's name resonates with the voyeur's strategic interest in dead women that this novel examines. In her essay *"The Blithedale Romance,"* Nina Baym has made a persuasive case for the connection between Fuller's characterization of woman's "electric" nature and Priscilla's mesmerized femininity. See, in this connection, Margaret Fuller, *Woman in the Nineteenth Century* (New York: Norton, 1971), 103–4.

46. Feminist readings of this novel have focused on Zenobia's death, taking it as either Hawthorne's sympathy with or his containment of nineteenth-century feminist critiques of domestic womanhood. See, for example, Judith Fryer, *The Faces of Eve: Women in the Nineteenth-Century American Novel* (New York: Oxford University Press, 1978), 207–19; Mary Suzanne Schriber, "Justice to Zenobia," *New England Quarterly* 55 (March 1982): 61–78.

47. In both novels it is clear that women—their bodies and their work—provide the conditions for making individuality possible. Domestic individualism thus amounts to an "institution of ho(m)mo-sex-

uality." I take this phrase from Luce Irigaray. Reading Marx's account of the commodity as an account of woman, Irigaray powerfully analyzes the deployment of women in the consumer relations I have discussed here within the frame of nineteenth-century American culture and the particular perverse practice *The Blithedale Romance* presents. It seems to me that the structure of erotic relations in Hawthorne's novel—an encounter between two men played out through two women who are essentially interchangeable—exemplifies precisely what Irigaray has identified as the dynamic among men in which women figure. See Irigaray's "Women on the Market," in her *The Sex Which Is Not One*, trans. Catherine Porter (Ithaca: Cornell University Press, 1985), 170–91.

Chapter Five

1. Herman Melville, *Pierre; or, The Ambiguities;* ed. Harrison Hayford, Hershel Parker, and G. Thomas Tanselle (Evanston: Northwestern University Press and the Newberry Library, 1971), 244. All subsequent references to this text will appear in parentheses in the text.

This chapter (without its treatment of *Ruth Hall*) first appeared as part of my 1985 dissertation, "Domesticity and the Nineteenth-Century American Imagination." Portions of it have been presented in talks at Princeton University (1985), the MLA (1985), and the University of Massachusetts at Amherst (1988).

2. My treatment of *Pierre* and domestic individualism is much influenced by Michael Rogin's insightful and intriguing discussion of the connections between nineteenth-century politics, the sentimental family, and Melville family history: *Subversive Genealogy: The Politics and Art of Herman Melville* (New York: Knopf, 1983), 155–86.

3. The figure of the writer struggling against society dominates conceptions about American literature. Richard Poirier identifies the prominence of this archetype when he writes that "[t]he classic American writers try through style to temporarily free the hero (and the reader) from systems, to free them from the pressures of time, biology, economics, and from the social forces which are ultimately the undoing of American heroes and quite often of their creators" (*A World Elsewhere*, 5). For an exposition of the gender distinctions operating in this American mythology, see Baym, "Melodramas of Beset Manhood."

4. On the development of nineteenth-century American literary sales techniques and the puffery system, see Kelley, *Private Woman, Public Stage*, 3–27. In writing about the literary careers of nineteenth-century women writers, Kelley has coined the term *literary domesticity* to signify the "integration of private individual with published writing"that she believes

these sentimental writers achieved. It is this integration of individual with literary commerce against which *Pierre* sets literary individualism.

5. The most forcefully articulated account of *Pierre* and the masculine literary career as a critique of sentimentalism and suffocating "feminine sensibility" is Ann Douglas's "Herman Melville and the Revolt against the Reader," in *The Feminization of American Culture* (New York: Avon, 1977), 349–95. In this chapter I shift from her focus to investigate what is at stake in anti-sentimentalism: the issue here is not how sentimentalism constrains but how it creates and sustains literary individualism.

6. On Melville's career difficulties see Leon Howard, "Historical Note, I," in Melville's *Pierre; or, The Ambiguities*, 365–79. The popularity of domestic literature is documented in James D. Hart, *The Popular Book: A History of America's Literary Taste* (New York: Oxford University Press, 1950); Mary Ryan, *The Empire of the Mother: American Writing about Domesticity, 1830–1860* (New York: Haworth Press, 1982), 1–43.

7. William Braswell describes Melville's satire of sentimentalism in *Pierre* in "The Early Love Scenes in *Pierre*," *American Literature* 22 (November 1950): 283–89.

8. Melville himself, in a letter to his English publisher, considered anonymous publication for *Pierre*: letter to Richard Bentley, April 16, 1852, in *The Letters of Herman Melville*, Merrell R. Davis and William H. Gilman (New Haven: Yale University Press, 1960), 150–51.

9. Herman Melville, "Hawthorne and His Mosses," *The Literary World*, August 17 and 24, 1850, reprinted in Herman Melville, *Moby-Dick*, ed. Harrison Hayford and Hershel Parker (New York: Norton, 1967), 536.

10. Ann Douglas provides an illuminating discussion of the professional and economic aims (and necessities) of women sentimental writers in "'The Scribbling Women' and Fanny Fern: Why Women Wrote," *American Quarterly* 23 (1974): 3–24. The benefits of the strategy of anonymity for seventeeth-century French woman writers are delineated in Joan de Jean, "Lafayette's Ellipses: The Privileges of Anonymity," *PMLA* 99 (1984): 884–902.

In a much-debated essay ("What Is an Author?" in Josue V. Harari, ed., *Textual Strategies: Perspectives in Post-Structuralist Criticism* [Ithaca: Cornell University Press, 1979], 141–60) Michel Foucault links the rise of the "author-function" with bourgeois society, with individualism and private property. In this society the author regulates "the fictive" by limiting "the proliferation of meaning." With change, Foucault writes, this "constraint" on fiction "would then develop in the anonymity of a murmur." In other words, the agency of regulation would be less recognizable. In his effort to imagine a discourse about literature that would be attentive to political questions, Foucault advocates an "indifference" about questions of authorship and the author. Underlying this scenario of "fiction and its polysemic texts" more freely circulating and proliferating meaning is the myth of an autonomous text: the author-function does not disappear but is displaced onto the text, to which motives are now ascribed. Foucault's desire for unimpeded circulation of meaning bespeaks a new individualism—that of the text. The same vision of literary freedom that underpins Melville's myth of the anonymous author emerges in Foucault's post-structuralist myth of authorship fading into anonymity.

In a careful study of the institution of copyright, Mark Rose offers some astute qualifications to Foucault's account of authorship and individualization: "The Author as Proprietor," *Representations* 23 (Summer 1988): 51–85.

11. Fanny Fern, *Ruth Hall and Other Writings,* ed. Joyce W. Warren (New Brunswick: Rutgers University Press, 1986), 206. Subsequent references to this novel will be given in parentheses in the text.

12. Joyce Warren details Willis's treatment of his sister in her informative Introduction to *Ruth Hall and Other Writings*. This volume includes another satiric sketch Sara Willis wrote about her brother, "Apollo Hyacinth," 259–60. A much more favorable portrait of Willis emerges in Harriet Jacobs's autobiography, where, under the name of Mr. Bruce, he appears as one of Jacobs's supporters in gaining her freedom: *Incidents in the Life of a Slave Girl.*

13. Quoted in Joyce Warren, Introduction to *Ruth Hall,* ix.

14. Even though Ruth tells her daughter that "God forbid" she grow up to become a writer because "no happy woman ever writes" (175), the book emphasizes that the domestic situation that allows women not to earn money is never a certain fate.

In an unpublished essay on *Ruth Hall* (delivered as a talk at the American Studies Association in 1986), Richard Brodhead proposes that the novel represents shifting accounts of domesticity—specifically, the shift from an agrarian domestic economy to domestic consumerism. Brodhead treats the novel's representation of literary celebrity in "Veiled Ladies: Toward a History of Antebellum Entertainment," *American Literary History* 1 (Summer 1989): 273–94. This essay, which was published after this book was written, contains interesting parallels also to my discussion of domestic values and *The Blithedale Romance.*

15. Susan Sontag traces the emergence of photography and its relation to the aesthetics of individuality and the logic of consumption in *On Photography* (New York: Farrar, Straus and Giroux, 1977), 153–80.

16. For Douglas, Melville exemplifies the serious writer's plight in a

commercial culture. My reading does not presume that literature could ever be independent of socioeconomic trends. *Ruth Hall* demonstrates that the crucial issue is who controls or succeeds in commerce.

17. Jane Tompkins also analyzes the critical bias against popularity for a literary work: *Sensational Designs,* xi–xix.

18. Ahab's leg is the most memorable example of Melville's play on the relation between labor and the body; another instance is the ghostly disappearance of female physicality in the production of paper depicted in Melville's story "The Paradise of Bachelors and the Tartarus of Maids," in *Harper's Magazine* 10, no. 59 (April 1855): 670–78, reprinted in *Great Short Works of Herman Melville,* ed. Warner Berthoff (New York: Harper and Row, 1969), 202–22. Sharon Cameron has powerfully explicated the issues of body definition enacted in *Moby-Dick* in *The Corporeal Self,* 15–75.

19. "Hawthorne and His Mosses," 550.

20. In Melville's imagination, the goal of shared genius is the emergence of the individual talent. In this respect his cannibalistic brotherhood of genius distinctly differs from the myth of impersonal authorship familiar to us from T. S. Eliot's formulation of literary tradition as transcendence of history and personality: "The progress of the artist is a continual self-sacrifice, a continual extinction of personality" ("Tradition and the Individual Talent," in his *Selected Essays* [New York: Harcourt Brace Jovanovich, 1964], 7).

21. The image of a male society of privileged consumers of culture is much more fully detailed in "The Paradise of Bachelors and the Tartarus of Maids," where he considers the class and gender hierarchies of production and consumption.

22. "Hawthorne and His Mosses," 548.

23. Melville's horror of publishing practices stemmed from his own experience. Perry Miller describes Melville's literary education after the success of *Typee* as the process of learning that the publishing world was "a literary butcher shop": *The Raven and the Whale: The War of Words and Wits in the Era of Poe and Melville* (New York: Harcourt, Brace, 1956), 6–7.

24. For Melville, cannibalism also figures as the threat to subjectivity, as a sign that "individuality is a mirage." See Mitchell Breitweiser, "False Sympathy in *Typee,*" *American Quarterly* 34 (Fall 1982): 411–13.

25. William Alcott, *The Young Housekeeper, or Thoughts on Food and Cookery* (Boston: G. W. Light, 1839), 43.

26. Sarah Josepha Hale, *The Good Housekeeper, or the Way to Live Well* (Philadelphia: B. Otis, 1844), 144.

27. Hale, *The Good Housekeeper,* 144.

28. Orson S. Fowler, *Maternity* (New York: Fowler and Wells, 1855), 206.

29. The way breast-feeding can operate as a governance technique is even more explicit in the case of nineteenth-century France. Jacques Donzelot, in *The Policing of Families,* explicates how the state deployed its authority through normalization of child-nursing practices. Limiting wet-nursing to a family practice, Donzelot argues, the state invested the family with childcare responsibilities and thus internalized in the family the control of individuals.

30. Melville describes the opposite of this benign literary ecology in his portrayal of the nineteenth-century literary economy in "The Paradise of Bachelors and the Tartarus of Maids." There, the mechanical workings of the publishing industry are exposed as violations of nature. The health and beauty of the female paper-mill workers are subsumed into the paper they produce. Industry, replacing nature, does not merely alienate the worker's labor but incorporates the worker.

31. My thinking on the connections between selfhood and "thingness" has benefited from William James's discussion of subject-object relations in "The Self" in his *Psychology: Briefer Course* (1892; rpt. Cambridge: Harvard University Press, 1984), 159–91.

32. Barbara Johnson has explored the relation between mothering and autobiography with reference to the woman writer, describing the particular complications that arise in a female subject's relation to authority: the sense of monstrosity associated with female projects to mother the self in literature: "My Monster, Myself," *Diacritics* (Summer 1982): 2–10. In *Pierre,* motherhood itself is the monster preventing self-expression. The troubled relation to the mother Johnson identifies with female autobiography is in my view an effect of any autobiographical project.

33. I am following here Mary Ryan's account of the rhetoric of motherhood: *The Empire of the Mother,* 45–95.

34. William Alcott, *Advice to Young Men* (Boston: Perkins and Marvin, 1838), 135.

35. Michael Rogin suggests a Melville family model for the figure of the father's illegitimate daughter, arguing that in *Pierre* Melville is exploring the possibilities of a premarital affair his father may have had or contemplated: *Subversive Genealogy,* 192–201.

36. For a provocative discussion of other deployments of daughters by a patriarchal order, see Sandra Gilbert, "Life's Empty Pack: Notes toward a Literary Daughteronomy," *Critical Inquiry* (March 1985): 355–84.

37. This association of foreign lands and cultures with freedom from

nurture is perhaps most poignant in *Typee,* where the words the traveling hero teaches the native, the characteristics by which the man of
society identifies himself to the native, are *home* and *mother.*

38. Note, for example, Melville's description of Pierre's proposal to
Isabel that they pretend to be married: "Over the face of Pierre there shot
a terrible self-revelation; he imprinted repeated burning kisses upon her;
pressed her hand; and would not let go her sweet and awful passiveness"
(192).

39. The incest intimations shocked many readers of the novel. An
anonymous reviewer called *Pierre* "an unhealthy mystic romance"; Julian
Hawthorne characterized the story as "a repulsive, insane, and impossible romance." Both reviews are reprinted with other contemporary and
subsequent assessments of *Pierre* in Brian Higgins and Hershel Parker,
Selected Essays on Melville's "Pierre" (Boston: G. K. Hall, 1983), 73, 82.

40. Frances Ferguson elucidates the ways that individuation emerges
in experiences and environments of self-vitiation: "Edmund Burke's
Sublime, or the Bathos of Experience," *Glyph* 8 (1981): 62–78.

On incest and sublimity, see Thomas Weiskel, *The Romantic Sublime:
Studies in the Structure and Psychology of Transcendence* (Baltimore: Johns
Hopkins University Press, 1976). Michael Fried traces some relations
between the sublime and family romance in his fascinating study "Realism, Writing, and Disfiguration in Thomas Eakins's *Gross Clinic,*" *Representations* 9 (Winter 1985): 73–76, reprinted in his *Realism, Writing, Disfiguration: On Thomas Eakins and Stephen Crane* (Chicago: University of
Chicago Press, 1987).

Myra Jehlen also treats the relation of incest to the logic of individualism and *Pierre*'s autotelism in *American Incarnation: The Individual, the
Nation, and the Continent* (Cambridge: Harvard University Press, 1986),
185–226. For yet another recent reading of *Pierre* and individualism, see
Wai-chee Dimock, *Empire for Liberty: Melville and the Poetics of Individualism* (Princeton: Princeton University Press, 1989), 140–75.

41. I elaborate on eating disorders as responses to commercial culture
in my discussion in the next chapter of another Melville work, "Bartleby
the Scrivener."

42. Sharon Cameron points out that the distinction between self and
others, individualness and relation, is itself a confusion, since if "the self
cannot adequately or stably be defined, neither can distinctions between
selves." Cameron reads *Moby-Dick* as a quest for self-definition through
extensions of the body. I am reading *Pierre* as a different though related
movement, the search for self-definition in the elimination of others, an
infinite regress from connections. See *The Corporeal Self,* 56.

43. Michael Rogin also sees Isabel as figuring the return of the mother. See *Subversive Genealogy,* 192–201.

44. Many of the feminist critics published in the collection *Writing and Sexual Difference,* first published as a special issue of *Critical Inquiry,* would disagree, arguing that sexual difference determines different subjectivities and different relations to writing. But this attempt to define and even legislate a specific female subjectivity reenacts the myth of self as prior to symbolic systems, the very myth *Pierre* epitomizes and problematizes. In her astute commentary on the volume (included therein) Jane Gallop observes that this myth takes the form of a confusion about the body's relation to language, an effort to differentiate between body and language as if language did not constitute bodies, male or female: Elizabeth Abel, ed., *Writing and Sexual Difference* (Chicago: University of Chicago Press, 1982).

45. William Fletcher, "The Robber and Little Ann," *The Little Grammarian* (New York: W. B. Gilley, 1829), quoted in Clifton Johnson, *Old-time Schools and School-books* (New York: Dover, 1963), 268–270. Karl F. Kaestle and Maris A. Vinovskis explore the connections between family and education in "From Apron Strings to ABCs: Parents, Children, and Schooling in Nineteenth-Century Massachusetts," in Demos and Boocock, eds., *Turning Points,* 39–80.

46. In *The Little Grammarian,* reprinted in Johnson, *Old-Time Schools,* 370. The now standard statement on the constitution of individuality through discipline is Michel Foucault, "Docile Bodies," in his *Discipline and Punish: The Birth of the Prison,* trans. Alan Sheridan (New York: Vintage, 1977). The role of the family as an organ of authority for the socialization of individuals is delineated in Donzelot, *The Policing of Families;* David J. Rothman, *The Discovery of the Asylum: Social Order and Disorder in the New Republic* (Boston: Little, Brown, 1971), 206–36.

47. Alcott, *The Young Housekeeper,* 43.

48. Alcott, *The Young Housekeeper,* 40.

49. Alcott, *The Young Housekeeper,* 25.

50. Reverend John C. Abbott, *The Mother at Home; or, Principles of Maternal Duty* (Boston: Crocker and Brewster, 1833), 15–16.

51. Abbott, *The Mother at Home,* 20.

52. The hostility toward mothers and mothering operating in the tradition of domestic womanhood has been explicated by feminist investigations of socialization. See Nancy Chodorow, *The Reproduction of Mothering: Psychoanalysis and the Sociology of Gender* (Berkeley and Los Angeles: University of California Press, 1978); Dorothy Dinnerstein, *The Mermaid and the Minotaur: Sexual Arrangements and Human Malaise* (New York: Harper and Row, 1977).

53. In a different reading of *Pierre,* Emory Elliott attributes Pierre's failure to the fact that "he takes himself and his American heritage too seriously": "Art, Religion, and the Problem of Authority in *Pierre,*" in Sacvan Bercovitch and Myra Jehlen, eds., *Ideology and Classic American Literature* (Cambridge: Cambridge University Press, 1986), 346.

Chapter Six

1. Herman Melville, "Bartleby the Scrivener: A Story of Wall Street," *Great Short Works of Herman Melville,* 39–40. Subsequent references to this work are cited in parentheses in the text.

2. For an account of the icons of home and mother in popular nineteenth-century discourse see Mary Ryan's discussion of the 1850s rhetoric of domestic isolation and rest in *The Empire of the Mother,* 97–115. One invalid, the housebound Alice James who welcomed the "divine *cessation*" (her emphasis) of death, represents in extremis the ethic of immobility recommended by the nineteenth-century American cult of true womanhood: *The Diary of Alice James,* ed. Leon Edel (New York: Dodd, Mead, 1964), 232. The resemblance between female invalidism and the domestic ideal of woman at home is explored in Jean Strouse, *Alice James: A Biography* (Boston: Houghton Mifflin, 1980) and Ruth Yeazell, *The Death and Letters of Alice James* (Berkeley and Los Angeles: University of California Press, 1981).

3. The images of hysterical postures became publicly available with the publication of D. M. Bourneville and P. Reynard's *Iconographie Photographique de la Salpêtrière,* 3 vols. (Paris: Bureaux du Progrès médical, 1877–1880). On the discourse of hysteria in America, see Smith-Rosenberg, "The Hysterical Woman." Although paralysis represented only one symptom in the multifarious symptomology of hysteria, which includes aphonia, depression, fatigue, nervousness, numbness, and epileptic-like seizures, it is preeminently emblematic of hysteria, I am suggesting, because of its continuity with domestic prescriptions. Hysteria in nineteenth-century America, in Smith-Rosenberg's words "the disease of the Victorian bourgeois family," caricatures domesticity; in the sociological account of hysteria developed by American doctors and recently politicized by feminist investigators such as Smith-Rosenberg, the hysteric suffers mainly from reminiscences of that domesticity. Whereas current feminist reformulations of hysteria, such as the provocative rereadings of Dora collected in Bernheimer and Kahane, eds., *In Dora's Case,* identify hysteric gestures as a female language, I am more interested in how the visibility of hysteria historically underscores what is already visible about woman: her removal from the public sphere. In this

exposition, the dynamics of motion and stasis in the photographs of hysterical seizures and poses elaborate the antinomy between movement and repose upheld by nineteenth-century domestic ideology.

4. William James, *The Principles of Psychology*, vol. 2 (1890; rpt. New York: H. Holt and Company, 1950), 421–22.

5. D. C. Westphal coined the term *agoraphobia* in an article discussing a case of fear of open places: *Journal of Mental Sciences* 19 (1873): 456. An earlier version of this article appeared in Germany in *Archiv für Psychiatrie* 1 (1871).

6. William A. Hammond, *A Treatise on Insanity* (1883; rpt. New York: Arno, 1973), 419–22.

7. *Préface aux oeuvres de Blaise Pascal* (Paris: Bossut, 1819), xxxii, and *L'amulette de Pascal* (Paris: F. Lelut, 1846); quoted in Hammond, *A Treatise on Insanity*, 419–20.

8. Alexis de Tocqueville, *Democracy in America*, trans. Henry Reeve, vol. 2, ed. Phillips Bradley (1840; rpt. New York: Knopf, 1980 [1945]), 146.

9. George M. Beard, *American Nervousness*, 96–129.

10. Hammond, *A Treatise on Insanity*, 422.

11. S. Weir Mitchell, *Wear and Tear, or Hints for the Overworked* (1887; rpt. New York: Arno, 1973), 63.

12. See Drinka's chapter on railway neuroses in *The Birth of Neurosis*, 108–22.

13. For example, Andrew Jackson Downing declared "the true home" a "counterpoise to the great tendency toward constant changes" in American social and economic life. His house and landscape designs accordingly stressed privacy and isolation, the home as a retreat from the world. See *The Architecture of Country Houses* (1852; rpt. New York: Dover, 1972), 269.

14. Mitchell, *Wear and Tear*, 30. Mitchell described his rest cure in "The Evolution of the Rest Cure," *Journal of Nervous and Mental Diseases* (1904): 368–73. On the sexual politics of the rest cure, see Douglas's pioneering essay "The Fashionable Diseases," and Ellen L. Bassuk, "The Rest Cure: Repetition or Resolution of Victorian Women's Conflicts?" in Suleiman, ed., *The Female Body in Western Culture*, 139–51.

15. Charlotte Perkins Gilman, *The Yellow Wallpaper* (1894; rpt. Old Westbury, N.Y.: Feminist Press, 1973), 30. Subsequent references are cited in parentheses in the text. Gilman recorded her nervous illness and unsuccessful experience of Mitchell's rest cure in her autobiography *The Living of Charlotte Perkins Gilman*. Walter Benn Michaels offers an intriguing analysis of the relations between "The Yellow Wallpaper," hys-

teria, and selfhood in a market economy in *The Gold Standard and the Logic of Naturalism,* 3–28.

16. As Sandra Gilbert and Susan Gubar explore the rebellion implicit in Charlotte Brontë's Madwoman in the Attic figure, feminist historians similarly trace a history of feminism from the subversive or proto-feminist features within domesticity. See, for example, Berg, *The Remembered Gate;* DuBois, *Feminism and Suffrage;* Barbara Epstein, *The Politics of Domesticity: Women, Evangelism, and Temperance in Nineteenth-Century America* (Middletown, Conn.: Wesleyan University Press, 1981).

17. Charlotte Perkins Gilman, *Women and Economics* (1898; rpt. New York: Harper and Row, 1966) and *The Home: Its Work and Influence* (New York: Charlton, 1910).

18. Beecher, *A Treatise on Domestic Economy,* 268–97. Beecher's and Gilman's contributions to architectural history are described in Hayden, *The Grand Domestic Revolution.*

19. In nineteenth-century sentimental literature, Nina Baym writes, "Domesticity is set forth as a value scheme for ordering all of life, in competition with the ethos of money and exploitation that is perceived to prevail in American society": *Woman's Fiction,* 27.

20. Sarah Josepha Hale, "Editor's Table," *Godey's Lady's Book* (February, 1852): 88.

21. Hale, "Editor's Table," 88. For an informative analysis of biological models invoked by late nineteenth-century anti-feminism, see Rosalind Rosenberg, *Beyond Separate Spheres: Intellectual Roots of Modern Feminism* (New Haven: Yale University Press, 1982).

22. Hale, "Editor's Table," 88.

23. Hale, "Editor's Table," 88.

24. A Retired Merchant, "My Wife and the Market Street Phantom," *Godey's Lady's Book* (September 1870): 339–42.

25. "My Wife and the Market Street Phantom," 340.

26. "My Wife and the Market Street Phantom," 341, 342.

27. "My Wife and the Market Street Phantom," 342.

28. Alan Trachtenberg, *The Incorporation of America: Culture and Society in the Gilded Age* (New York: Hill and Wang, 1982), 130–39. In *The Bon Marché* Michael Miller treats the emergence of kleptomania as an effect of the department-store display of abundant goods; in "selling consumption," the department store seemed to incite theft by offering *"apéritifs du crime."* Cases of kleptomania escalated with the emergence of the great store, and the store itself became the most common site of kelptomaniac thefts. I am stressing a similar complementarity between agoraphobia and the escalation of consumerism. Both agoraphobia and

kleptomania might be considered diseases of sentimentalism: conditions arising from desires in a sense invented and institutionalized by market capitalism; conditions linked to woman and her sphere, the respository of selfhood within consumerist culture.

29. Veblen, *The Theory of the Leisure Class*. On the transformation of housekeepers into consumers, see Susan Strasser's indispensable study of housework, *Never Done,* 243–62; Matthaei, *An Economic History of Women in America;* Cowan, *More Work for Mother.*

30. Philip Fisher brilliantly elaborates the features of this "conspicuousness" in late nineteenth-century American culture in "The Life History of Objects: The Naturalist Novel and the City," in his *Hard Facts,* 128–78.

31. Robert Seidenberg and Karen DeCrow, *Women Who Marry Houses: Panic and Protest in Agoraphobia* (New York: McGraw-Hill, 1983), 22–30; Alexandra Symonds, "Phobias After Marriage: Women's Declaration of Independence," in Jean Baker Miller, ed., *Psychoanalysis and Women: Contributions to New Theory and Therapy* (New York: Brunner/ Mazel, 1973), 288–303. These studies of agoraphobia depart from standard psychoanalytic accounts which, following Freud's analysis of Little Hans, view agoraphobia as a form of castration anxiety: Sigmund Freud, "Analysis of a Phobia in a Five-Year-Old Boy" (1909), trans. James Strachey, in Philip Reiff, ed., *The Sexual Enlightenment of Children* (New York: Collier, 1974), 47–184. According to subsequent Freudian analyses, agoraphobia in women also signifies an unresolved Oedipus complex—the anxiety of repressed libido manifest as "promiscuous urges in the street." The traffic and publicity of streets evoke in the agoraphobic her fears of her illicit, incestuous desire: Miller, "On Street Fear," *International Journal of Psychoanalysis* 34 (1953): 232. Helene Deutsch notes in female agoraphobics a "dread of parturition"—the dread of being "away from home and outside in the world" masks a dread of defloration or parturition: Helene Deutsch, "The Genesis of Agoraphobia," *International Journal of Psychoanalysis* 10 (1929): 69. More recently, Julia Kristeva rereads psychoanalysis and the case of Little Hans, viewing Hans's anxiety as the surfacing of the underlying fear of castration anxiety: "the frailty of the subject's signifying system": Julia Kristeva, *Powers of Horror: An Essay on Abjection* (New York: Columbia University Press, 1982), 35. The account of agoraphobia I develop here (from the imagery of public and private space recurring through psychoanalytic as well as pre- and post-psychoanalytic representations of agoraphobia) locates agoraphobia in the social rather than the psychic register (and locates the psychic in alignment with the social). I am not exploring agoraphobia as a disease but as an organization of specific social anxieties, as the structure of domestic ideology, and thus as the structure of selfhood in a market

economy. In this account the psychoanalytic exegesis of agoraphobia, staking out a psychic territory, would be another instance of how the agoraphobic imagination works—a denial of the agora in agoraphobia to advance a radically privatized model of self.

32. Seidenberg and DeCrow, *Women Who Marry Houses*, 47–48.

33. The self-sustaining female culture of Gilman's 1915 *Herland* is also the goal of earlier feminist elaborations of domesticity such as Catharine Beecher and Harriet Beecher Stowe's vision of "the Christian Neighborhood" in their popular manual *The American Woman's Home.*

34. Elizabeth Hardwick, "Bartleby in Manhattan," in her *Bartleby in Manhattan and Other Essays* (New York: Random House, 1984), 217–31. Another intriguing aspect of "Bartleby" as an urban tale is its contemporaneous appearance with articles describing the emerging phenomenon of the urban poor and homeless. I am indebted to Hans Bergmann for this point.

35. For a different interpretation of Bartleby's feminine position in the tale, see Patricia Barber, "What If Bartleby Were a Woman?" in Arlyn Diamond and Lee Edwards, eds., *The Authority of Experience* (Amherst: University of Massachusetts Press, 1977), 212–23. The possibilities of a "what if" school of literary criticism are limitless, but I am here suggesting only that nineteenth-century culture defines the scrivener's mode as feminine. Bartleby's femininity, insistently encamped in the public sphere, draws attention to the public peformance of the domestic. That Bartleby is a man makes his discontent with Wall Street an especially strong critique of both the market and domesticity. That is, though free to be in the world, Bartleby prefers not to.

36. Another reading of the lawyer-copyist relationship particularly suggestive for my own is Michael Rogin's interpretation of the tale as an exposé of false familial claims by employers of wage labor. In Rogin's reading, Bartleby attacks the lawyer's attempt to establish worker-employer bonds; he resists the boundaries of a sham familial relationship. In my reading, Bartleby redresses the falsity of the family, not because he is "boundaryless and insatiable" as Rogin characterizes him, but because the family, like the economy, is voracious and ignores boundaries. Bartleby insists on the set boundaries and self-sufficiency associated with an ideal domestic economy. See Rogin, *Subversive Genealogy*, 192–201.

37. Ira L. Mintz, "Psychoanalytic Therapy of Severe Anorexia: The Case of Jeanette," in C. Philip Wilson, ed., with Charles C. Hager and Ira L. Mintz, *Fear of Being Fat: The Treatment of Anorexia Nervosa and Bulimia* (New York: J. Aronson, 1983), 217–44.

38. Hilde Bruch, *The Golden Cage: The Enigma of Anorexia Nervosa* (Cambridge: Harvard University Press, 1978), 75–77.

39. The case of the anorectic against the coda of conventional femininity is persuasively presented by Kim Chernin, *The Obsession: Reflections on the Tyranny of Slenderness* (New York: Harper and Row, 1981); Susie Orbach, *Fat Is a Feminist Issue* (New York: Berkley, 1978), and *Hunger Strike: The Anorectic's Struggle as a Metaphor for Our Age* (New York: Norton, 1986); Seidenberg and Decrow, *Women Who Marry Houses,* 88–97; John Sours, *Starving to Death in a Sea of Objects* (New York: Aronson, 1980).

40. Hilde Bruch, *Eating Disorders* (New York: Basic Books, 1973), 211–25. William Gull and Charles Lasegue introduced the nomenclature *anorexia nervosa* for eating disorders in 1873, but Gull had already recorded cases of female refusals to eat in 1868. Reports of similar cases date back to medieval times; Rudolph Bell and Caroline Bynum have identified anorectic behavior in the fasting of saints. See Rudolph M. Bell, *Holy Anorexia* (Chicago: University of Chicago Press, 1985); Caroline Walker Bynum, "Fast, Feast, and Flesh," *Representations* 11 (Summer 1985): 1–25, and *Holy Feast and Holy Fast: The Religious Significance of Food to Medieval Women* (Berkeley and Los Angeles: University of California Press, 1987).

41. Susan Sontag, *Illness as Metaphor* (New York: Random House, 1979), 63.

42. Sandra Gilbert treats literary representation of the feminist politics of anorexia in "Hunger Pains," *University Publishing,* no. 8 (Fall 1979), pp. 1, 11–12. Two more recent feminist analyses link anorexia to the problematics of female identity following from mother–daughter relations. In *Starving Women: A Psychology of Anorexia Nervosa* (Dallas: Spring, 1983), analyst Angelyn Spignesi characterizes the anorectic as "our twentieth-century carrier" of the repressed female psyche (13). In denying the "principles of matter," she "enacts in her disease the interpenetration of the imaginal and physical realms" (59). This lack of demarcation between body and psyche, self and others, returns her to "the realm of Mother" (63). Similarly focusing on the relation of the anorectic to the maternal, Kim Chernin reads anorexia as a matricidal act, "a bitter warfare against the mother," enacted on the daughter's body: *The Hungry Self: Women, Eating, and Identity* (New York: Times Books, 1985), 93. Taking the anorectic as the protagonist in a history of female experience or placing anorexia in a maternal tradition, in a chronology of the constitution of identity and difference, suggests a fundamental relationship among maternity, anxiety, and the definition of bodily borders. My purpose here is not to dispute or advance the claim of archetypal female anxiety but, rather, to demonstrate how a nineteenth-century cult of

motherhood and domestic mythology shaped particular discourses of border anxiety: the nullifications of Bartleby, the negotiations of agoraphobia, and the negations of anorexia.

43. Ann Douglas has aptly termed this sentimental cult of death "the domestication of death" and has characterized it as a gesture by which women claimed a real estate society denied them: *The Feminization of American Culture*, 240–72.

44. Job 3:11–16.

Afterword

1. Henry James, *The Notebooks of Henry James*, ed. F. O. Matthiessen and Kenneth B. Murdock (London: Oxford University Press, 1947), 46–47.

2. Henry James, *The Bostonians* (Harmondsworth, England: Penguin, 1986), 84. All subsequent references to this work will be cited in parentheses in the text.

Index

Compositor: Braun–Brumfield, Inc.
Text: 11/13 Bembo
Display: Bembo
Printer: Braun–Brumfield, Inc.
Binder: Braun–Brumfield, Inc.